Kife

Kife

THE LIVES AND DREAMS
OF
SOVIET YOUTH

NANCY TRAVER

With a foreword by Yuri Shchekochikhin
Editor of *Literaturnaya gazeta*

ST. MARTIN'S PRESS
NEW YORK

Design by Robert Bull Design.

All interior photographs by Valery Schekoldin.

Library of Congress Cataloging-in-Publication Data

Traver, Nancy.
    Kife : the lives and dreams of Soviet youth.
      p. cm.
    ISBN 0-312-02938-1
    1. Youth—Soviet Union. I. Title.
    HQ799.S69T73–1989 305.23′5′0947—dc20 89-34834

First Edition

10 9 8 7 6 5 4 3 2 1

For Andy, who took me to Russia

CONTENTS

FOREWORD

I have written about youth problems for many years and it seems I should already know everything about the subject. My two sons are growing up and their future is my future as well. It's often difficult to find answers to the questions they raise. I can only imagine what questions are still ahead and how I will agonize to find answers for those. That is why I understand the complications that any Westerner faces when he or she tries to understand not only a new generation of young people, but the generation of a foreign country across the ocean, during the time of *perestroika*.

Who are they, these children of *perestroika*? How are they proclaiming themselves? What can be expected from them in the future? And finally, how do I see them?

In my time, society has often shifted blame for its own errors and miscalculations onto youth. "Materialism," "callousness," and "laziness" were among the faults of which they were accused.

It was easier for people to point a finger at a bunch of teenagers noisily crossing the boulevard, than to take a look at themselves in the mirror. For to look is to see a crisis in the economy, corruption, the political decay of leaders, and the blood of the thousands of kids thrown into the senseless war in Afghanistan.

I recall my amazement at an event that occurred near the end of the Brezhnev era. On an ordinary weekday evening in the very center of Moscow, on Gorky Street, I saw a demonstration of noisy young football fans. Today, when demonstrations, meetings, and street speeches have become habitual attributes of our life, no one would be surprised to see a crowd of teenagers marching in a column along a central street. But that's now, at the end of a decade. Back then, our elderly leader was merely dreaming of giving himself yet another medal of honor!

I thought about it for a long time, trying to understand what kind of generation had appeared in our country. Even if they only shouted idiotic football slogans, who could bravely march through the center of the city?

It came to me: A new generation, devoid of social fear, had stepped into life. The nightmare of Stalin's terror was not in their genes because they were the first generation in our country whose innocent fathers had not been arrested. And for this reason it was easier for them than for us when we were their age.

All sorts of youth groups began to appear in the early 1980s. Hippies, punks, nationalists, rockers, even monarchists. They cropped up every day, and immediately announced themselves by means of slogans and calls, which decorated walls, telephone boxes, and even the public entrances of government buildings.

"Everything creeps from the West, everything—from the West," our despairing, thick-headed officials repeated over and over. But it became apparent that only the external symbols came from the West. Underneath the outlandish hairdos, ribbons, and loud, bold voices was a true youth movement. Young people were protesting against hypocrisy, lies, and the suppression of personality.

These unfamiliar voices had to be heard. That was why I published in *Literaturnaya gazeta* a telephone number for a hot line connecting the editorial office with those new voices. Every Thursday I sat near the telephone and gradually came to understand why it was constantly ringing until late at night, why I saw my telephone number written on the walls of houses, why the janitors stopped being surprised when they let in more and more peculiar visitors to see me.

I remember well a dialogue I had for many hours with a seventeen-year-old Moscow punk, Sergei. He first came to the editorial office in a jacket pinched with a couple of dozen safety pins. A little jangling bell was attached to his knee.

"Showing off is a principle of our group. We want to turn heads, be noticed. It's fun to stroll down the street and see perplexity in the faces of passersby. When a respectable-looking man looks at you arrogantly, you feel that by your appearance alone you've somehow insulted him." Sergei stressed the word *insulted*.

I asked him if he took pleasure in insulting such a man.

"Not a man," he corrected me, "a Philistine. . . ."

"Whom do you consider a Philistine?"

"Those who live in banality, produce banality, and defend it."

He meant those slogans which surrounded us, and the countless speeches of the leaders. It was impossible to make out what these smooth phrases were about. Sergei also spoke of the war in Afghanistan, and the idiotic struggle against rock music. In a word, he talked about everything that would have made me hang a little bell on my pants if I'd been younger. "Hear us. Understand how we live!" his bell said.

My article on Sergei was published under the title "For whom the little bell tolls." His little bell heralded a new life for all of us, a new life when all voices would be heard. I will honestly admit that I didn't think such a time would come. But unlike Sergei, I came from a different generation: Our fathers were still startled by the late-night knock on the door. I am talking not of the distant past, I am speaking about recent times.

Those who were seventeen at the beginning of the eighties are now only eight years older. Those who were twenty still have not reached thirty. And it is their clear, brave voices that are ringing today through the country joining those of people who preserved the ideals of freedom since Khrushchev's short spring.

Already another new young generation is appearing in our life: It's composed of the ones who are growing up during *perestroika*. These are the children of *glasnost*. They don't have to look for the words of truth in samizdat (illegally published literature). *Glasnost* is not an unexpected gift for them, as it is for us, the older generation. *Glasnost* is an integral part of their lives and they will never let anybody destroy it. I meet them in school and student sections of the anti-Stalinist society, Memorial. I see them picketing near new atomic power stations that are still under construction. It's their voices I want to heed.

That's why it is with pleasure that I am introducing this book. *Kife* is about the children of *glasnost*, and about young people who've known both the days of fear and the flowering of freedom. Ultimately, this book is about the future, which is in the hands of those who will dwell in it the longest.

Yuri Shchekochikhin
Editor
Literaturnaya gazeta
Moscow, U.S.S.R.
June 1989

ACKNOWLEDGMENTS

WITHOUT THE patience of many young Soviets who sat up late into the night telling their life stories, this book would not have been written. Many cannot be thanked here; they would not want their names mentioned in a book like this. But most of them know they are here, and if change is allowed to continue in their country, eventually they may be able to buy a book like this from their own state stores.

Many former Soviets who emigrated to the West also helped tremendously with the writing of this book. Lyuda Yevuskov, formerly of Moscow and now a resident of Washington, D.C., gave very generously of her time and read every chapter as it was completed. Nina Raben, her husband Mark Belenky, and their daughter Masha Belenky, former Moscow residents who now live in Washington, D.C., also offered advice and carefully combed through the finished manuscript for errors. Lena Kaplan, another former Muscovite living in Washington, spent many hours of her time helping me. These friends deserve special thanks.

For their help on the first chapter about education, Kathy and Lisa Guroff of Washington, D.C., were especially helpful. In the section in Chapter 3 about counseling programs for Afghan vets, I would like to thank Dr. Charles Figley of Purdue University for taking the time to talk with me. For her help in arranging my interviews with visiting Soviet exchange students, I thank Zita Dabaras, a teacher at the Friends School in Baltimore.

Catherine Henry, a tireless chronicler of religious freedom in the Soviet Union, allowed me to use her library and collection of materials from Keston College in London for Chapter 6 on religion and atheism.

For Chapter 7 on culture, I owe many thanks to Joanna Stingray of Los Angeles. I also thank Alexander Kan, a rock critic from Leningrad, and Thom Shanker, a former Moscow correspondent with the *Chicago Tribune*.

For their help with the section on film in Chapter 7, I would like to thank Joan Ellen Delaney of the International Film Exchange in New York and Jutta Jensen of the Museum of Modern Art. I would also like to thank Justin Friedman at Columbia University's Harriman Institute in New York for his help on the television section in Chapter 7.

A special word of thanks to Murray Feshback and his wonderful library at Georgetown University.

Also, I would like to thank my editor at St. Martin's Press, Michael Sagalyn, who had faith in me, got me started, and helped me every step of the way.

Finally, the biggest bouquet of thanks must go to my husband, Andy Rosenthal, for his steady encouragement, occasional words of praise, thoughtful advice, and careful editing. I never gave up, because he didn't.

INTRODUCTION

WHEN I moved to Moscow in 1983, I joined the ranks of foreign correspondents who watched for clues about what happened behind the Kremlin's walls. We studied the rare public appearances of a frail Yuri Andropov and his aged allies from the politburo. Occasionally, an American reporter was fortunate enough to receive a leak from a party spokesman or foreign ministry source. But such tidbits of information were generally reserved for the senior members of the press corps. Soviet statesmen who were authorized to speak had little use for a woman reporter in her 20s.

So I directed my attention toward other segments of Soviet society. It seemed natural to focus on young people. Since I was one of them, I reasoned that they would readily accept me. I was convinced they could not be very different from my Western friends.

But penetrating the youth culture proved difficult. Andropov's ascension from KGB chief to party leader had cast a pall of gloom over the city. The media blamed America for most of the world's ills, and few Soviets felt it was safe to strike up an acquaintance with an American correspondent.

Gradually a handful of young Soviets began to introduce me to their friends, and the small circle of "refuseniks" I'd known at first gave way to a group more representative of Soviet society. Over the course of nearly four years in the Soviet Union, I was able to meet a variety of young people. Their generation was comprised of the children of soldiers who had proudly defended their motherland from the invading Nazis, and the grandchildren of revolutionaries who had passionately helped build Lenin's dream. This younger generation became alienated during the Brezhnev years. Most ignored the steady drumbeat of pro-Soviet propaganda.

Mikhail Gorbachev is out to change all that. Gorbachev has introduced a whole new vocabulary to Soviet life. People now relish the chance to form opposition groups, to meet openly, to print their own small alternative newspapers and become players in the political process.

Among Soviet youth, the reaction to Gorbachev is often determined by age. Those who were in their teens when he came to power are hopeful. But their older brothers and sisters—members of the generation that came of age under Brezhnev—remain largely indifferent. Their skepticism is already so ingrained that they can hardly be induced to dream Gorbachev's dream.

As the government has moved toward *perestroika*, one of Gorbachev's gravest challenges is to overcome this skepticism. A 1989 poll conducted by a Moldavian newspaper among youth from age seventeen to twenty found that 89 percent of the respondents believed their country would still be poor and underdeveloped in twenty years. Ninety-three percent said economic reform was needed, but they were not prepared to make sacrifices at work. The poll reinforced what many educators say about Soviet young people: they may have an idea of what should be done to improve their society, but they would rather not get their hands dirty to do it.

A 1987 poll conducted by the Communist party's youth newspaper *Komsomolskaya pravda* offered even more evidence of the profound skepticism among young people. The respondents, from 157 cities and towns all over the Soviet Union, were under twenty-eight years of age. Asked what they thought about communism, one-third said they did not believe in it. A twenty-nine-year-old railroad worker from the Ukraine said, ''I think communism is a bluff, a fairy tale. It is easy to sit in Moscow and discuss communism. But take a poll in a line of people waiting at a store. Ask what's more important for people—communism or butter and sausage. That's your answer.''

Like the railroad worker, most young people are focused on the pursuit of *kife*, a slang word that has slipped into the vocabularies of Soviets all over the country. *Kife* means catching a buzz, or having it all. When a Soviet has achieved *kife*, he's got it made.

Kife is the centerpiece of many Soviet jokes, but one well-known tale is particularly apt in its illustration of the word. In the joke, three young men are locked in conversation, trying to define *kife*. One of them says, ''*Kife* is when you wake up in the morning with a terrible hangover. You go to the kitchen, open the refrigerator, and find a cold beer there waiting for you. That is *kife*.''

The second man says, ''*Kife* is when you come home and find two hundred rubles on the kitchen table and a note from your wife that says, 'Gone on a business trip. See you in two weeks.' That is *kife*.''

The third man says, ''*Kife* is when you hear a knock on the door in the middle of the night, you open it and a KGB agent says, 'Is this apartment 23?' And you have the pleasure of saying, 'No, this is apartment 25.' Now that, my friends, is *kife*!''

Like the three young men in the joke, this book tries to define *kife*.

As I sat around kitchen tables, drinking tea, listening to young friends talk and sharing their dreams, I searched for the answers to my questions: what do they want in life, and how do they go about getting it? I found their aspirations were not unlike my own, yet their social system made the pursuit of these goals radically different.

Now Gorbachev wants to recast his people into a more Western mold. He wants them to be self-starters rather than social dependents and he asks them to believe in their system rather than cynically dodge it. Can the society transform itself? Like any Western correspondent, I can only observe its progress. But it's certain that Soviet youth will play a key role in their nation's future. What they become, the nation will also become.

CHAPTER 1   EDUCATION AND INDOCTRINATION

 THE FOREIGNER first submitted her request for permission to visit a Moscow school during the dark, cold days of January 1986. It seemed like a small enough request, but one would think she'd asked to visit some top secret military facility in the frozen steppes of Siberia. As she followed up with calls and letters throughout the winter and spring, hoping that some Soviet bureaucrat would find it in his heart to make the necessary pen stroke and grant his approval, the Soviet Ministries of Foreign Affairs and Education demanded to know what questions the visitor from abroad, a journalist, intended to ask, what she wanted to see, and what her goal was in visiting a Soviet school.

The journalist's purpose seemed so obvious that she wondered whether the authorities were trying to wear her down, hoping she'd give up. Over and over she explained: "I simply want to see a Soviet school and talk with the students and teachers." She didn't even care if the school turned out to be one of downtown Moscow's showcase schools reserved for visiting foreigners.

After trying for five months, the foreigner knew that if she didn't get inside a Soviet school soon, classes would adjourn for the summer and she wouldn't have another chance until fall. Finally, on Monday of the last week of classes, one of the Foreign Ministry press officers designated to "facilitate" her work—he was referred to with irony by the press corps as a "handler"—called to say that the visit had been approved. The journalist was to be allowed to visit two kindergartens and two schools, one a regular school and the other a *spetzshkola*, a special school for students learning English.

The visit to the special school, Number 36, started out badly. The director, an elderly man who undoubtedly had terrified thousands of students over the years, refused to allow an accompanying photographer to take photos of the school because he was not officially accredited by the Soviet Foreign Ministry. Although Kolya, the photographer, had been working with foreigners in Moscow since his marriage to a British woman three years earlier, his semiofficial status was not enough for the school director. So while the visitor toured the school, he sat forlornly on the front steps, his cameras and lenses tucked away in his bag.

The building's neatly painted corridors were decorated with the words of V. I. Lenin. "You can become a Communist only when you enrich your mind with the knowledge of all the treasures created by mankind," said one sign. The visitor was taken to the Lenin Room, which, she later learned, all Soviet schools are required to have. The room was adorned with a gilded bust of Lenin and posters charting his childhood and youth, his revolutionary activities, and his work as founder of the Communist party.

Outside the Lenin Room, little girls in brown dresses, black pinafores, and the red scarf of the Young Pioneers (a children's Communist party organization) skipped rope and laughed. But inside the classrooms, the students seemed tense and constrained. Under the watchful eyes of the director and their teachers, they gave unswervingly loyal responses to all of the visiting journalist's questions. When a class of seventeen year olds in the tenth grade, or "form," as it is known in the Soviet system, was asked if they wanted to fight in the war in Afghanistan, the boys all replied that they were eager "to fulfill their internationalist duty."

Then, asked what they did after school in their free time, a blond-haired, blue-eyed boy answered mechanically, "We study the teachings of Lenin and take part in activities to help build communism." Nothing about hanging around with friends, listening to rock music, or even studying something other than Lenin's works.

The other encounters with students were depressingly similar. One would not have expected any of them to call for the overthrow of Mikhail Gorbachev or the Communist state, but it seemed that they had gone far beyond obeisance. No matter how hard she tried, she wasn't able to connect with any of the teenagers in that school, and so the journalist left, thinking that her visit had only confirmed an earlier notion: that many Soviets carefully craft for themselves an officially approved public personality for use in formal occasions. The students must have found theirs especially handy in the face of a foreign correspondent.

Outside, where Kolya was waiting, the journalist was surprised to learn that a girl had slipped the photographer a note on a small scrap of paper and asked that he pass it along to the visiting Westerner. It simply said, "The Bolshoi, 8 P.M." She wondered briefly if the note had been written by a student who wanted to exchange rubles for dollars, or even if it was a KGB plot to entrap a foreigner in some sort of embarrassing scheme—such thoughts can come unbidden into one's mind while living in the Soviet Union. But she decided that she would go to the Bolshoi that night. After all, the meeting was sure to be more interesting than the closely monitored conversations that had taken place in the school.

Later, she stood next to a fountain in front of the towering pastel-pink walls of the theater, feeling a little foolish, not even knowing whom she was supposed to be meeting. Suddenly, a slender, smiling girl with long dark hair bounded up. She was one of the students who had kept silent and looked on sympathetically from the back of the classroom as the correspondent had attempted to dredge up some human emotions among the students.

The girl said her name was Tanya and that she was ashamed of the way the visitor had been treated in her school. The two spent a couple of hours together that evening, strolling along the streets of downtown Moscow and enjoying the warm weather that comes to the capital for only a couple of months a year. Tanya was not looking to change rubles or buy Western clothing; nor was she a KGB plant. She was a Soviet girl who, despite seventeen years in a system that discouraged individual expression, had disregarded the inherent dangers and made contact. For Tanya, curiosity about the world beyond the Soviet borders and a strong desire to make friends had outweighed any risks of being seen with an American correspondent.

Her honesty, her ingenuousness, and her willingness to criticize her government's policies were a surprise. In the first meeting, she explained how the students in her class had been prepared for the visit—how they had been coached on what to say and threatened with punishment if they deviated. There was to be no spontaneity, they had been warned; everything was carefully planned, and they were to follow the script. Just to make doubly sure that the visit came off as planned, one hooligan was ordered to stay away from classes that day, for fear that he would speak up and embarrass the school.

In contrast to her classmate's rote answer on Afghanistan, Tanya later described how her mother, a surgeon, had arranged for a physician friend to write a document stating that Tanya's older brother had an illness which would prevent him from serving his two years in the Soviet army. "Ask any Soviet guy and he'll tell you he thinks the war in Afghanistan is filthy and he doesn't want to go there," Tanya said.

At the time, Tanya's bravery and daring in seeking out a Western correspondent was unusual. When she unobtrusively slipped her tiny, handwritten note into the photographer's hand it was mid-1986, and for a girl who aspired to a rewarding career as a translator or teacher, seeking out a Westerner, especially a reporter, was risky. The more tolerant policies of Mikhail Gorbachev had yet to sweep the nation; *glasnost* (openness) and *perestroika* (restructuring) were not yet household words, and Soviet society had only just begun to open itself to Gorbachev's "democratization." Soviet propaganda remained blisteringly negative about capitalism and all things American, and the line between simple friendship with a foreigner and dangerous contact with a capitalist enemy was frighteningly thin.

Many Soviets regarded the world beyond their borders with suspicion and mistrust. Officially, there were two worlds: the foreign one and *nash*, Russian for "ours." *Nash* was supposed to be unquestionably superior; schoolchildren were taught that it would lead to a socialist paradise on earth and the eventual triumph of communism over Western governments.

Tanya's parents and grandparents were inclined to go along and get along. These older generations had always found plenty of cause to be patriotic; they had helped build their country during the Russian Revolution and had fought off the invading German army in World War II. Many had lived through the forced collectivization of Stalin. Each of these eras had brought starvation, violence, prison camps, death. In comparison, the 1970s and 1980s were the good times.

But the youth of today's Soviet Union are neither impressed nor satisfied with that view of the world. Tanya's generation has not known war or deprivation on the scale of Stalin's political purges. It has had no hand in building Soviet society and has no patience for the vague promise that someday it will be a paradise. Tanya and her friends are less inclined toward obedience. They want their reward now. For most young Soviets, the goal is to achieve what they call *kife*—a Russian word that, roughly translated, means having it all, grooviness, or catching a buzz.

For some, *kife* means fashionable clothing, a comfortable apartment, a dependable car, and a videotape collection. It means having enough of everything, whether it be food, alcohol, or marijuana. For others, it means singing in a rock band with instruments good enough to produce world-class music. Unlike previous generations, who were forced to make a choice between life in their own country or abroad, today's Soviet youth want to travel to the West—and then come home again. In short, they want everything their Western counterparts have and they want it now, not in some far-off Soviet utopia that party organizers only preach about while living in a style that far exceeds the meager hopes of ordinary Soviet workers.

Since their state jobs pay pitifully low salaries and their stores offer little of what they want to buy, many young Soviets set about acquiring amenities through connections and the black market. Actually, they are following a time-honored Soviet tradition: if the system fails you, work around it. They move through the system, taking advantage of what it has to offer and ducking its penalties, yet not playing an active role in it as they move through their teen years and into young adulthood.

That is not enough for Gorbachev, who dreams of a superpower respected and influential because of its economic might, not just feared for its arsenal of nuclear missiles. Gorbachev wants the Soviet Union to compete on a world stage with Japan, West Germany, and the United States. To push his nation into the twenty-first century, he needs the participation of all of its citizens, particularly the young people of Tanya's generation, who will one day be its leaders. His goal of building a better country will be realized only if indifference can be replaced with a commitment to hard work and innovation. Instead of dropouts, Gorbachev and his allies need people who are actively involved in transforming Soviet society.

He is encouraging a generation of young Soviets, like Tanya, to boldly take the initiative. Tanya was an ideal candidate for the task of helping to rebuild Soviet society. There was no cynical wish on her part to induce the journalist to buy her some Western shoes; Tanya was not jaded enough to have become a black marketeer. She was bright, creative, and curious. Despite years of conditioning designed to make her a creature of the collective, she was at times assertive and independent.

Yet she possessed all of the traits one would expect her to have acquired in seventeen years in a collective society. Tanya often displayed the pessimism and fatalism that some Westerners find so maddening among their Soviet friends. Having grown accustomed to complying with a centralized government, at times she would instinctively become docile in the face of authority. Why, when she had the courage to violate the norm by contacting a Western correspondent, did she put up with the artificially imposed rules so much of the time? The answer was simple: she had never been taught to question the established order, and she had little understanding of individual rights.

This type of meekness may undermine Gorbachev's plan of restructuring. Generations of Soviets have learned that obedience in the face of authority reaps richer rewards than risk taking. Most people view the state as the principal provider of life's necessities. As one Soviet economist put it, seventy years of socialism has produced a nation of social dependents. To change that, the government will have to reverse years of conditioning. In creating a new mind-set, the Soviets will need to overcome two national character traits: cynicism and passivity. The skepticism that is so widespread will be difficult to neutralize; no one knows better than the Soviets that their country's system is inept. Gorbachev has to convince his compatriots that their bumbling economy can be made to work, if only they will grab hold of it and shake some life into it.

Even more important, the rewards must be there for them to earn.

Young people must be made to feel confident enough in the future that they will commit themselves to reform. An authoritarian government that lurches forward toward reform and then suddenly backs away will not encourage many young people to sign on. Teenagers and young adults in the Soviet Union need to be convinced that what they build cannot suddenly be taken away from them at their government's whim. They must also become confident that the state's cumbersome bureaucracy will not block their attempts to be innovative. Young people in the Soviet Union are anxious for change; it is now up to their government to step out of the way and allow it.

The second trait, passivity, will be equally hard to counteract. After years of reinforcing a collective conscience and squelching individuality, some young people are reluctant to strike out on their own. Instead of doing their best to prove that they are number one, Soviet children have always been told that they should excel for the good of society. Altruism is not such a bad trait, and some would argue that Western society could use a few more unselfish people. But emphasizing such characteristics has failed to encourage the Soviets to think of themselves as active players; they haven't been told that they can change things. This submission to authority takes over in most Soviets almost as their mothers carry them home from the hospital.

CONFORMITY AND THE *KOLLEKTIV*

As soon as a baby is born, cultural influences begin the process of transforming him into a docile Soviet citizen. Instead of the loose-fitting, comfortable clothing worn by American newborns, the Soviet child is diapered and wrapped in white sheets like a little mummy. Called a *pelyonka*, the wrapping keeps his arms pressed close to his sides and his legs held firmly in place. This is the way many Soviet children, especially those in rural areas, spend the first year of their lives.

Younger couples avoid swaddling these days, especially if they can find Western playsuits for their children. But the practice remains common. Soon after her baby girl was born, one young Russian woman proudly invited her friends over, one by one, to see the baby and drink tea. Her mother was there looking after the newborn. As they gazed down at her in the crib, the baby started to cry and thrust her tiny hands outside her swaddling clothes. "Cover her hands—she'll catch cold," the older woman cried out. The *pelyonka* was necessary to safeguard the child's health against a drafty apartment and the cold Moscow climate. But the mummylike wrapping acted almost as a straitjacket.

Mothers are also careful about the way they hold their babies. In the Soviet Union, people believe that bouncing a child on one's lap and allowing him to look around will permanently injure his backbone. Instead, mothers are taught to keep their young babies either flat on their backs or suspended in the air by grasping them under their arms. Soviets are often shocked when they see foreigners handling a baby. One young Soviet woman reacted with alarm as she watched a British correspondent she was visiting dandle his six-month-old baby on his knee. Nothing could convince her that allowing the child to sit up and gaze around was good for him just because it helped him learn about the world.

Another young Soviet woman was horrified to see that an American mother had accidentally allowed her baby to fall off a bed. She looked on in disbelief as the baby happily played on the carpeted floor. Soviet children, she explained, are never left to move around so freely that they might fall from a bed or play on the floor. They spend most of their time in their mothers' arms or neatly swaddled in bed.

The practice of wrapping a baby in a *pelyonka* and holding him in a passive position are the first steps toward preparing a Soviet for a passive life. Even before he can walk, it is easy to distinguish a Soviet from a Western child. The Soviet's muscles are less developed and his movements uncoordinated—the result of having spent many months with his legs and arms tightly bound. The Western child moves more independently and already is exploring his world.

As soon as he is old enough to walk outside, the Soviet child is taken to the neighborhood park, usually by his grandmother. While the children of foreigners are allowed to yell, run, and splash in mud puddles, Soviet toddlers are strictly supervised. Instead of being allowed to act like children do in the West, they are expected to behave like forty year olds.

One young Soviet recalled an episode that illustrates the society's tendency to control even the very young children. When she was five years old, a group of children in her neighborhood found a large rubber ball and began bouncing it against the wall of an apartment building. "We were screaming and racing around and having a marvelous time. But the grown-ups appeared and made us be quiet," she said sadly, remembering the scene. The adults grabbed the ball and cut it in half with a kitchen knife, putting an end to the children's game and leaving them in tears.

"They couldn't allow us to do something wild and uncontrolled," she remembered. "It seemed to us that every game was forbidden. We wanted to shout, fight, scream, run in every direction—everything normal for children. But we were forbidden to do these things, and we felt that we could be punished at any moment."

Although most parents begin teaching their children the Soviet life-style before sending them off to school, it is the task of the educational system to see that people learn to live comfortably in their society and become loyal to the regime. Most government-run schools in the West claim to be ideologically neutral (and at this they succeed in only varying degrees). The Soviet school system is an instrument of indoctrination, and unabashedly so. It shapes the national consciousness to fit the official ideology.

One of the most important goals of the educational system is the teaching of collectivism. Students learn that a collectivist works to improve society, not to further his or her own well-being. They are taught that an individualist selfishly seeks personal benefit, not the good of the whole. Children are not praised for being different from their classmates; rather, they are told that it is impolite to show off what they know. Anyone who does attempt to stand out is asked, "Are you better than the others?"

Games also emphasize the group rather than the individual. Children are taught to help fellow students who are slow learners. Most competition is organized between groups, and the winners are told to use their victory to teach the other children how to succeed, not to bring glory to themselves.

Children get their first taste of the *kollektiv* when they enter kindergarten at the age of three or younger. In kindergarten, collective behavior is imposed through strict discipline, which is justified by the fact that there is usually only one teacher, or "upbringer," for twenty-five small children. All children are required to play the same games, follow the same schedule, and behave the same way.

They take a nap for one and one-half hours every day. During this time, it is *Nyelzya!* (Forbidden!) to get up, even to go to the bathroom. One youngster of twelve once recalled that his strongest memory of kindergarten was of having been forced to lie on his right side, facing the wall, during his daily nap, which seemed to last an excruciatingly long time. His kindergarten teacher would stand over the class to make sure nobody moved.

The food in most kindergartens consists of kasha, served lukewarm at best. Some children find this rough buckwheat cereal distasteful, but they are required to eat every bit of their meals. Afterward they must swallow a spoonful of cod-liver oil.

The concept of uniformity dominates almost all of their lessons. During a visit to one kindergarten by a Western reporter, a teacher proudly looked on as her students filed past and handed the visitor the presents they had made in art class. All of these little creations of construction paper and glue were exactly the same: yellow and orange tulips with green stems and the Russian words *Miru—Mir*, "Peace to the World," printed on them. The only deviation was a drawing with crayon on a piece of wood of a papa bear admonishing a baby bear. On the back the little artist had written, "To Grandma on her birthday, from Sasha." The child had been forced to give up his carefully made present to impress the foreign guest. In kindergarten, there are no specific political lessons. However, teachers do try to lay the foundation for a communist worldview by telling stories about "Grandfather Lenin" and his childhood and by telling their little charges how fortunate they are to live in the greatest country on earth.

The skepticism that greets these lessons surfaces in a joke passed around by Soviet people. In the joke, a kindergarten teacher tells her students that in the Soviet Union, all children are happy, with the best toys and games, sweet candy, and red apples. Everything, the teacher says, is best in the Soviet Union. But one little girl bursts into tears. "Mashinka," the teacher asks, "what's wrong?" The little girl whimpers, "I don't want to live here—I want to go live in the Soviet Union." The joke is a caustic commentary on the propaganda that portrays the Soviet Union as a utopia.

The first day of school begins with the military-style *linyeika*, or "line." The class stands at attention for roll call—all except for the *dezhurnii* (duty officer), who positions himself two steps ahead of the rest and announces the day of the week, the month, and how many pupils are in the line. It is the first line of many that the Soviet child will join during his lifetime, and it represents the departure from home and the private and entry into a public, official existence. When he stands at attention in the *linyeika* a Soviet no longer belongs to himself. He is now part of the collective.

From the first day of school, a child becomes a member of various collectives. A group of up to ten students forms the basic collective, which is called a *zveno*, or "link." The class forms a larger collective, called an *otryad*, or "detachment," and the whole school is an even larger collective, called a *druzhina*, or brigade.

A collective that operates effectively will motivate its members to put pressure on one another to do the right thing. But a collective does not form spontaneously; it takes time and requires the work of a skilled and sensitive teacher. The first step in forming a collective is taken when the teacher makes demands on students and orders the more conscientious ones to counsel those who are discipline problems. Soviet students are made to feel responsible for one another much more than American students are. A young woman who had been a good student and received marks of 5, the Soviet equivalent of an A grade, in most of her courses recalled how she had resented having to look after one of her classmates. Because he didn't do his homework, she had been sent to his apartment to help him in the evenings. She often found the student's father sitting drunk in front of the television set and her classmate absent. Later, when he did poorly on a test, she was accosted by her teacher. "Why doesn't Seryozha know anything?" her teacher asked. "It's your fault."

In one visit by a group of Westerners to a Moscow school, a class in the tenth form was asked what they did when classmates refused to study. A boy wearing a Lenin pin and a blue-and-white button that read *Nyet Voinye*, "No to War," explained that when children refused to learn their lessons, other students would tutor them after school until their study habits improved. Were the volunteers rewarded? "No—it's not necessary," he said. "We know that to help is the duty of every person."

Soviet children are supposed to live by the slogan, "The collective is always right." Anyone who steps out of line is told by the teacher, "Be like the rest. Don't stand out." Children recognize that an attempt to step outside the *kollektiv* might result in punishment. A young Russian woman from Moscow recalled that at age fifteen, she met a girl in one of her classes and the two became fast friends. They were inseparable during lunch, in the brief periods between classes, and before and after school. Eventually, their relationship drew the attention of their teacher, who organized a meeting and denounced the two in front of the class. "You don't respect the *kollektiv*. You should learn to spend time with everyone and have equal friendships with all," the teacher said angrily. "Why can't you be with the rest of us? We are just dirt for you." It was a bitter lesson that taught her to moderate her friendships and not focus her attention on only one person.

But the *kollektiv* is not always so harsh and punitive. Lisa Guroff, whose father, Greg Guroff, was a diplomat at the American Embassy in Moscow from 1982 to 1985, attended a Soviet school, where she was part of the *kollektiv*. Lisa recalled the approach her class took with one boy, a heavy smoker who earned low grades and had been caught stealing from other students. The teachers voted to expel him, but the director of the school called a meeting and asked the boy's classmates what should be done. His mother pleaded that he be allowed to finish school. Although the class fiercely denounced her and judged her to blame for the short-comings of her son, they elected to let him stay on—a collective decision made with a democratic show of hands. The boy remained in the class and, with the help of the *kollektiv*, his marks improved. Their decision was a lesson in benevolence that taught Lisa's class that they were re-sponsible for bringing their comrade into line.

Naturally, the *kollektiv* is not airtight. Like so much in the Soviet system, it is weakened by disorganization. Overworked teachers are some-times too tired to enforce the *kollektiv* philosophy or discipline their students.

Kathy Guroff, Lisa's mother, said she was appalled by the confusion and disorganization in the special English school where her two children studied. "Children stand at attention when the teacher enters the room and stand at their desks to recite when called upon. After that, chaos breaks out," Kathy said.

Her children's teachers often came down with severe colds and flus every winter and stayed home for weeks to recuperate. Even though absenteeism was high, there was no safety net of substitute teachers. Kathy said her daughter once went without biology class for six weeks because the teacher was ill. "The children in the class skipped school and went to the movies or roamed the halls, and no one did anything to stop them," she said.

One tradition in the Soviet school system that prevents children from expressing their individuality and reinforces the *kollektiv* is a process known as "leveling." In the era of the American superbaby, with parents pushing their children to overachieve, Soviet parents encourage their youngsters to bury their talents, lest they miss out on some of their childhood. In addition, according to a 1987 article in the newspaper *Sovietskaya kultura* (Soviet culture), teachers are annoyed by "know-it-alls" because they are more demanding as students. "Gifted children soon learn to hide their talents under a bushel basket to avoid conflict with classmates, teachers, and uncomprehending parents. Their lives improve, they feel comfortable, but society suffers a loss," said the article.

While the Soviet Union has its stars in many fields—its prima ballerinas and its brilliant scientists—the "leveling" process has kept millions from pushing themselves to excel. Gifted students have been held back by the absence of what are known in the West as advanced placement classes. In the Soviet Union, all children are considered to have the same potential. Only the most severely retarded are sent to schools for the handicapped; the rest remain in the general education system, where they attend classes with both average and talented children. A 1986 article in *Uchitelskaya gazeta*, a Soviet newspaper for teachers, estimated that in a class of thirty-five students, up to nine are handicapped because of alcoholic parents, birth defects, or congenital diseases. The newspaper also said that the brighter students resent the slower ones, who have trouble competing and are often humiliated by their teachers. Yet they are all forced to study together.

The most pervasive teacher of mediocrity is the overuse of memorization and rote learning. Independent thinking is not often encouraged. Beginning in the first grade, Soviet children learn that their teachers and textbooks hold the answers; questioning these established authority figures is not tolerated. Under Gorbachev's reforms, students are being allowed to dispute some previously held truisms, but this shift has not found its way into the educational system all over the country.

In many schools, the teachers and their prescribed lessons control millions of children. An article about the tyranny of the school system was published in 1985 by *Literaturnaya gazeta*, the nation's leading literary newspaper. Headlined "Letter from an angry mama," the story was written by a Moscow woman whose son had been assigned to write a composition about autumn. When she asked her son how he planned to begin, he replied, "But they already told us everything we should write." Then he proceeded to recite the composition: "The golden autumn has come. The leaves on the trees have turned yellow. It is rainy. It has gotten colder. People and animals are preparing for the winter." It was the same composition children in second-year classes all over the country had been ordered to write.

When the boy's mother pointed out that the leaves on the trees had not turned yellow, that the weather was not rainy in Moscow, and that no one was preparing for winter, the child became confused and troubled. His mother encouraged him to be more original. The boy's teacher objected, however, and gave him a mark of 3 (the equivalent of a C in the American system). After only a year and a half in school, this little boy was unable to think for himself. His confidence in the uniqueness of his own personality and opinions had been thoroughly shaken by the rote memorization forced on him in class. While such rigid control in schools has loosened since the 1985 article, tens of millions of young Soviets have grown up under similar conditions.

Children adapt quickly, but in the process they lose their individuality. The mother who wrote to *Literaturnaya gazeta* said of her son: "Imagination, fantasy, his own impulses—these real treasures of a child's psyche—are stored away in boxes at home. They are taken out only in the evening, before the child goes to sleep, after he has finished his lessons. He has become like a little office worker, suppressing everything that makes him different from others."

One 1986 segment of the popular television program for youth, "The Twelfth Floor," stated the problem bluntly: Soviet schools teach children to be boring. Students who appeared on the show, which is an approximation of a Phil Donahue program for young people, said flatly that the word *school* in the Soviet Union is synonymous with *boredom*. Said one young man, "The school has turned into a mechanism that stands over us and rules." Another asked school officials, "Who do you want to bring up—robots or real people?" One girl grumbled that "very little ever happens in school." The most common complaint on the show was that children were allowed only to memorize, never to question. It made their teachers' lives easier, but it also left the students alienated and dissatisfied instead of fully engaged.

Pressure to make all students alike is reinforced by the grading system. Each school is required to report its students' grades to a district educational committee, which compares them to those of other schools. It reflects badly on teachers if their students' grades are consistently lower. Because of this, most teachers dole out nothing lower than a 3. This obsession with the percentage of students receiving high grades has come to be known as "percentomania."

The problem has been discussed even at the pinnacle of Soviet power. In his keynote speech to the Communist party plenum on education in 1988, Yegor Ligachev, then the Kremlin's number two man (he was later demoted to overseeing agriculture), mentioned an engineering institute in northern Russia in which no student received a grade lower than 3. Meanwhile, 70 percent of the student body could not pass the math exam.

Grade inflation is also fueled by cheating on tests, which some people say is rampant in Soviet schools. What makes matters worse is that teachers tacitly condone cheating among their students. Lisa Guroff said she often watched as children brazenly copied from their schoolmates and used cheat sheets, which in Russia are known as *shpargalki*. "Almost everyone cheated and depended on other people for the answers," she said. "It seemed the Russian way of doing things—you learned to stand in line and you learned to cheat on tests."

In Lisa's classes, the teachers not only overlooked the cheating, sometimes they even gave students the correct answers themselves. Said Lisa, "One of my teachers stood at the back of the room next to the coffee urn where the worst students sat and told them all the answers on tests. She wanted them to get good grades—after all, she had her quotas, too."

"Percentomania" is demoralizing for teachers because they must give their students good marks just for appearances sake. Teachers who report the best marks are officially declared to be the most proficient—although often they are the most immoral. But the system is especially harmful to the students. When their teachers falsify grades and overlook cheating, students learn that they will receive high marks no matter what their performance, and it gives them little incentive to work. They lose faith in their teachers and schools, and many become cynical about society's values.

Until school reform was introduced under Gorbachev, children learned to repeat things they knew to be devoid of meaning. The schools taught Soviet children to recite slogans, such as "Communism is the Bright Future of All Mankind" and "The Party—Wisdom, Honor and Conscience of Our Epoch." Few paid much attention to what these slogans meant, but they recited them because they were what their teachers and school director wanted to hear. A young teenager once said, "My generation is worse than my parents' generation. It seems like my parents really believed. But I've never met one person my age who sincerely believes. We say what the teachers want, and later laugh about it among ourselves."

For many young Soviets, learning to be hypocritical became an important part of their education. Some were turned into play actors at the behest of the adults around them. The school authorities did not insist that each child sincerely believe the Communist party position; nevertheless, they required students to at least appear to believe. Students who learned to suppress their thoughts and parrot the official line knew that there was dishonesty all around them. It was not surprising that they turned skeptical. This cynicism was not a quality the Soviet school system set out to breed, yet it was often present.

During the years under Gorbachev, there has been a growing awareness that the emphasis on the *kollektiv* has certainly not created a society of forthright people ready to voice their own opinions. Neither are they independent thinkers. Education experts, teachers, and even Gorbachev himself have called for school reform to steer children away from the hypocrisy and formalism of the past. Students are being encouraged to ask more questions, voice their opinions, and discuss the shortcomings of Soviet society.

But millions of young Soviets now in their twenties and early thirties grew up under the old system. For years they were witness to, and active players in, displays of hypocrisy. Now, when they are being called on to take part in a system that in the past was riddled with lies, many young adults are too cynical and are choosing to remain on the sidelines. Gorbachev and his allies are discovering how difficult it is to build trust in a society whose foundation was once deception and insincerity.

The Soviet leadership has recognized that the educational system, in its zeal to build the *kollektiv*, has discouraged free thinking. In February 1988, Gorbachev presided over a Communist party Central Committee plenum, a gathering of the most powerful people in the Soviet Union, that focused on education. It was the first plenum on education in thirty years. Gorbachev spoke of the need for a change in Soviet education, calling it central to his program of economic and social reform. "We pin our hopes for the future largely on the work of the school—which is only natural—with its own restructuring, its own teaching talents and the creativity of the Soviet teacher," he said.

Yegor Ligachev called for the "democratization" of the school system by creating local, regional, and national councils of parents, students, teachers, and business managers to monitor their neighborhood schools.

The councils were supposed to mirror America's system of local school boards. Ligachev said that the quality of teaching should be improved and that teachers should be given the right to choose their methods of instruction. It was a radical departure from the existing system, which laid a blueprint for every teacher to follow throughout the school year. He also announced that young people would be given more freedom in choosing their career paths, rather than being shunted into vocational schools to fill the nation's need for more factory workers and engineers.

Many reform-minded educators found Ligachev's speech disappointing because it did not go far enough in addressing the Soviet school system's problems. Children were still to be brought up with socialist values. His critics said he focused on improving the indoctrination of children in party policy, with better classes in history and military training. It was only a first step toward making a change, for it was clear at the plenum that communist ideology would remain the core of Soviet education—and a central tenet of communist doctrine is the *kollektiv*.

The plenum was a sign that the leadership was toying with the realization that restructuring can take place only if people are pushed into more independent thinking in the workplace. But before adults can be made to change their behavior, Gorbachev and other reformers must reach into the schools and teach new attitudes to the nation's children. So far, crusaders for change in education make up only a minority, and teaching the *kollektiv* predominates.

THE *KARAKTERISTIKA*

In American schools, every high school student finishes with a grade point average and a diploma. Although family connections and wealth often have a hand in determining where students go to college, grades and entrance exam scores play a major role in college placement. These are a measure of intellectual acumen, not moral character or loyalty to the state.

The Soviet Union uses a different system of deciding who will go to the best schools. Known as the *karakteristika*, it is an official document that attests to a student's character. It is written in longhand by his or her teachers and signed and stamped by the school director and leader of the local chapter of the Komsomol, the party's youth organization. The document is a subjective analysis of the student's personality—his or her loyalty, patriotism, and ability to work within the *kollektiv*.

At many institutes and universities in the country, applicants must first present their *karakteristika*. A negative evaluation prevents them from being admitted to the most prestigious schools, even if they have been diligent students and received high marks. Because higher education leads to the most desirable careers, a *karakteristika* that contains something unflattering can block a student from following his or her chosen path. Under Gorbachev's school reform, the *karakteristika* has been discredited and attacked in the Soviet press. One teacher at School Number 79 in Moscow, a special school for students who wanted to specialize in foreign languages, told a visiting Western correspondent that the *karakteristika* now is no longer used. She told the Westerner that Soviet students are not required to present a *karakteristika* when they apply to enter an institute or university. Later, in the hallway when the students in the class won a few private moments with the correspondent, they laughed about their teacher's words. One boy named Oleg, who said his father was a diplomat, added, "A positive *karakteristika* is still necessary to get into a good school. Our teacher didn't want to admit it, but the system still exists."

The fate of one young man named Volodya, who grew up in a village outside of Moscow, illustrates the power of the *karakteristika*. Volodya received a negative *karakteristika* because of his refusal to go to a summer camp. Like teenagers all over the country, Volodya was dispatched to spend thirty days in a camp. Some young people look forward to their time at camp because it allows them to escape the watchful eyes of their parents and teachers; they can get away with things that are off limits at home, such as drinking, smoking, and sexual experimentation.

But Volodya deeply resented being assigned to a camp. He tried to obtain a medical deferral so that he could be excused, but the ploy did not succeed. Work there was supposedly "voluntary," but when punishment was threatened, he decided to put in his one-month term.

It is not difficult to understand why he disliked his time in the camp. Students were required to work for nine hours a day, picking weeds, preparing land for spring planting, and performing other menial work. What Volodya found most objectionable was that their work was unpaid. Conditions were primitive; they lived in rough cabins furnished with bunk beds and no showers or indoor toilets. After a long day of physical labor under the hot sun, the most they could do was sponge themselves off with cold tap water. They washed their clothes in a nearby stream or pond.

Volodya decided to leave and return home. "The first time I ran away, I was ten kilometers down the highway when the director drove up in his Zhiguli car and took me back," Volodya recalled with a nostalgic smile. "But the next day, I escaped again, and I never returned." His nonconformist behavior did not go unnoticed. Upon graduating, school officials wrote in his *karakteristika* that he had been rude, uncooperative, and argumentative. They also wrote that he was greedy and cared more about money than working for the motherland. Even worse, it said he did not respect the *kollektiv*. Volodya's school director predicted that the boy's career was ruined and advised him never to aspire to anything higher than a farm worker. Sure enough, Volodya ended up driving a cab in Moscow.

MISHA AND ZHENYA

Many young Soviets manage to break away from the *kollektiv* in countless little ways. Like much that it sets out to do, the state is not very efficient in socializing its young people. When called on, they appear to be loyal citizens; in reality, they are cooking their own soup. Despite social restraints and the political and economic pressure to conform, they rebel against the narrow definition of propriety.

Misha and Zhenya, both from Moscow, are two examples of young Soviets who managed to slip through the cracks of the collective consciousness. They were a couple of social misfits; the two placed as much distance as possible between themselves and the state, short of actually leaving it. In doing so, they walked a fine line. Although they had run-ins with the authorities, they had never been charged with anything more serious than hooliganism, the equivalent of petty juvenile delinquency in the United States.

The pair first showed up on a railroad platform in Sochi, a resort town on the Black Sea. It was the summer of 1985, only a few months after Gorbachev came to power. The sun was sweltering and the platform was jammed. With their punk hairstyles and Western T-shirts, Misha and Zhenya could have fit in easily in Greenwich Village or Times Square, but in Sochi they drew stares.

These two knew their way around. They drifted over to an elderly woman and began to haggle with her over the price of a room in her house. Such deals were illegal, but the authorities tolerated them because of the housing shortages in the towns along the Black Sea coast. Before long, they had found a cheap place to stay for two weeks.

Misha and Zhenya easily managed to pick their way around the system. Both in their early twenties, they were graduates of a Moscow vocational-technical school. They shared a two-room apartment with Misha's father, sister, and two-year-old nephew; the flat was not far from the Exhibition of Economic Achievements, a sort of proletarian Disneyland.

Misha was lanky and favored stark black clothing decorated with metal studs. Badly in need of dental care, he would cover his mouth with his hand whenever he smiled or laughed. Misha did not have a job, but he had persuaded a friend to sign a work document declaring that he washed dishes at a restaurant. Under this arrangement, Misha was not listed as unemployed, which might have gotten him arrested, yet he did not have to work. He was free to spend his time on his artwork; beyond that, he made money in the black market. Almost every day, Misha and Zhenya went to an area around the Kosmos Hotel in Moscow, where they asked foreign tourists to sell their Western clothing and audiocassettes. They would resell these goods to Soviets at much higher prices.

Zhenya, a short, stocky young man with an impish grin and a small silver cross dangling from his left earlobe, had already been in trouble with the authorities. Caught changing rubles for dollars, he had spent two weeks in a labor camp near Moscow on a charge of hooliganism. After he was released, Zhenya had taken an official job as a delivery boy for the business where his mother worked. The job paid only seventy rubles a month (about $115), but it did not require much concentration and his bosses allowed him to sleep or read much of the time. Most important, Zhenya said with relief, *Ya legalnii*—"I'm legal."

Although the two listened to Soviet rock groups like Akvarium or Zvukii mu, they much preferred the music of Western bands like Talking Heads. They spoke with sarcasm and distaste for everything Soviet, making fun of the ruling politburo and laughing derisively at party slogans and displays of patriotism on Soviet holidays. The two performed imitations of the poignant moment in 1984 when, as millions watched on Soviet television, the aging and sickly Konstantin Chernenko, the newly appointed Communist party general secretary, stood in Red Square and was unable to hold up his arm in a salute at the funeral of his predecessor, Yuri Andropov.

Outwardly, it seemed that these two young men were in for long, hopeless lives of hating a system they considered impossible to change. But instead, each had devised a long-range plan to find a way out. With his black-market earnings, Zhenya managed to buy a television and Western videocassette player and spent all of his time recording and selling black-market videotapes. It was a profitable business and one just dangerous enough so that he could not add the risk of hanging around foreigners. He dropped out of sight. But it is possible that Zhenya has turned himself into a young entrepreneur, under the new laws that allow Soviets to set up cooperative businesses.

Misha kept himself busy meeting with foreigners, hoping to find a Western woman who would marry him and help him out of the country. He didn't care if the marriage was fictitious or real—he was prepared to pay his way out. After finally marrying a West German woman, he managed to emigrate to Berlin. A short time later, he wrote an American friend a poignant letter:

Everything here is terribly interesting to me. . . . For the first time, I saw a demonstration that was organized by the people themselves. The press writes about every imaginable theme. People dress as they want, do as they want, say what they want. At first I felt as if I'd traveled to another planet, but now I'm beginning to get used to it. The opportunities are so great that it's even difficult to decide what I want to do. I'm studying German and not working. I don't have much money but I'm able to live. The only thing I really long for is my friends "back there." I'd like to help them leave, but so far, I don't know how.

Despite all their years of conditioning in Soviet schools, Misha and Zhenya had defied the system. Both regularly broke laws and lived as they pleased. They had quit the collective and relied on each other. Individualistic, alienated, and indifferent, the two had taken on attitudes and behavior that were considered more than just objectionable—they were deviant.

Their iconoclastic life-style challenges the stereotype of the Soviet Union widely held by Westerners: that Russia is one huge maximum-security prison, with KGB agents watching their captive citizens' every move. They imagine that each law in the Soviet Union is unfailingly enforced and that the slightest infraction draws a long sentence in a Siberian labor camp.

Clearly, that is an exaggerated, nightmarish version of Soviet life. But perhaps equally unrealistic is the new stereotype that many Westerners are forming with the advent of Gorbachev's reign. Because he uses words like *democratization*, many Americans believe that the Soviet Union is on its way to being transformed into a free-wheeling democracy in the Western mold. In reality, life there for most young people remains somewhere between the harsh repression of the past and the reformed society some optimistically envision for the future. There are abundant signs that Gorbachev cannot create a Jeffersonian state; nor does he have any desire to do so.

Instead, the Soviet leadership is seeking to modernize a ramshackle economy encrusted with years of ideology and sloth. Under this plan, the Mishas and Zhenyas in the Soviet Union will go to work; they will become players in the society rather than outsiders. The pent-up energy Zhenya used to found his illegal video parlor will be channeled into a profitable cooperative, fully legal under *perestroika*. It is Gorbachev's dream that millions of young people will find much in the reformed Soviet Union to excite them—more consumer goods, a captivating press, films, and discos. If his plan is carried out, young people will build a better society, but it will be one in the Soviet, not Western, tradition.

In the meantime, many young people like Misha and Zhenya are still defying the *kollektiv*. They look on *glasnost* and *perestroika* with some interest and even hope, but they decline to fully take part. This widespread reluctance to join in was dramatized in a 1988 opinion poll. While three-fourths of those surveyed said they believed more openness was needed, only 30 percent expressed any willingness to take an active role in the process.

Most Soviets live as they have always lived, by carving out a small world of friends and acquaintances and sheltering themselves against the harsh realities of shortages and long food lines. Learning this method of survival is part of growing up in the Soviet Union. While they may not leave the country as Misha did, countless young Soviets choose the path of passive resistance.

ONE SCHOOL FOR FORTY-FIVE MILLION STUDENTS

Although a primary purpose of the Soviet school system is to indoctrinate young people in the ways of the collective and the political rhythms of socialism, the schools also must educate their pupils. And when it comes to imparting knowledge, teaching scientific fact, and training youth in the basic skills, Soviet schools are wonderfully efficient. Teachers there have good reason to be proud. Before the Russian Revolution, 75 percent of the populace was illiterate. Today's literacy rate is better than 99 percent. At least 164 million of the nation's 280 million people have a high school or college education. Meanwhile, American schools are graduating young people who can neither read nor write.

Math and science are the Soviet system's strong points. Especially since the 1950s, after the Soviet Union launched its first Sputnik spaceship, the Soviets' heavy emphasis on math and science has prompted Americans to fear that in some respects their schools are substandard to Soviet ones. Many educators agree that the mathematics curriculum in the Soviet Union puts that in the United States to shame.

School is free of charge to everyone. The right to a free education is guaranteed in the Soviet constitution; even students at specialized schools and the toniest of universities pay no tuition. Soviet youth are shocked to hear that some American parents will end up paying twenty thousand dollars a year or more for their children to attend Yale, Harvard, or other elite schools. They are proud of their no-cost school system. The right to a free education is unlikely to change under Gorbachev. Like free health care and low-cost housing, the Soviet educational system is one of the center-pieces of socialism.

But Soviet schools have their drawbacks. Most of what goes on in them is still held in the grip of centralized control. As the 45 million students in the 130,000 general schools across the country move through the academic year, most students from eastern Siberia to urban Moscow, learn the same state-approved lessons from the same textbooks on the same day and even at the same hour. With one of the world's largest educational systems in the world, the Soviet Union has for years carefully orchestrated its schools at the Ministry of Education, which was renamed the State Committee for Public Education in 1988.

This rigid centralization has been relaxed under Gorbachev's school reform, as previously taboo themes, such as the crimes of Stalin, come under discussion and teachers are given more leeway in handling issues like religion or sex with candor. Fresh breezes of tolerance are wafting through the corridors of some Soviet schools, and they are being driven by *perestroika*. Under Gorbachev, Soviet schools have been charged with changing students from obedient sheep into energetic self-starters. To help children cope with the demands of a changing society, many teachers are trying to cut down on memorization in school, and instead spur more independent thinking.

But like many aspects of life in the Soviet Union, the nation's school system is in a period of transition. Skeptics are not confident that change in the vast Soviet school system will come rapidly. They say that the schools cannot lead the way toward reform; they can only reflect society, rather than shape it. Some of the harshest criticism comes from *Uchitelskaya gazeta*, the national teacher's newspaper, which blames the State Committee for Public Education for holding back reform. Parents fault the school system's five million teachers, who are trained by the Academy of Pedagogical Sciences. For years, teachers have been one of the most conservative elements of Soviet society, standing over their classes like drill sergeants, barking out orders and demanding quick obedience. Many of these teachers don't have the will to change, or they think the old methods are just fine. Until the reforms proceed further, old habits tend to remain.

Students go to classes four to six hours a day, six days a week in many areas of the country, which means that they spend more time per week in the classroom than their American counterparts. They attend school for ten months out of the year for eleven years, not twelve as in the United States. About 35 percent of their schoolwork is in science, 40 percent in the humanities, and the remainder in athletics and vocational training.

A few special schools have begun allowing students in the upper classes to choose electives and plan their own class schedules. Those who want to become translators or linguists can drop advanced science and math classes. But most pupils are stuck with the standardized curriculum mandated by the State Committee for Public Education. Students begin with five years of arithmetic, then move on to algebra and geometry, followed by calculus in the ninth and tenth grades. With few exceptions, students must take one year of mechanical drawing and astronomy, five years of physics, six years of biology, and four years of chemistry.

But many Soviet young people complain that they are forced to deal with too many subjects and are not allowed to concentrate on the ones they enjoy. During their last year of school, many Soviets study Russian language and literature, algebra, geometry, physics, astronomy, history, geography, biology, sports, technical drawing, and a foreign language. To keep up with their course work, they have to do four or five hours of homework every day; instead, many end up with only a superficial knowledge of each subject.

Soviet schools can be ranked into four categories, according to quality. At the pinnacle are the special schools, the *spetzshkoli*, which are reserved for the brightest students and the children of parents with connections. At the second level are the general schools, where students can get a broad education that leads them to either a white-collar or a blue-collar job; these make up the bulk of the nation's schools. Below them are the vocational-technical schools, known as "PTUs," for the less gifted. Their students usually go straight into factories or manual labor jobs after graduation. Also occupying the bottom rung are the schools in small villages, which attempt to follow the general school curriculum but are hindered by a shortage of teachers. In these rural schools, children from three or more grade levels often crowd into one room with the teacher, who may or may not have a higher education.

The quality of education in rural schools is reduced even further by the shortened school year. For millions of Soviet students, the ten-month academic year is reduced to seven and a half months because they spend every fall harvesting crops. Some young Soviets claim that their strongest memories of school involve the hours they spent stooped over, picking potatoes, sugar beets, or carrots in nearby fields. They speak with bitterness about being forced to do the work. Paid nothing for their efforts, they knew that if they had refused, they would have received a negative mark on their *karakteristika*.

Teachers say that such "lessons" are intended to teach children proper work habits. What is clear, however, is that the Soviet economy remains dependent on child labor. In 1986, one Soviet newspaper estimated that more than 30 percent of the tomatoes in Astrakhan, a southern region near the Caspian Sea, had been harvested by unpaid students.

Volodya was one young man with bitter memories of having to work the fields. Every year, he said, he would arrive on the first day of school in a new shirt and new shoes. "Our director started with a lecture about how important it was to study well. Then he told us our motherland needed us. He said digging potatoes in the field was our first patriotic duty and told us to show up the next day in work clothes," he said.

Volodya said students would arrive at 7:00 A.M. and cram themselves into a small bus to be taken to the fields. Children as young as seven were put to work. Each was shown a long row and told he would not be allowed to stop working until he had picked all of the potatoes in that row. His teacher poked around in the muddy fields with a long stick and scolded the children whenever she discovered a potato they had missed.

The work continued even in rainy, cold weather. Students brought their own lunches, but there were no tables and no places to wash the mud from their hands before they ate. There also were no toilets, showers, or fresh drinking water.

Millions of parents have resented sending their children off to toil in the fields, but for many years, no one spoke out publicly against it. In the more tolerant atmosphere of *glasnost*, however, parents and teachers have begun to voice their objections. In 1988, the newspaper *Trud*, or "Labor," published a surprisingly frank report by the state prosecutor's office, saying that exploitation of children in the fields had killed hundreds and crippled thousands every year. It said that children as young as ten were brought to collective farms, where they put in as many as twelve hours of work every day. *Trud* told about a fourth-grade boy who had fallen asleep inside a bunker and was buried alive by grain, and about how one hundred others had suffered dysentery when forced to clean potatoes in a filthy barn.

After the *Trud* article appeared, new child labor laws were introduced. But in some areas, unless the children and teens were mobilized, the crops rotted in the fields and farm managers were blamed for the losses. Because of economic pressure, the child labor laws were widely ignored. The popular television show "Up to 16 and Older" carried an investigative segment in 1988 on child labor practices in the central Asian republic of Uzbekistan, where the nation's cotton crop is grown. Pesticides and herbicides are widely used there, making field work particularly dangerous for children.

In the TV report, a group of teenagers stood on the edge of a cotton field and told a reporter that when their parents had complained that their children were being sent into the fields, the students were threatened with expulsion from school. The director of the school was fired as a result of their complaints. Despite the firing, the television reporter said he had found that in two regions, children and teenagers continued to harvest the crops, even on Saturdays and holidays.

THE SAINTED MEMORY OF LENIN

While American school lessons have always carried heavy doses of political indoctrination opposing communism, Soviet instruction has been even more overtly propagandistic. The goal of the Soviet school is to teach the communist worldview and bring up loyal Communists. As Lenin once said, ''The purpose of training, educating, and teaching youth today should be to imbue them with Communist ethics.''

In the first grade, children are given the red plastic Lenin pin they will wear until they pass into the upper grades. The small, five-pointed star carries a picture of Lenin, supposedly as a baby, with flowing blond locks and a cherubic, even Christlike, expression. Every child is required to wear one, and anyone who goes to class without his Lenin pin is sent home, and his parents are summoned to school.

The students' first political lessons are about Lenin, who is presented as a kindly grandfather. He is portrayed as simple, kind, modest, and devoted to the good of the people. Children memorize such phrases as, ''Lenin created the Communist party. The party continues the work of Lenin. It leads our people to a bright and happy life.''

Children are indoctrinated so thoroughly that Lenin becomes a godlike figure. Even the slightest hint of disrespect toward him is seen as blasphemy. Once, when a young woman from a provincial city was visiting a family in Moscow, she was shocked to see another woman using a small metal bust of Lenin as a weight to exercise her arm. ''I just can't stand to see you treat Lenin this way,'' she wailed, pleading with the woman to stop.

Lack of respect for Lenin could have been at least partly to blame for one Western correspondent's problems with the Soviet authorities. Peter Millar, who went to Moscow in 1983 as a correspondent for the British news service Reuters, made comical use of a hollow metal bust of Lenin. He drilled holes in the eyes and placed a red light bulb inside the small sculpture, giving Lenin a demonic glare that Peter and his Western friends found hilarious. The authorities were not so amused. Peter was denounced in the press and for two years was refused permission to reenter the Soviet Union. Many of the other correspondents thought Peter's Lenin bust had contributed to his problems. Soviet officials take their demigod seriously and do not appreciate foreigners who poke fun at him. For some Soviets, there is still resonance in the slogan, "Lenin lives."

There are also plenty of jokes told at his expense, however, especially among the school children who are forced to memorize his pronouncements on every subject. One anecdote was inspired by an ideological tract entitled *Mother*, which was written by the revolutionary author Maxim Gorky. Schoolchildren are repeatedly taught that Lenin himself had pronounced the novel "very necessary and very current." In the joke, Lenin is sitting on the toilet when the doorbell rings. His wife, Nadezhda Krupskaya, calls out, "Who's there?" The reply: "It's Gorky. I've written a novel, called *Mother*." And Lenin replies from the bathroom, "Great, hand it over. It's very necessary and very current."

POLITICAL EDUCATION

By the time students reach the end of their third year of studies, they should have accepted the policies of the party and feel pride in their *rodina*, the Russian word for motherland. Early indoctrination is designed to make them receptive to the official line they will hear throughout their adult lives. Almost every course involves at least some ideological instruction. For instance, during art classes, films of artists selling their works on the sidewalks of Western cities are used to point out the drawbacks of capitalism. In biology, lessons about evolution are used in the battle against religion. In foreign language classes, students read the speeches of Communist leaders, such as Cuba's Fidel Castro.

The benevolence of the Soviet system is brought up in language lessons. An eight-year-old boy in one Moscow school stood to recite during his English class. "Every citizen in the Soviet Union has a right to education," he said. His teacher asked, "And how do you understand this, Sasha?" And the boy replied earnestly, "We can all study and study for free." The teacher praised his answer and added that Soviet people begin studying at the age of six and can go on, free of charge, to a vocational school or university.

The propaganda is often so artfully disguised that children don't notice it. One young Soviet woman called such classes "propaganda through fun." She described a special school pageant celebrating the Soviet Union's fifteen republics. During lessons that lasted several weeks, every class was assigned to learn a song in the language of another republic, study its dances and native costumes, and create a program for the whole school. The director concluded the celebration with a long, flowery speech about the nation's one hundred ethnic groups unified under communism. It was propaganda skillfully blended with the fun of dressing up for a masquerade party.

Political education classes for generations of young Soviet children once presented a simplistic worldview. Before reforms under Gorbachev, the schools made no attempt to show the diversity of the world; countries were all either communist or non-Communist, and the latter were portrayed as threats to the Soviet Union. A young woman named Masha said that one of her earliest memories of school was hearing her teacher reassure the class that they could sleep quietly at night because Soviet border guards were defending them from invaders and spies. "It made me believe that everyone beyond the Soviet borders was an enemy," she said. Under the school reform, lessons for young children are not so openly hostile toward foreigners, but many Soviets in their twenties and thirties recall the lessons in mistrust they were once taught.

Toys for young children served to reinforce this feeling of paranoia. One such toy was a cardboard pop-up book entitled *Our defenders*, with brightly colored cutouts of tanks, ships, airplanes, missiles, and KGB border guards. The book was designed for children from six to nine years old, but it dwelt on mature themes—the perceived threat from foreign countries and the goal of making the motherland's borders inviolable. Its illustrations were accompanied by a cheerful verse:

> Our peaceful country is well defended,
> With automatic rifles, with machine guns,
> The brave fighters—our glorious infantry
> Our brothers and fathers.
> Our vigilant intelligence services—
> Here today, there tomorrow!

The Soviet victory in World War II has long been used in school lessons to shape this paranoia. Known as the Great Patriotic War, this tragic period is given much more attention in the Soviet Union than in the West, because Soviet losses in the conflict were far greater. Even children in the lower grades learn about individual battles from special maps on which they are required to diagram troop movements and losses.

One young Soviet said she still could remember many of the heroic war tales, even ten years after graduation. She recited the legend of the young girl Zoya Kosmodimyanskaya, who had fought with the Soviet army to help liberate a western portion of the Soviet Union that had come under German control. Zoya was captured by the Nazi army, raped repeatedly, and forced to walk naked in the bitter cold to the town square, where she was hanged. Before her death, Zoya turned to the townspeople who had assembled to watch and bravely shouted at them to defy the Nazis and free their nation from German control.

The schools' emphasis on such stories of heroism is understandable; twenty million Soviet people were killed in the war and the nation's economy was devastated. But the Soviet authorities go beyond patriotism and use the war to instill a siege mentality. Every town in the Soviet Union has a war monument, and children as young as five years old are taken there by their teachers to learn the lessons of war. They visit veterans, set up exhibits of "combat glory" in their schools, and tend the graves of soldiers killed in the war. Today more than forty years after the war's end, monuments are still being built and veterans are being awarded new medals for their bravery. The war is over, but the Soviet people keep reliving it.

Of all of the political indoctrination lessons that Soviet children undergo, the "peace" lesson most closely mirrors the leadership's fluctuating attitude toward the West. It is taught in every school on September 1, the first day of school, when the teachers, students, and parents gather in school courtyards all over the country for ceremonies and speeches. As with the first day of school anywhere, there are mothers dabbing at their eyes and children sobbing because they don't want to be separated from Mama. Most of the little girls wear stiff white bows in their hair and many children carry flowers for their teachers. It is a touching scene—until the school director begins the official program.

In 1983, U.S.–Soviet relations reached a low point. U.S.–built Pershing II and Cruise missiles would soon be deployed in western Europe. The Soviets were smarting from the insults of President Reagan, who had derided their country as "the evil empire" and predicted it would end up "in the dust bin of history." As the opening day ceremonies unfolded in the schoolyards, the world began to come to grips with the horrible knowledge that the Soviet Union had shot down a South Korean airliner, killing all 269 passengers on board. The tragedy sent U.S.–Soviet relations into another downward spiral.

America was enemy number one that year, so the peace lesson was tailored to fit that ideological bias. In the playground of one school in a Moscow suburb, violent posters were passed out to children depicting the American eagle, its claws dripping blood, screaming for nuclear war. Children as young as seven held up posters showing blacks and Hispanics being smashed under the heels of their capitalist oppressors. Some older students staged a short skit about the Soviet Union's quest for peace.

The hate-filled peace lesson was disturbing and offensive. But it was a typical example of the overkill that was used in Soviet propaganda of the past. It was most effective when directed toward people who are young and impressionable. Since 1983, U.S.–Soviet relations have improved and the annual peace lessons have been altered to reflect Kremlin policy. But many generations of Soviet schoolchildren have grown up on similarly negative lessons about the United States.

THE "BLANK SPOTS" IN SOVIET HISTORY

In 1987, the Communist youth league's newspaper, *Komsomolskaya pravda*, printed a letter from a Soviet schoolboy with the headline, ''I want to know everything.'' The boy said in his letter:

> One of my concerns is to hear or read the truth, without distortion. The changes taking place in our country now do not mean that the past was all bad and we must forget about it, cross it all out. Let my parents, my teachers and my older comrades talk to me as an equal. I will understand them on one important condition—they must speak honestly with me. And then young people who are 17 and younger will walk confidently and build a new life here.

The boy's letter must have sent a chill through the ranks of teachers and school directors as well as the party leadership. If in fact the party was sincere in its talk of *perestroika*, it had to meet the demands of young people like the author of the letter. After all, how could students read critical articles about Stalin in their newspapers and then be handed a wholly different version of events in their schoolbooks?

While *glasnost* was taking place all around them, children were learning history from books that were evasive about some eras and downright dishonest about others. Textbooks focused on Soviet successes—the victory in World War II and the launching of Sputnik—but shed little light on the darker moments of Soviet history. A tenth-grade textbook, for example, made no mention of the suffering under Stalin; nor did it touch on the Moscow purge trials of the late 1930s. The book referred to the old dictator only twice, as representative of the Soviet Union at the Tehran and Yalta conferences. Nikita Khrushchev was not mentioned at all.

Periods of Soviet history that escaped the spotlight of *glasnost* were given the name "blank spots." Gorbachev began calling for these blank spots to be filled, and his supporters took up the crusade.

As the Soviet Union became more accessible to the West and relations with capitalist nations improved, the leadership realized that textbooks also had to be altered to reflect the changes that were taking place in the media. Soviet schoolbooks, in their sections on life in the West, had always painted a dismal picture of poverty, racial discrimination, and crime. "Typical traits of American society, which is founded on social inequality, are violence and terror," one book said. On the assassination of John F. Kennedy, another text read: "'International opinion viewed this 'crime of the century' as the deed of ultrarightists linked to the CIA and carrying out the will of the oil magnates of Texas.''

This particular book was removed from the shelves of Soviet schools in 1987, after the authorities decided that the official version of history had to be rewritten. It was a step taken several times before, whenever the Soviet leadership determined that history books no longer reflected the Kremlin's view of history. During Stalin's rule, he was depicted as a hero who had guided the Soviet Union through a period of massive industrialization and as a brilliant tactician who had led the country to victory in World War II. After Khrushchev denounced him at the 1956 party congress, these glowing passages of praise for Stalin were excised; some texts carried only a mention or two of him. Later, after Khrushchev was ousted, his name was also expunged from the official record of events. The successes of Leonid Brezhnev loomed large—until Gorbachev came to power and declared Brezhnev's eighteen years of rule to have been a "period of stagnation."

Under Gorbachev, teams of writers set about revising the texts to make them correspond with the new ideology under *glasnost*. The approved list of topics acceptable for inclusion was expanded. As the work progressed, the press promised that the new books would include chapters on the power struggles that preceded the 1917 revolution, the repression of the Stalin era, and Khrushchev's fall from grace. The names of Nikolay Bukharin, Leon Trotsky, and other old Bolsheviks were to be mentioned. There was sure to be disparaging reference made to Brezhnev's rule. Lenin's New Economic Policy, with which the Gorbachev reforms were positively compared, would be praised. Once the new textbooks were written, each teacher was to be offered two or three versions from which to choose.

In the meantime, Soviet schoolchildren began to learn history and current events from newspaper clippings enlivened by the candor of *glasnost*. Once-banned classics of twentieth-century Russian literature, such as Mikhail Bulgakov's *Master and Margarita*, found their way into classrooms. Teachers found themselves free to talk about epochs of history they had long avoided. For the first time, lessons were not clearly defined by the State Committee for Public Education.

At the end of the 1987–88 school year, written history exams, which had been a staple for so many generations of students were canceled. The reason was simple: students across the country could not be tested on history when no official version existed. History was in the process of being rewritten. It had been revised to suit Stalin, then Khrushchev, and later Brezhnev; now, under Gorbachev, it was being rewritten again. Many people hoped that this time, the textbooks would take a more candid approach that actually corresponded with the truth.

During a visit by reporters to school number 29 in downtown Moscow, one shy seventeen-year-old girl, dressed in the navy blue school uniform worn by girls in the senior grades, put it simply: "They've canceled our history exams because of *glasnost*. History is changing." Her girlfriend echoed her remarks. "Now we feel we have a voice," she said triumphantly. "We can say what we feel and understand." Another student said he had been able to learn only bits of information about Leon Trotsky, such as the fact that his real name was Bronstein. But, the boy added, "We were never told what role he played in the revolution and why he fell into disfavor. Now, we hope we'll be able to talk about these things."

In place of the exams, teachers and students had "conversations" which went ungraded. Instead of the forty-six-question exam that had been given the year before, students discussed twelve questions of current events based on selected newspaper clippings. Portions of a book by Gorbachev were required reading. Students were asked to analyze how *perestroika* differed from Lenin's New Economic Policy, which had given Soviet entrepreneurs a measure of independence that was quickly taken from them after Stalin assumed power.

The textbook revision project continued throughout 1988. On September 1, with millions of Soviet students returning to school, the new books still were not ready. Until the full-scale revision was completed, the State Committee for Public Education could only issue supplements as a stopgap measure. In the supplement for ninth graders, the "blank spots" in the period after the Russian Revolution were filled in. Even more important, the slim text urged students to "know the facts" and added, "You're welcome to argue." Young people were permitted to disagree with their teachers and textbooks, without receiving lower grades. It was a major departure from the past, when the authority of the Soviet textbooks went unquestioned and students learned mainly by rote.

But many students remained cynical about the extent of the government's candor in its revised version of history. In a brief conversation with three schoolboys in the courtyard outside of school number 29, one boy wearing a red leather tie asked if the new textbooks would really touch on all aspects of Soviet history. Would they, he wanted to know, present an honest account of the ouster of former Moscow Party Chief Boris Yeltsin, who was silenced in 1987 for his attacks on bureaucrats who stood in the way of reform? The Soviet press, he pointed out, had not been totally frank about the internal struggle that led up to Yeltsin's firing. "We're still listening to the 'Voice of America' for some of our information," he said sarcastically. "Why should we be convinced that our new schoolbooks will tell us everything?"

PATHS IN LIFE

One possible path selected for Soviet students by their elders is the PTU —the polytechnical school, or vocational school. For generations, the Soviet educational system has been strongly vocational. Unlike Western students, Soviets do not have the luxury of attending school merely to broaden their minds or to satisfy their curiosity about the world; only one-fifth of all high school grads go on to a higher education. The rest go to work. Many begin their careers at the tender age of fifteen, when they decide whether to attend a general school or a PTU.

The reasons for this emphasis on vocational training are both ideological and practical. One of the most important responsibilities of the Soviet educational system is to raise children to be "builders of communism." Vocational training plays a major role in teaching this concept, because, as Marx and Engels said, communism can exist only in a fully industrialized society.

On the practical side, the nationwide shortage of skilled laborers has forced the schools to produce more workers. In 1984, the labor shortage reached such a crisis that the leadership introduced a school reform to steer students away from general education and into the vocational schools. This was spearheaded by Konstantin Chernenko, then number two at the Kremlin and later Gorbachev's predecessor as general secretary. Under Chernenko's reform, openings in the general schools dropped. The number of students in vocational schools was then supposed to double, with the goal of requiring up to 70 percent of the nation's school population to train in vocational skills. Chernenko's reforms were widely unpopular; many parents resisted having their children forced into the less prestigious vocational schools.

During the 1988 Central Committee plenum on education, the goals espoused by Chernenko were soundly rejected. One reason, it was said, was that the Chernenko proposal "was conceived before April 1985," meaning the beginning of Gorbachev's rule. Instead, it was announced, children would be allowed to finish a course of general studies and then decide whether to try for entry into an institute or attend a vocational college. Computers and other high-tech fields would be emphasized. Although the plenum put an end to the Chernenko reform, it did not address the problem of most students' eagerness to attend either an institute or a university, leading to a white-collar job.

Most students enter a PTU after they have completed eight grades in a general school. Choosing to go to a PTU forces entry into the working class and a low-prestige job. Even if they are workers themselves, many parents try to keep their children out of the PTUs, in the hope that their offspring will achieve a higher rank in society than they did. But many children opt for a PTU because the monthly stipend of thirty rubles provides at least the semblance of economic independence from their parents.

PTU graduates often find themselves poorly prepared to do the work for which they supposedly have been trained. One young Soviet entered a radio electronics PTU, where he studied four days a week. He devoted much of his time to ideology classes, military-style drills, and physical exercises on a nearby football field. Every Friday and Saturday, he worked in a radio assembly plant. But instead of being put on the assembly line, where he would have been given on-the-job training, he unloaded bricks from trucks or did other menial work unrelated to the skills he was supposed to be learning.

After one year at the PTU, he was given a certificate and taken to the factory where he was assigned to work. But the boss there realized that the young man and his classmates knew nothing about assembling radios, so he immediately put them to work hauling bricks up and down stairs. Eventually the students were trained to build radios, but it was a skill they learned on the job, not in the PTU, where they had wasted countless hours of their time.

Instead of helping the Soviet economy, PTUs cut into the nation's productivity by keeping students in unproductive classes when they could be working. If Gorbachev's plan of economic restructuring is to succeed, vocational schools should be geared to the requirements of tomorrow's industry. Specialized colleges must be set up in large cities to train qualified workers in sophisticated skills. The PTUs should be made into training grounds for young workers, not stopping-off points where students gather their monthly stipends and delay their entry into the work force.

★ Special schools are what is known in the West as the fast track; they are reserved for the children of the privileged elite. When a child enters a special school, he has taken his first step toward joining the upper class of professionals and party officials. His parents make sure that he takes this first step early in life, by using their connections, known in Russian as *blat*, to get him placed in a specialized kindergarten.

Most of these special schools are showcases whose facilities far outshine those for the less privileged. One specialized kindergarten, located in a quiet section of downtown Moscow not far from Mayakovski Square, was more modern and attractive than the other fading, rundown buildings in the neighborhood. It was encircled by well-designed playground equipment; in front there was a small circular driveway, painted with lines to look like a city street, where the children learned how to practice crossing in imaginary traffic.

The kindergarten had the feeling of a well-ordered, hushed sanctuary. It boasted the finest facilities. There was a shallow swimming pool, specially built for small swimmers, with tiled walls decorated with cheerful designs of ducks and flowers. Each classroom was well furnished, its walls covered with drawings and paintings as well as the ubiquitous portrait of Lenin. Staff members, all dressed in clean white smocks, spoke calmly. No one seemed frazzled from having too many little charges to account for and no one lost his patience. Many of the children wore Jordache and other Western designer-brand clothing and shoes. To attend such a kindergarten, they were most likely the sons and daughters of ministerial officials or others with a great deal of *blat*.

Most of these children would probably go on to one of Moscow's special schools. These are distributed unevenly around the city; very few are located in working-class sections, and most are in the center, where many of the more privileged people live. When one of Moscow's daily newspapers conducted a survey in 1987 of special schools in the capital, a reporter asked pupils where their parents worked. Answers included:

In the Council of Ministers.
In an institute—both my mommy and daddy.
Father works in a ministry.
Father works in a secret job and Mother is a Ph.D.

The survey discovered that only six out of every hundred first graders had parents who were blue-collar workers. Nearly 20 percent of the children's parents were managers or ranking officials in ministries.

Teachers in these special schools say they would prefer that more truly gifted children were allowed to enter, whatever their parents' rank. A woman who taught at one of these schools called the children of privileged people "phone callers," because their enrollment came about through a call to the right person. She said such children were often more difficult to teach because they never let anyone forget that their parents had influence. At the end of the school day, the teacher said she would watch from the window as her students left in black Volga sedans driven by chauffeurs from their fathers' enterprises.

Students in special schools are more sophisticated than their counterparts in the PTUs or general schools, and they are often contemptuous of the rest of Soviet society. Tanya, the young woman who had arranged the clandestine meeting with the Western journalist outside the Bolshoi Theatre, later introduced the journalist to some of the boys in her class. When no longer under the watchful eyes of their teacher and director, they dropped their deferential talk of world peace and internationalist duty and spoke freely about their true concerns.

For most of these boys, the primary goal was *kife*. They were interested in careers that would give them access to foreign goods or, even better, to travel abroad. Each dreamed of becoming a minister or director, or even the foreign trade representative in a factory—a job that would allow travel. The prospect of becoming a lowly worker, or even a doctor, didn't interest them.

Once they had shed their standard school uniforms, they were far better dressed than the average child. They wanted imported clothing, records, and tapes, which they traded and sometimes stole from each other. The boys had their own private language, much of it based on English words: *spikat* was "speak," *stripovoy* was "striped," *voch* was "watch," *leibl* was "label," and *fazer* was "father." Their style was reminiscent of the London street toughs in Stanley Kubrick's movie *Clockwork Orange*, who used bastardized Russian words like *horror show*, which is actually *khorosho* (good). Like Kubrick's characters, the students from the special school had devised a way of communicating that shut others out of their small, privileged world.

✳ A graduate from a special school must go on to an elite institute or university if he is to continue his climb up the social ladder to the intelligentsia. Unless the student is unusually gifted, getting into one of these requires special tutoring and perhaps even a bribe to the school authorities.

The practice of tutoring is much more widespread in the Soviet Union than it is in the West. Instead of saving for years to pay their children's college tuition, Soviet parents count their kopecks to hire special tutors, who charge up to twenty rubles, or thirty-three dollars, an hour. The fees can add up to the equivalent of $250 a month—a huge burden when the average monthly wage is only about $360.

Tutoring gives the children of richer parents a head start in life. There are occasional press campaigns to wipe out private tutoring—it clashes with the official propaganda that attempts to portray the Soviet Union as a classless society—but the practice is tough to eradicate. Tutors rely on the extra work to supplement their incomes, and students turn to them for help in passing exams.

Tutors are often teachers at the institutes or universities that their young clients are trying to enter. Private lessons with these teachers are especially helpful because they cover the material the students will need to pass the entrance exams. Tutors can also smooth the way by putting in a good word for their students with the examination committee or institute director.

HIGHER EDUCATION

The next step toward entry into an institute or university is the entrance exam—a traumatic event for young people because so much rests on it. A high score may earn them a place in a prestigious school, with the promise of a rewarding career. Failure means disappointing their parents, who may have paid a great deal of money in tutors and bribes. More important, failing to get into a university or institute in the Soviet Union can mean that their chosen careers are closed off to them.

On the morning of the exam, the students stand in a line for hours before entering the testing room, where they sit before a commission of professors. After answering a preliminary set of randomly selected questions, they face two additional queries formulated by the professors. It is at this point that students can be eliminated if there is anything questionable about their backgrounds. One professor who sat on an examining commission said he was given a blacklist of students who were to be barred from the school and a white list of pupils who were exceptionally talented or whose parents had offered bribes or worked in ministries. The commission could easily exclude certain students by asking them impossibly difficult questions.

Few schools in the country are more difficult to enter than Moscow State University. Set atop Lenin Hills, the vast university can be seen from every part of the capital. Constructed under Stalin, who wanted to prove that the Soviet Union could compete with the developed world in feats of architecture, the thirty-two-story university building, with its monstrous towers of red and gray granite, proved instead that Soviet architects were resourceful in designing eyesores. Although many Westerners consider the Stalinist skyscrapers grotesque, Soviets look to them as landmarks that set off the different sections of their capital.

It is this university that students all over the country dream of entering—only the best are allowed to apply. Moscow State boasts some of the best equipment and the most talented professors, and its graduates are among the nation's most gifted and loyal students. Competition to enter is so stiff that of the twelve hundred who take entrance exams for the mathematics department each year, one thousand are eliminated after the first test. Uniformed police stand at every entrance, barring anyone without proper identification. Students fortunate enough to attend this school undergo a rigorous schedule of course work. Many structure their own studies and attend classes when they choose, but they can be expelled if their grades are too low.

Standards at other places of higher learning are not nearly so lofty. Professors often consider themselves lucky if their students complete half of their assignments. Students are not often allowed to design their own curriculums, and attendance is required in all classes.

Expulsion from the less prestigious schools is rare, but it is becoming more common. Before Gorbachev came to power and began talk of restructuring the nation's economy, students who managed to enter an institute were practically assured of graduating. Even if a student realized that he had chosen the wrong field, he could spend the next five years comfortably, doing a minimum of work. If he received low grades, his professors did not expel him. When he graduated, he knew little about his specialty, but he was assured of a diploma and job.

In a step designed to prod students out of their lethargy, Gorbachev's reforms reached into institutes and universities around the country. The government newspaper *Izvestia* announced in 1987 that teachers would be allowed to fail students for poor marks or bad behavior and that students who could not pass their annual exams would be expelled. The newspaper also said that students' monthly stipends, previously averaging 50 rubles (about $80), were to be increased by 50 percent for students who received 5's and by 25 percent for students who received 4's. It was a step toward holding young people accountable, rather than just guaranteeing them a five-year free ride with pay.

Another change under Gorbachev was the reform of ideology classes, which focus on the history of the Soviet Communist party, communist theory, political economy, and scientific communism. In the past, these were taught from poorly written textbooks laden with ideological phrases that students were required to recite—like third graders repeating chunks of poetry by Pushkin. Attendance was mandatory; each week, students had to sit through two hours of lectures and a seminar. The seminar was supposed to be a spontaneous discussion, but students would orchestrate these sessions by dividing the material among themselves in advance and deciding who would respond to the professor's questions. Most students disliked the ideology courses and tried to earn passing grades by doing minimal work. If they were caught cutting classes or received low marks, they were lectured by the dean on the importance of a "communist conscience." Those who ignored his advice could be expelled.

In 1987, educators moved to make the classes more engaging. Like high school history exams, ideology classes were now based on clippings from the newspapers about subjects previously considered off limits. College students were eager to fill in the blank spots. Many called for an end to all ideology classes. In 1989, Soviet newspapers received letters from young readers all over the country calling on the government to free students from ideology classes and let them concentrate on their specialties.

But Soviet university students didn't always push their call for democratization as far as Americans might expect. Protests and rallies became more common among students under Gorbachev; students at some campuses demonstrated on behalf of former Moscow party boss Boris Yeltsin after he was removed from the politburo in 1987. But activism on Russian campuses has not reached nearly the same level that Americans saw on their own college campuses in the 1960s.

Before President Reagan's speech to two thousand students and faculty at Moscow State University in 1988, several young Soviets talked to Western journalists about reform in their country under Gorbachev. They praised the general secretary but made it clear that they didn't expect to see, and weren't interested in having a Western-style democracy.

Peter Skorospelov, a twenty-one year old studying American history, said, "Democracy is important in our country, but it won't be achieved through Western methods." One reporter asked if it would be difficult to transform the Soviet Union into a Westernized democracy, and Peter responded that it was not a matter of difficulty, but of necessity. Repeating a notion that was often heard among elite Soviets, he said that a participatory democracy was not necessarily the goal. "Not everyone needs to get involved—just the people who are well informed," he said.

As he stood on the steps outside the main entrance of the vast university building, Peter spoke bitterly of Western misconceptions about the Soviet Union. With a note of disdain in his voice, he said, "Reagan thinks about our people as he does about his own people, but we have different historical traditions and these are difficult for him to understand. We won't be like the West; we have a vast country, with many different people, and lots of them scattered over a great territory.''

Another young man, Mikhail Vasyanin, a student of linguistics and literary criticism at the university, said he was active in Komsomol and was also president of an independent political organization called the Breakthrough Club that was unaffiliated with the party. Mikhail pronounced himself unimpressed by Reagan's talk of human rights and offended by the president's meeting in Moscow with dissidents and refuseniks. ''When the president comes to a host country, he had better do what everyone wants him to do,'' he said resentfully. ''Reagan didn't meet the men who are best in our country—he met the troublemakers, the ones who make our country look bad. I don't feel sorry for them. They are just complainers.''

These students' comments made it clear that while they would like to have a hand in pushing their university, and their nation, toward greater democracy, neither was sold on the idea of sweeping change that most Westerners imagine for the Soviet Union. Like their government, Peter and Mikhail resented unsolicited advice and pressure from the West. If the Soviet Union is to become more democratic, its own people will find the way. With people like these two young students involved in the process, the brakes are sure to be liberally applied.

DESTROYING MYTHS AND LEARNING CYNICISM

When students graduate from their institutes or universities, they are supposed to be fully formed Soviet citizens. As they look at their fellow students on graduation day, they can imagine where each will end up. The bright ones, who have earned high marks and been active in Komsomol, may enjoy prestigious careers. Perhaps they will work in a ministry or even overseas. Others, whose grades were not so high, will have unspectacular jobs. They will be average Soviets—forced to struggle for the most-sought-after things in life, to wait in lines, and to cultivate acquaintances who may help them obtain goods through the black market.

By the time they are ready to graduate, Soviet youth distinguish themselves by the number of myths they believe. It is the task of the Soviet educational system to indoctrinate students in these myths, but most tend to disbelieve at least some of them, depending on their level of sophistication and cynicism. As they pass through childhood, the more worldly stop believing the myth that the Soviet Union is on the verge of achieving true communism. They drop the myth about the purity of the party as well as the myth that the Soviet Union is a worker's paradise. Most stop believing the propaganda that life in the West is unbearably hard. Instead, they yearn to travel abroad—if only long enough to get a glimpse of life there. As they strip away these superficial myths, Soviet youth increasingly take on the appearance of their Western counterparts. They wear jeans and enjoy Western music.

But some of the myths endure, and it is these that make a young person distinctly Soviet. Even the most cosmopolitan among them continue to hold certain traditions they consider inviolable. Lenin is held up by many as a saintlike figure. Many believe that the Soviet Union single-handedly defeated the Germans in World War II. Some think that Russia was transformed into a great nation because of communism. The Soviet educational system has, for the most part, successfully inculcated a minimal faith in these beliefs among many of its young people.

Unlike their Western counterparts, Soviet youngsters have not been taught to think independently or question openly in school. They have learned to memorize their lessons and regurgitate so-called knowledge as their teachers demand to hear it. Above all else, they have been channeled toward the *kollektiv*.

But the schools are far from infallible in their goals. Many young Soviets express cynicism—at times even contempt—for the system. However, instead of trying to change what they believe should be improved, many learn to live outside the system, at least in part. They soften the harshness of everyday life by occasionally buying things in the underground economy and forming small worlds of closely knit friends within the larger world of Soviet society.

Gorbachev demands that they do much more. He understands that if the Soviet Union is to succeed in rebuilding its economy, it must have the full participation of today's youth. But most young people are unlikely to join in—unless they can be convinced that there is something in it for them. So Gorbachev has taken steps to win them over to his side, calling on teachers to make political education classes more interesting and revising textbooks to fill in the blank spots. He must also find a way to engage the nation's young minds in lessons that will make them think rather than simply follow a mechanical routine.

Young people are now encouraged to devise ways to improve their country while staying within the confines of a *kolletiv* that will take years to undo. They are told that the blank spots will be filled in, yet some of society's myths have remained untouched. Many young people point to contradictions in Gorbachev's approach; unless there is more radical change in the system of education and indoctrination, Soviet youth will not be swayed. Many, sticking to what is safe and familiar, will look to others to devise ways of rebuilding their society. Or they may simply decide that it is more interesting to sit back and watch as others play out the scenario of reform.

CHAPTER 2 SEX, COURTSHIP, MARRIAGE

ONE OF the chilling realities of Soviet life is that the government interferes in people's most intimate and private decisions. Directly or indirectly, the state and the socialist economy play a part as each young person falls in love, selects a mate, gets married, finds a home, and starts a family.

When a teenage Soviet boy first begins thinking about girls, he has little access to books or magazines about sex because the state's tough antipornography laws prohibit the publication of even the most tame literature and photographs. When he begins dating, he is faced with the problem of where to take his girlfriend, since long lines form outside most restaurants and there are few discos or other places where young people can gather. Salaries and student scholarships are so low that it may be impossible for him to buy even a glass of wine and a simple meal for two in a cafe. And, in a nation where 20 percent of the population still lives in communal apartments, escaping the watchful eyes of parents is difficult.

An unmarried couple cannot simply go out and rent an apartment together, because the state assigns housing and priority is given to families with children. Most couples find that the only way they can be together is to get married—in a state ceremony at a government office building—and then place their names on a long waiting list for an apartment.

Because birth control products are difficult to buy in the Soviet Union, most new couples quickly become parents and face the additional burden of finding child care. By the time they reach their mid-twenties, most Soviets have already shouldered the drudgery of a low-paying job, hours of waiting in lines to shop, and the daily chore of transporting a child to a day care center. The morass of rules that pervades every aspect of life in the Soviet Union and the hardships caused by an inefficient economy can turn love and marriage into a tiresome struggle.

Gorbachev's vision of rebuilding his nation's economy has had little impact so far on people's intimate lives. If he truly hopes to make a change, new factories will have to be built to manufacture birth control products and dozens of other necessities that make raising children easier, such as disposable diapers and plastic pants. But housing will be his biggest challenge, for the difficulties of finding a suitable apartment puts more of a crimp on sex, courtship, and marriage than any other shortage a young Soviet faces.

THE DATING GAME, SOVIET STYLE

Masha grew up in the faceless tracts of massive prefabricated apartments that ring Moscow in a series of gray suburbs. A tall woman of twenty-five, she had long brown hair and a small wardrobe of fashionable Western dresses scraped together over the years. No spoiled child of the elite, Masha was the daughter of a working couple who lived far from the effete intelligentsia or central party apparatus of the Soviet Union. Once, after a late dinner followed by strong coffee and cognac, she related to a Western journalist friend the tale of her sexual coming of age.

She was sixteen years old when she decided to have her first sexual experience. Most of the other girls in her class had already experienced sex and she was beginning to feel left out. Besides, her boyfriend was pressuring her. She knew little about sex, since she had never read any books about it or discussed the subject with her parents, but her girlfriends had assured her that she wouldn't get pregnant if she had sex on the day following her menstrual period. That day came, and she invited her boyfriend over when she knew her parents would not be home.

When he arrived, she was freshly showered, wearing her best perfume and her nicest dress. Apprehensive, she sat on the tattered old fold-up couch in the living room that her parents used as a bed every night. "I remember my boyfriend was a bit startled, but pleased, just the same," she said. "He seemed to enjoy himself, but I remember how strange it was making love on my parents' bed. I was scared they would come home in the middle of everything." Afterwards, Masha felt let down, but she was glad to have the experience behind her. She continued seeing her boyfriend, and they made love regularly, while her parents were away at work.

A few months later, they were having sex in the apartment her boyfriend shared with his father and mother. It was the middle of the day and they thought no one would come home. Suddenly, the boy's father arrived unexpectedly and burst into the front room, where they were lying together on the couch. "I was so embarrassed, I wanted to die," Masha said. "Both of us were naked. I pulled the blanket over myself, but it was too late. He saw everything.''

The boy's father backed out of the room and went into the kitchen. ''I wanted to leave, but my boyfriend insisted everything would be all right, that we should have some tea and pretend nothing had happened. Can you imagine sitting and drinking tea with someone who's just walked in on you while you're making love?'' But she said the man's face was expressionless—''as if he'd seen us eating soup, not making love.'' Masha's boyfriend told her later that his father had confessed that the same thing had happened to him as a boy, and that after his father punished and taunted him mercilessly, he vowed that if he ever found his own son in the same situation, he would show more understanding.

Masha went on to have many more boyfriends, and her biggest problem in all of these relationships was birth control. The pill was considered dangerous and the IUD and diaphragm were not available, so she used the rhythm method. At the age of nineteen she discovered herself pregnant and had her first abortion in a clinic not far from her home. The operation was free, but painful, because the doctor used no anesthesia. Most unpleasant was the lack of privacy. ''Everyone in my town knew each other and there was a lot of gossip. The doctor didn't try to keep things quiet and all my neighbors knew I'd been pregnant and that I'd had an abortion,'' Masha said.

After that, she resolved to be more careful about birth control. She tried many methods, but the one she said was most effective was to insert a lemon wedge in her vagina before sex. This method was as unreliable as the others, however. In a city where foraging through stores for food is a time-consuming chore, finding lemons was often a problem. Although Soviet condoms were readily available, Masha steadfastly refused to use them because they are known to be especially thick and clumsy. ''I hate them—they're like sleeping in shoes,'' she said, her voice rising. Most of the time, she relied on the rhythm method.

It was not surprising, then, that she discovered she was pregnant a second time at the age of twenty-three. ''I couldn't believe it. I was furious with myself for my bad luck,'' she said. But this time a girlfriend recommended a doctor who agreed to perform an abortion, illegally and secretly, in his office. It cost 100 rubles (about $160), nearly an entire month's salary from her office job.

Masha also learned about male impotency when she was in her twenties. She was attracted to a young artist—a handsome but delicate, almost frail man a few years older than Masha. She became frustrated and annoyed when nothing further developed in their relationship. Then she discovered that her friend Olga was in the same situation—she too was strongly attracted to a man who hardly seemed to notice her. Commiserating with each other, the young women decided one night that the best way to seduce such a man was to wear their finest clothes, jewelry, and French perfume and appear on his doorstep. They each carried out their plan, only to learn that both men were impotent.

"6:30," Masha explained, using a common slang expression and holding both of her fingers pointed downward to demonstrate the man's problem. "I remember coming home and feeling very dejected," said Masha. "About an hour later, Olga showed up at my apartment, also very depressed. The same thing had happened to her—6:30!" Masha said she believed that the problem of male impotency is widespread in the Soviet Union because men face so many problems and pressures at home and at work.

As she grew older, Masha became more demanding of her lovers. She slept with young men who knew nothing about foreplay and she tried to teach them how to make her happy. "I felt good about teaching men a few things—it meant they would be better for some other woman," Masha said. "But I have always been careful about acting too freely." She said many young Soviet couples have oral sex only after they have known each other for a long time. Gravely lowering her voice, she said, "A woman thinks very, very carefully about doing that thing to a man, especially the first time she sleeps with him, because some men think that only prostitutes do that." She also said that few men perform oral sex on women. "When a man does it, it means he is more sophisticated and imaginative. Or perhaps he has had sex with Western women who have taught him to do it," she added wistfully.

Like other young Soviet women, Masha complained that most of the men she knew satisfied themselves quickly and rarely considered her needs. They hardly ever experimented, sticking to the tried-and-true missionary position, known in the Soviet Union as "the working peasant position." "For most people, that's what sex is—five minutes, working peasant position, disco beat—and usually in total darkness!" she said. Eventually, Masha found herself more and more irritated by unskilled, insensitive men, and she became less willing to educate them. During her last experience with a man her age, she found herself growing angry with his roughness. "I thought to myself, *Oh, why not—another pupil.* But I couldn't make myself go through with teaching him. I let him do what he wanted and then I fell asleep," she said.

The only exceptions Masha had found were Jewish men, who were more sensitive and attentive to her needs. This perception is common among young Russians. Many believe that Jews are more emotional, warm, and demonstrative—more attuned to their own and others' feelings. Masha later decided to confine her sex life to an older, married Jewish man—an artist who was the father of a young man she had once dated. He was a pleasant-looking man in his mid-fifties, with a round face, balding head, and dark-rimmed glasses. Although finding time alone with him was sometimes difficult because of his wife and family, Masha obviously enjoyed his company.

This man was not wealthy, but he had a good job and had once offered to rent an apartment for Masha so that she could move from the suburbs into the capital. She had been seeing him steadily for three years and said he had spoiled her for any other man. He showed no signs of leaving his wife for Masha, but that did not bother her. "He doesn't need to get a divorce, because I'm not sure I'd want to marry him. He brightens up my life and I do the same thing for him," she said. Even before the age of thirty, Masha was fed up with the Soviet-style dating game. She was content with her older, married man and said she had no desire to look for a husband.

Many of Masha's experiences are typical among Soviet young people. Almost everyone agrees on the need for informative, up-to-date sex education and sex manuals, but only the government has the authority to provide them. A nationwide prudish mentality often undermines attempts to make Soviet society more sexually aware. Parents who call for better sex education classes in their childrens' schools are often accused of attempting to destroy the morals of Soviet youth. Because of the shortage of information and the government's reluctance to address the subject, most Soviet youth grow up with fewer opportunities to learn about sex than their Western counterparts. Couples have no place to go on dates because the state does not build enough cafes, nightclubs, and discos. Their attempts to steal a few moments alone in their parents' apartments often end in embarrassing scenes, when someone arrives home unexpectedly. Women lack reliable birth control methods because there are not enough factories to manufacture them. Many seek illegal abortions because anesthesia is not generally used in state clinics and because they are afraid that their co-workers and neighbors might find out.

★ Masha was clearly uninhibited in talking about her sexual experiences, but only because she was sharing them with a close friend. Many Soviet youths are more reluctant than Westerners to discuss sex because totally frank discussion in public and in the press is taboo. There has been a trend under Gorbachev toward slightly more open talk, but books and magazine articles that mention the subject continue to be edited, and, once word spreads of their existence, difficult to find. Sexual references in song lyrics remain almost childishly romantic and sentimental. Unlike the graphic sex scenes in American films and frank discussion of sex on American television, Soviet movies and television are mild and full of allusions and euphemisms. Copies of *Playboy* are confiscated from foreigners at customs, and what might be defined in the United States as pornography is strictly outlawed, punishable by a lengthy jail term.

While many American teenagers are not as well informed as they should be about sex and birth control, Soviet teens tend to be especially ignorant, since many have not had sex education in schools. Until recently, such classes were absent from the Soviet school curriculum. As late as 1980, only the more progressive Baltic republic of Estonia offered a class in "personal hygiene."

In 1981, a pilot program of sex education was introduced for fifteen and sixteen year olds in the Moscow area and in 189 schools around the country. The course was supposed to deal with the psychological, moral, and physiological aspects of sex and offered pointers on how to achieve a happy marriage. It was considered experimental at first and was not widely offered. A 1982 article by a Soviet sociologist concerned about the nation's plunging birthrate said, "Almost no serious, scientifically based sex education takes place in our country—in the home or in the school. This means that sex education is left mainly to the street."

In a 1983 speech, even Soviet leader Yuri Andropov acknowledged the urgent need for sex education, although he restricted himself to only a delicate allusion to the subject. Andropov called for "a certain minimum of knowledge in the fields of hygiene and medical care." In response to his call, Soviet school administrators scrambled to find trained teachers willing to discuss the troublesome topic with their students. Sex education finally became mandatory for all Soviet eighth graders. The course, entitled "The Ethics and Psychology of Family Life," is offered to students in a forty-five-minute class once a week. But Soviet teenagers who have taken it complain that it does not offer enough practical information. A seventeen-year-old named Lena said her teacher used only flowery euphemisms to describe sex. "She was embarrassed and that made us embarrassed. Everyone started giggling, then she got angry and turned red. After class, we were all in hysterics," she said.

The proper approach to teaching sex education came under heavy debate in the Soviet press. The author of one letter printed in a newspaper said that teenagers were not interested in lessons on how to bring up children and that the course should focus on themes "closer to the heart of the average seventeen-year-old."

But the author of a textbook entitled *Family* responded in a moralistic tone resembling the calls of southern conservatives for a ban on *Catcher in the Rye*. In *Uchitelskaya gazeta*, the author wrote that the goal of the course should be to fill youngsters' heads only with "general, philosophical themes on life and love," claiming that any more explicit discussion might "descend to the level of street talk." If the approach of even the sex educators in Soviet society is so restrictive, it stands to reason that the young people are going to be kept ignorant about sex and birth control.

The absence of practical information has kept generations of Soviets ignorant about the subject of lovemaking. Among young people raised outside of the major cities, lack of knowledge about sexual technique is widespread. Irina, a young woman in her late twenties who was born in western Siberia, said she had never experienced oral sex and didn't expect to, because it wasn't a common practice among Soviet couples. "But," she said, "I think it's also not so common among Americans as well, isn't that right?" When she was told that, according to some polls, the majority of American couples engage in oral sex at least occasionally, she refused to believe it. Irina also said she much preferred to make love with the lights off: "We only have sex in the dark—who wants to see what's going on?" She seemed a little shocked that other people might view things differently.

Lyuda, a nineteen-year-old from Rostov, was clearly unimpressed by sex. She had had several boyfriends and was engaged to be married, but when asked if she had a satisfying sexual relationship with her future husband, she replied disdainfully, "Oh, I let him have sex with me whenever he wants. It only takes five minutes and then he leaves me alone for the rest of the night."

DATING SERVICES

Young Soviets often complain that meeting other eligible single people is difficult, largely because of the severe shortage of cafes, restaurants, and recreation areas where teens and young adults can gather. In the mid-1970s, thousands of women began writing to newspapers to complain about their difficulties in meeting men. After ten years of public debate, in which some officials condemned dating services as a capitalist "transaction," the authorities relented. Government dating services were given the official stamp of approval.

The Ministry of Domestic Services agreed in 1984 to take on the project, and dating bureaus were set up in thirty-seven Soviet cities. Meanwhile, the authorities in twelve Soviet cities began printing newspapers with personal ads. Since then, the Kremlin has become the matchmaker for millions.

Masha, the young woman who had given up on men her own age and was seeing an older, married man, decided to try out a dating service after reading an article in a Moscow newspaper announcing the opening of the capital's first dating bureau in 1986. She took along her friend Olga, who had also been having difficulties meeting eligible young men. The article said that the service had been created after years of research by scientists, psychologists, and sociologists, so the two young women concluded that it would be professional, confidential, and efficient. They even had visions of being matched up with men by a computer.

The two discovered on their first visit to the dating service that couples were unlikely to be matched up by a computer anytime before the year 2000. When they arrived at No. 40 Pyatnitskaya Street, they found a dilapidated building marked with a plaque that read, "Moscow city consultation on the question of families and weddings." The dating service was perched atop a cafe, from whose doors stretched the obligatory long line of young people waiting to enter. Masha joked to Olga, "Well, if we don't meet anyone upstairs, we can come back here and maybe we'll meet a man in line."

After climbing the well-worn steps, the two found themselves in a reception room with a threadbare carpet, a sagging couch, and walls of cheap plastic paneling plastered with official notices, such as: "Psychological investigation of personality: 7–11 rubles" and, "Initial consultation: 4–6.50 rubles."

Located off the reception area were consultation rooms with numbered doors. The office was silent except for the nervous whispers of waiting women—there were about ten standing around, all aged thirty to forty, neatly dressed, and plain in appearance. Each had come with a girlfriend, perhaps not having had the courage to visit a dating service alone.

After waiting more than an hour, the two were invited into separate consultation rooms. They were interviewed by a woman dressed in a white jacket who identified herself as a psychologist. A look of distrust crossed her face as she asked Masha, "But you're so young and pretty, can't you meet a man on your own?" She explained the ground rules: only people over eighteen were allowed to use the service, and numerous documents would be required to establish residency in Moscow, marital status, education, and employment.

They were told that after a "short wait," they would be invited back for an interview to determine whether they were "suitable" to join the "club." They would be charged 4 rubles (about $6.50) for the interview and 11 rubles ($17.50) to join. There were additional charges for a questionnaire and for searching through a card catalogue of men's photos. Compared to their salaries, these fees were high; obviously, this was a rather exclusive club. Olga was a specialist in restoring works of art at the Kremlin and Masha was a secretary, but each earned a monthly salary of only 120 rubles (about $190).

Their short wait stretched into nine months. "In that amount of time, I could have produced a child," Masha joked. But the two waited stoically—Soviet people are accustomed to spending time in lines. Finally, they received cards in the mail inviting them to return to No. 40 Pyatnitskaya Street. Armed with all of the proper documents, the two spent three hours there talking to a psychologist named Vera Petrovna, an attractive blond in her mid-thirties, who provided more details about the service. She apologized for the delay, but explained that it had been necessary because women applicants outnumbered the men eight to one. "If we allowed all women to join immediately, we'd have nothing but women here and no men at all," she added.

Masha and Olga were asked to supply photos of themselves and were given a questionnaire, in which they provided such vital statistics as age, height, weight, and marital history. There were 154 questions in all. Their answers were placed alongside their photos on a card, which men could sort through in their search for a date. They were assigned a number, and all contacts were to be arranged through the service.

For a fee of 3 rubles an hour, an assistant at the dating service would help them sort through the cards. Vera Petrovna assured them that looking through the cards was not difficult, since they would not have to pay any attention to the men's responses to the questions. She nonchalantly advised them, "Men never answer sincerely. You should just look at their photo, age, profession, education, and whether they have children. Also, make sure you pick a guy with a separate apartment, not someone in a communal flat. And make sure he doesn't live with his mother!" Masha thought to herself, *This is like standing in line at a liquor store—you see a face, you pick him out. Why go through all this bother and expense if it's just a matter of looking at photos?* But she decided there was no turning back and went on to complete the questionnaire.

Some of the questions were difficult to answer, but many were banal. For example: "What do you like to do in your spare time?" Possible answers were (a) go to the movies, (b) stay at home and read books, (c) visit friends, and (d) take a walk. Only two questions on the survey dealt with sex. One question was, "What level of sexual desire would you prefer in your mate?'' The possible answers were: (*a*) one with normal interest in sex, (*b*) one with greater than normal interest in sex, and (*c*) one not interested in sex at all. The second question was, ''What would you do if you were not satisfied with your sex life?'' The answers: (*a*) not pay attention to the problem, (*b*) recognize the problem but not become upset, and (*c*) seek a divorce.

When Masha complained that many of the questions were silly, Vera Petrovna simply advised her not to waste her time answering them carefully. ''Don't take too long over your replies,'' she said. ''No one reads them. The men only look at your photo. Just get through the questionnaire as quickly as possible.''

The combined fees were the equivalent of twenty-four dollars. Masha objected to the prices, which were high by Soviet standards. ''I can't afford all these services. But I suppose if a woman is eager to get married, she shouldn't spend money on a new pair of shoes or sexy new clothes; she should come to the dating service,'' she said.

Masha and Olga were told that they could look at the card file, select up to three cards, and turn these cards over to an attendant, who would call each man. The men would then come down to the dating service, look at their cards, and, if they liked what they saw, the young women would be given their phone numbers. If the men did not want to meet them, Masha and Olga would receive a card in the mail politely saying they had been rejected.

The two discovered several alarming trends as they searched through the card files. They estimated that, in response to questions about preferences among prospective dates, 70 percent of the men said firmly, ''No Jews.'' Olga, who was Jewish, spoke bitterly of the men's openly anti-Semitic attitudes. Many others wrote that they didn't want to date women from central Asia. Most of the men wrote that they wanted a woman who would take a secondary role to her man. Masha said she remembered reading one card that said, ''I'm not interested in any woman who thinks she can be equal with me.'' For some men, housing was an important consideration. Many men said they were not interested in dating women who lived with a mother or other relative. Consequently, any single women who had the good fortune of living in their own apartments would list their housing situation prominently.

After paying her 3 rubles and searching through the card files, Masha selected a thirty-eight-year-old restaurant chef who said he was divorced; his only child, a son, lived with his former wife. The chef said he lived alone in a one-room apartment. In his photograph, the man stood with his arms crossed, gazing over one shoulder in what was apparently meant to be a seductive pose. He was wearing a turquoise jumpsuit, Adidas running shoes, and an imported watch and eyeglasses. "The photo was meant to show that he had access to Western goods," Masha explained.

When she called the man, he curtly asked what she looked like and what her dating service number was. "I've selected so many women, which one are you?" he asked. Then he told her to call back on the following Sunday at ten o'clock in the morning. Masha considered that a rather odd time to call, but she agreed. When she dialed his number, a woman answered and said the chef was out buying a newspaper. Masha thought the ploy was deliberate. "He wanted to make it clear that he had a lot of women and I shouldn't think that I would be important in his life," she said. The next time she called, he sounded harsh and uninterested. "It seemed to me that he was using the dating service so that he would have a large number of women to sleep with," she said. "At three rubles each, it's a lot easier—and safer—than visiting prostitutes."

The experience was enough to put her off the dating service. She began to refer to it as the *sluchka*, the Russian word for the process of mating a stud and a female dog in heat. But she continued to accompany her friend Olga, who was rejected by her first choice with a card in the mail that read, "Dear comrade, the one you have chosen from the card file has refused to get acquainted with you."

Olga was hurt, but her second choice, a thirty-seven-year-old divorcé named Alexander, did want to meet her. Their first obstacle was what to do on their date. Olga lived with her elderly, disagreeable father in an uncomfortably close apartment, and she knew it would be impossible to bring anyone there. Alexander said he had one room in a communal flat —also not the ideal spot for a first encounter. Finally, the two decided to rendezvous at an art exhibit in a large hall near Gorky Park.

Olga and Alexander spent several hours talking and looking at art. He was a disaffected man who, after graduating from the elite Moscow State University, had quit his job as a psychologist in animal behavior. His voice full of disgust, Alexander said he had watched the way others won their promotions: "If you want to reach a high position, you have to ruin other people's careers." Instead, he had gone to work as a janitor, a job that allowed him plenty of free time to read books about his beloved pastime, philosophy. After strolling around the art exhibit, the two walked to the post office in the rain to pick up a package from her relative in America.

Olga, a striking young woman with rosy cheeks and a vibrant smile, flushed when she recounted their first date. She said, "He told me he liked me better than the other women who called because I'm not interested in material things''—meaning Alexander's low salary and simple life-style. She didn't suggest to her date that they go anywhere for a meal, since she knew that ''a man on such a salary lives hand to mouth.''

Alexander called her again and arranged for a second meeting in the apartment of an artist friend who had a large collection of paintings. But their second date didn't go as well as the first. ''There was nothing there—no feeling for me at all,'' Olga said. ''It was like he was just talking to a friend, not a woman he really found interesting.''

She later invited him to a private evening lecture on history. Such events are usually organized among a small circle of friends who know each other well. On this occasion, an expert was to discuss events in Soviet history that had not yet been covered in the official textbooks. Organizers told participants not to bring tape recorders to the lecture, since what they were doing was illegal at that time and thus slightly dangerous. But Olga's date brought along a friend and a tape recorder. ''That was the end for me. I had a strong feeling that I couldn't trust him after that,'' she said.

But Olga met a second man at the dating service who fell in love with her. Sasha was a geologist and frequently traveled on long business trips around the country. When he was in Moscow he tried to spend all of his time with Olga. He brought her flowers and insisted on cooking elaborate meals for her from a cookbook, which he pored over carefully. A large, red-haired man, he was so embarrassed by the freckles that covered his chest and back that he wore an undershirt to bed so that Olga couldn't see them.

The two occasionally spent the night together in the flat Olga shared with her fussy, quarrelsome father. On one occasion, the old man burst into the room while they were making love, only to back out hurriedly, muttering apologies under his breath. The next day, Olga noticed that her father had installed a small lock on her door.

While away on his frequent travels, Sasha sent her long, loving letters. ''His letters are sickeningly sweet—a mixture of sugar and snot,'' Olga said. He begged her to marry him, but she refused, saying she wasn't in love with him. Even then he kept after her, calling and writing; she didn't have the heart to tell him to stop. Besides, Olga had no other dates and Sasha was at least someone with whom she could pass the time.

Both Olga and Masha stopped relying on the dating service when they saw that they could not realistically expect to meet anyone there who would interest them. Because the service was primitive and difficult to use, it was hard to believe that many people were actually matched up with someone compatible. Most young Soviets say they meet people at work or at school, but once the possibilities there are exhausted, the search becomes more difficult.

SEX, COURTSHIP, AND MARRIAGE

For Soviets fortunate enough to find someone new, the problem becomes one of where to go. After that it is finding the privacy to enjoy their first sexual experience. Many share cramped apartments with parents, a sister or brother, and sometimes a grandparent who is almost always at home. While both parents usually work full time, there is still the constant fear that one of them will come home unexpectedly, as was sixteen-year-old Masha's experience.

Unlike some of their American counterparts, Soviets do not have their first sexual encounter in the backseat of the family station wagon. Car ownership is a luxury reserved mainly for the elite. A car is considered precious, the result of many years of careful saving; some Soviets even refer to their Russian-made *Zhiguli* as their "third child." Parents can hardly be expected to turn their treasured automobiles over to their teenage sons and daughters for a Saturday night date.

Hotels are off-limits to unmarried couples. Under Soviet law, people who share a hotel room must be either married or members of the same sex. Couples are required to present their government documents proving they are married when they check into a hotel—a far cry from simply signing in as "Mr. and Mrs. Smith." The law also forbids people to take a room in a hotel in the town where they are officially registered to live.

Masha told about taking a two-day car trip with a boyfriend. When the two checked into a hotel the first night of their journey, the desk clerk, seeing that they were unmarried, assigned Masha a room on the fifth floor with an overweight, elderly woman who snored all night. Meanwhile, her boyfriend shared a room on the second floor with a drunken man who kept him awake by snoring and bellowing in his sleep.

Lest Masha or her friend had any thoughts of sneaking into each other's rooms in the middle of the night, there was a woman known as a *dezhurnaya*—the Soviet Union's more threatening version of the traditional concierge—posted outside the elevator on each floor, as they are in every hotel, to see that only registered residents are allowed inside. Visitors must leave the hotels by 11:00 P.M.; the *dezhurnaya* sees that the rule is strictly enforced.

During the warmer months, Moscow's park benches provide further evidence that young lovers often have a hard time finding a place to be alone. As soon as the snow melts and temperatures begin to rise in the spring, young couples sit together on benches, kissing and embracing, especially in spots unlit by streetlights. It can be awkward and embarrassing to come upon such couples, but where can they go? Home, for them, is a small apartment with Mom, Dad, and maybe even Grandma. It is easy to understand why they would prefer the romantic intimacy of a park bench.

The taxi driver Volodya, a towering, spare man in his twenties who always seemed bemused by the vagaries of life in his native country, once told a poignant story about a couple who climbed into his cab one day and asked to be driven to a neighborhood on the outskirts of Moscow. When they reached their destination, the man gave him twenty rubles (about thirty-two dollars) and asked him to leave for half an hour. Volodya was happy to spend the time strolling in a nearby forest. "Besides, twenty rubles—I think it's not so bad," he said cheerfully. After he returned from his walk, they asked him to drive to a spot on a busy street in downtown Moscow, where they gave him a big tip before disappearing into the crowd.

Many young Russians tell of making love under even more trying conditions. Another young man related the story of how, during one of Moscow's long winters, he and a girlfriend became frustrated in their search for privacy. Unable to borrow an apartment for even a few hours from any of their friends, they ended up making love in the forest not far from their homes. "You know, it wasn't bad," he said philosophically. "I think every Russian, by the time he gets to be very old, has made love in the snow at least once."

While the notion of making love in a snowbank might seem romantic, it is also a measure of the Russian's stamina—his strength to endure hardship and the patience he needs to stand in life's endless lines, all for the purpose of a few occasional pleasures. Because of the state's sloppy management of the economy and the attendant waste and deprivation that its inefficiency breeds, the average Soviet is forced to develop endurance at an early age. Even as a child, he begins to learn that Soviet life is full of limitations. By adolescence, he knows that this is as true of sex, courtship, and marriage as it is of other pursuits.

The effect of meager salaries on dating and courtship in the Soviet Union also cannot be underestimated. Wages are set artifically low by the government to keep prices down; many of the necessities, including rent, some kinds of food, and utilities, cost only a small fraction of what Americans pay. But the low wages, an attempt to meld all of the social classes into one, result in a standard of living most Westerners consider pitiful and associate more readily with the Third World than with a superpower.

Dating and courtship are followed by marriage, which the government has a hand in as well. If a Soviet couple wants their marriage recognized by the state, they must undergo a state ceremony. Marriages are performed at the local government wedding palace, or ZAGS, as it is known by its Russian acronym. After registering and paying a fee of one ruble and fifty kopecks, couples wait three months, until the date officially designated for their ceremony.

Many of the wedding palaces are housed in what were once czarist mansions. On a typical wedding day, several couples wait in line with their families and friends in a large, ornate gallery until an employee comes by with an ancient 8mm black-and-white movie camera, offering to record the big event. First the men and then the women are led into an adjoining room. There, having been instructed to act naturally, they pretend to chat with one another as they sit around a large table and are filmed by the photographer. The completed work is presented some months later to the couple, who, if they are like most Soviets, has no movie projector with which to watch it.

The actual ceremony takes place in a large, wood-paneled hall with a string quartet and pianist arranged opposite a large white plaster bust of Lenin atop a five-foot pedestal. The couple's friends and relatives watch from the back of the room. With their witnesses, the two step up to a large wooden desk and are greeted by a middle-aged woman functionary, a member of the local Communist party council. She wears an ornate brass chain around her neck and carries a two-foot plexiglass pointer. Speaking in a stentorian sing-song born from years of reciting the marriage speech by rote, the *deputat* proclaims the birth of ''a new Soviet family.'' As the *deputat* gestures to the proper spot with her plexiglass wand, the couple and their witnesses sign a ledger recording their marriage vows. The quartet strikes up, flowers are given by the guests to the bride, the entire wedding party moves on to more private surroundings.

Some newly married couples keep to Soviet tradition by riding around town in a rented black *Chaika* limousine with two large gold wedding bands mounted on the roof. They lay a wreath at the tomb of the unknown soldier or the Lenin mausoleum at Red Square and have their photos taken in Lenin Hills overlooking a panoramic view of Moscow. Then they head back to the home of the bride or groom, or perhaps to a local restaurant, where they sit down to a traditional wedding feast of champagne, caviar, vodka, and other delicacies. It is not unusual, even among poor families, for the parents of the bride to spend large sums of money on the wedding party, especially if it is their daughter's first wedding. During the party, the guests call out *gorko, gorko*, the Russian word for ''bitter.'' It is a signal for the newlyweds to kiss, since, according to tradition, only something sweet—a kiss—can rid one's mouth of a bitter taste.

The wedding ritual is much the same throughout the Soviet Union, although many ethnic groups add their own customs. In Soviet central Asia, where many people are Muslims, young couples appear briefly at the ZAGS for their official Soviet ceremony, then travel in a procession of *Chaika* limousines to the World War II monument that can be found in every Soviet city. After a moment of silence before the monument's eternal flame, the wedding procession continues to the home of the bride, where the mullah, a Muslim holy man, reads verse from the Koran and pronounces the two husband and wife.

In central Asia, marriage is a costly proposition. Families of brides must finance huge banquets; some fathers have written to central Asian newspapers complaining of having to pay between five thousand and nine thousand rubles, or eight thousand to fourteen thousand dollars, for these sumptuous feasts. Grooms are required to pay *kalim*, a dowry given to the bride's family.

Although the payment of *kalim* has been outlawed by the government, people tend to ignore the law. In ancient times, *kalim* usually consisted of livestock or a plot of land. In the central Asia of today, the groom's family must provide a refrigerator, a television set, and thousands of rubles so that the newlyweds can start life comfortably. In 1987, the Soviet press reported that *kalim* was paid by almost every central Asian family who had an eligible son.

Many families have to scrimp on food to save up the thousands of rubles needed for the payment; the Soviet press has speculated that this is one reason so many young men are in poor physical condition when they show up for the draft. Lavish wedding celebrations have had a similarly harmful effect on young women. Some central Asian newspapers reported a rash of self-immolations in 1988 among would-be brides whose families could not afford to pay for a costly wedding banquet.

After the wedding ceremony, many young Soviets quickly find that living with a spouse is more difficult than they had imagined. They must share either a cramped apartment with their parents or an uncomfortable communal flat with strangers. Only the most fortunate are able to move into their own apartments immediately after their weddings. For the rest, the difficulties presented by inadequate housing mean that the odds are stacked against keeping their relationships happy.

People in the Soviet Union are tending to get married younger than their parents did and younger than their Western counterparts. The Moscow University Center of Population Studies reported that the average Soviet married three years earlier in 1986 than he or she did in 1966. The study found that one in four women were only eighteen when they married, and their husbands were age nineteen or twenty. In comparison, the average age at which Americans wed has been on the rise; in 1987 it was twenty-three.

The population center offered no explanation for the drop in the age that Soviets marry, but one factor surely must be teenage pregnancy. Although there are no reliable surveys, the press has reported that many teenagers in urban areas begin having sex at the age of fifteen. Since they cannot buy reliable forms of birth control, many become pregnant and decide to marry.

Other young people are forced into early marriages by the official morality, which is taught in schools, the media, and party organizations and translated into everyday life by people who take on the regime's ethics. If a girl finds herself pregnant and complains to the party committee at the institute where she studies, the authorities there may threaten her boyfriend with expulsion or military service. A young man facing punishment can often be bullied into marriage.

Certainly, the nationwide housing crunch contributes to the tendency of Soviets to marry earlier than Westerners. Unlike their highly mobile American contemporaries, young Soviets cannot simply pack up, leave home, get a job, and find a cheap apartment. The government has control over most of the living space in the Soviet Union, through a housing authority that places families at the top of the waiting lists. Young Soviets know that so long as they stay single, it is nearly impossible to get a new flat and be rid of their parents. So, even if they don't have a solid basis for a long-term relationship, marriage often seems like the only ticket to independence. Ironically, many newly married couples are not fortunate enough to receive their own apartments after their weddings, and many wind up moving in with the families they were trying to leave. But they know that if they wait long enough, and if they have children, they will eventually receive a place of their own.

Others get help from their parents. The process works like this: after a couple marries, one set of parents goes to the housing authority. If the parents have a three-room apartment, they are allowed to break it up into two apartments—one with two rooms and the second with only one room—and turn the smaller flat over to the newlyweds. It is a protracted legal procedure, but one that many families choose over waiting for years to be assigned to an apartment or jamming several generations together into a small, cramped living space.

Inevitably, sharing uncomfortably close living quarters leads to tension and quarrels. In 1986, one sociological journal reported that 28 percent of the arguments between newly married couples were caused by interference from parents. The article said that nearly half of those surveyed lived with their relatives, but only 13 percent of the brides and 19 percent of the grooms were happy with the arrangement. A significant number of people said they would like to live as far away from their parents as possible.

But many experience conflicting desires; while they want to flee from their parents, they also need them. Many young marrieds depend on parents for help with child care, shopping, and housework as well as money to pay for food or other expenses. Parents often provide sizable monthly allowances to their married children; many automatically pay for and prepare the younger couples' meals. The survey in the sociological journal reported that half of the grooms and a third of the brides had never been asked by their parents to do housework before they married and that they continued to seek parental help long after their weddings. "For this reason," the survey prophesied, "in their married life, they are bound to encounter a great deal of daily problems."

One young couple well illustrates the survey's depressing prediction. They separated after having been married for less than two years because the husband refused to share housework or child care. Johan, a bearded saxophone player from Moscow, was the only child of parents who spoiled him and gave him his foreign name to distinguish him from the Russians around him. He married Vera, a traditional young woman who was attracted to his colorful personality and striking wardrobe. Before they married, she was his most ardent fan and accompanied him to all of his late-night jam sessions.

But their relationship soured almost immediately after their wedding. She became pregnant and gave birth to their daughter. While Vera did the housework and shopping and cared for their child after a full day's work as a secretary, Johan spent every evening with his musician friends. "I can't sit around with her all the time," Johan said contemptuously. "I have to keep up with my music."

Soon he was coming home only to eat, to change clothes, and, occasionally, to sleep. His wife complained bitterly, but that only prompted Johan to come home even less frequently. Finally, she forced him to move out of the apartment they shared with her parents. Johan began sleeping at the homes of various friends. After less than two years of marriage, the two filed for divorce.

Vera and Johan's problems are typical among young marrieds. Even as many American men in their twenties and thirties are beginning to take on more household and child-care responsibilities, their Soviet counterparts resist such a change. Certainly, there are some young Soviet men who try to share the housework equally with their wives, but they are extremely rare.

Despite the sexism in Soviet society, many young women do not recognize what people in the U.S. might term their second-class status. A married woman in her early thirties who tutored foreigners in Russian ridiculed the American feminist movement. She parroted the official line that Soviet women had reached full equality with men and were far ahead of their American counterparts; yet she did not recognize a contradiction when she added that Soviet women needed to be "feminine." For her, Soviet women had become too strong and needed to return to the traditional housewife-mother role. She pointed to her own life as proof that women's liberation had ruined relations between women and men. She said sadly that her husband, an English teacher and poet who was plagued by periods of depression, spent many evenings drinking with his friends. When she woke in the mornings, she found empty bottles and broken crockery all over the floor. The teacher believed that it was her strength—her willingness to work a full-time job and still be a good wife—that had caused her husband to become dependent and weak.

FAMILY PLANNING

Soviets' attitudes about female and male roles reveal just how difficult it is for a woman to balance home and career in the Soviet Union. The balancing act becomes even more demanding when a woman has a child, and most women are unable to avoid pregnancy soon after they marry. An article published in 1985 in *Komsomolskaya pravda* said that one-fourth of the young people surveyed had had a child within a few months of marriage and that a third had become parents within nine months.

Although the survey did not address the issue, it seems reasonable to add that many of those surveyed probably felt unprepared to have a family so quickly. But because effective forms of contraception are all but unavailable in the Soviet Union, these new parents had little choice. Certainly, there are no family planning centers to provide ready information about birth control.

It is not surprising, then, that the abortion rate is extremely high. In the Soviet Union, abortion is available on demand. Except for the central Asian republics, abortion is a primary form of birth control, and the popularity of the procedure has spawned some alarming statistics. Some researchers estimate that there are as many as three abortions for every live birth, and that nine out of ten first pregnancies end in abortion. Even though Soviets account for only about 6 percent of the world population, more than 25 percent of all abortions in the world take place in the Soviet Union. In fact, abortions are in such great demand that half of the country's gynecologists do nothing but perform abortions.

Although the state provides abortions at no cost, government clinics have their disadvantages: crowded wards, long waiting lines, unsanitary conditions, and typically no anesthesia. Irina, a young woman who had moved to Moscow from a provincial town, said she had had an abortion at the hands of a woman doctor who apparently was more interested in speed than quality care. At home, Irina began experiencing severe pain. The next day, she saw another doctor, who discovered that the first doctor had failed to remove the entire fetus. The second doctor completed the operation and told Irina that she was fortunate not to have developed an infection that might have left her sterile or even killed her.

Many women prefer to have private, illegal abortions, performed by doctors after hours, in part because they can request the use of a painkiller. But private abortions have serious drawbacks as well. Many doctors charge up to 100 rubles (or $160). In fact, one reason for their popularity is the fact that doctors see them as a stable source of income and often urge their patients to undergo them. Also, they can be very dangerous. One Soviet newspaper reported in 1988 that each year, six hundred women die during abortions in the Russian republic.

In an effort to cut down on the deaths and infertility caused by illegal abortions, the abortion law was made even more liberal in 1988. Under the new law, Soviet women can get abortions until their eighth month of pregnancy. Minors are entitled to abortions regardless of the fetus's age. Private abortions remain popular, however; one news story said that they make up one-fourth to one-half of all abortions.

✶ Many Soviet youth are ignorant about contraceptives; a 1987 survey of newly married couples in three cities showed that nearly 60 percent of the men and 70 percent of the women were unaware of the best methods of birth control, and that only an estimated 10 to 15 percent of the Soviet population were using contraceptives.

The contraceptive most commonly used among young Soviets is the condom. Following abortion and condoms, withdrawal is ranked by Soviet researchers as the third most widely used form of birth control. Articles in the Soviet press regularly advise against using withdrawal and warn that it can make both men and women "nervous." The rhythm method is recommended by many doctors for young couples. The journal *Zdorovye* (Health Care) reported a study that found that as many as one-fourth of all couples regularly use the rhythm method by the fifth year of marriage.

Birth control pills have never gained much popularity among young people because of fears about the side effects. The pills are produced not in the Soviet Union but in Hungary and Bulgaria. One woman named Irina reported that she had once taken the Hungarian pills, whose brand name was Infecudin. They made her so nervous and irritable that her husband insisted she stop taking them. Buying them in Moscow had never been a problem for her and several times she had persuaded pharmacy employees to sell them to her without a prescription, but she wondered whether they would be so easy to find in rural areas.

★ Because many women cannot find a form of birth control they consider acceptable, fear of becoming pregnant is a frequent topic of conversation. Among those who already have children, the talk often turns to childbirth. They complain that the doctors in maternity wards are cruel and uncaring, the nurses are poorly trained, and the buildings are dangerously filthy. Any young Soviet woman can recite horror stories about giving birth. Irina related the story of a friend who was a diabetic and had the misfortune of going into labor on May 1, a major holiday in the Soviet Union. When she arrived at the hospital, she immediately told the nurses on duty that she was a high-risk patient and asked them to call her doctor. The nurses, who had been drinking, told her that her doctor would be at home celebrating. They promised to call him later. "She couldn't convince them that there would be complications. My friend gave birth attended only by nurses, who weren't able to save the child," Irina recalled.

Such experiences are typical in Soviet hospitals. *Sovietskaya Rossiya*, the newspaper of the Russian republic, published a lurid report in 1986 about conditions in Soviet maternity wards. The story said that although most women give birth at night, doctors did not work in maternity wards after 4:00 P.M. It was not until the Ministry of Health issued a decree calling for doctors to be on duty at all hours in maternity wards that hospitals began requiring physicians to work at night.

Other accounts in the press have described the lack of modern equipment, poor organization, and bad diagnoses given in most Soviet maternity wards. Articles have told how a single hospital nurse may be required to care for twenty-five newborns at once, and how after delivery, 30 percent of new mothers are found to be suffering from illnesses that went undiagnosed during their pregnancies.

Tanya, who was in her late twenties when she had her first child, said her labor was difficult and painful. Her husband had tried to calm her in the taxi on the way to the hospital, but she was paralyzed with fear by the time they arrived. She had never heard of any classes to prepare women for childbirth, such as those offered in the West. Her labor lasted fourteen hours. She received nothing to ease her pain, even though she begged for an anesthetic. There were about half a dozen other women alongside her in the labor room, and most of them were suffering also. When the doctors determined that she was ready to give birth, Tanya had to get up and walk into the delivery room. After the delivery, she was placed in a ward with about a dozen other women.

Tanya remembered her week-long recovery at the hospital as a pleasant time in which she was able to relax while the nurses took care of her newborn daughter. Her family name was written in ballpoint pen on her baby's arm, from his shoulder to his wrist. Tanya laughed about the superstitious beliefs of some of the elderly nurses in the hospital. "One told me, in all seriousness, that whenever I was breast-feeding, I should keep a silver spoon wrapped in a ribbon nearby. She said it would keep me from losing my looks," Tanya said.

She recalled longing for her husband, who was not allowed to be with her during either the delivery or the week she spent recovering. Delivery rooms are never private, so this may be one reason that men are excluded. But the real explanation lies in the feeling among many Soviet people that childbirth is not "aesthetic." Many young people are horrified that in Western hospitals, a father may look on as his child is born.

Supposedly, the reason for not allowing fathers to visit after their children are born is to check the spread of disease. Because of this rule, young men can be seen standing in the street outside, their wives waving to them from the windows and occasionally lowering baskets filled with letters. The men place presents or food into the baskets and the women haul them back up. Tanya said some of the men had stamped out the words *I love you* in the snow outside the hospital where their wives had given birth.

After a week in the hospital, mothers are allowed to go home with their children. Parenthood is demanding in any society, but it is especially so in the Soviet Union because parents lack many of the consumer products Westerners take for granted. While the Soviet Union produces diapers (which are similar in appearance to a sanitary napkin), plastic pants are not available, and without them, there is no way to protect a baby's clothing. Soviet mothers are reduced to washing their children's clothes out many times each day. Because many in rural areas do not have washing machines, everything has to be rinsed out by hand and hung to dry on balconies or, during the winter months, in bathrooms. There are no disposable diapers or laundry services.

Raising a child in the Soviet Union is very expensive. Tanya, who related her experience of giving birth in a Soviet hospital, complained of having to spend 70 rubles, or about $115, for a new pair of boots for her daughter. Since her monthly salary was only 150 rubles (about $240), the purchase was a terrible hardship for the family. The costs of clothing and children's furniture, in relation to salaries, are much higher than the prices American families pay. In 1987, the Soviet press estimated that disposable income drops by one-half to two-thirds after a child is born into a Soviet family.

Most families in the Soviet Union are dependent on women's incomes, so many mothers return to work when their children are toddlers. They often feel torn about turning their children over to the state system of child care. Many mothers complain about the quality of care offered by the state-run day-care centers. Parents often use their *blat* and pay small bribes to win a place for their children in better facilities. Tanya said that when she wanted to place her daughter in a prestigious child-care center, she asked a friend with connections there to make an appointment for her. She wore her best dress, took along a bottle of imported cognac, and acted in a very officious manner so that the center's director would think she was dealing with someone important. "I was successful," she said. "I got my daughter in. But I saw another woman there who looked like a worker. Her child was not allowed to enter."

Although she considered the day-care center better than most, Tanya often worried about the conditions there. She said that as many as forty children were sometimes attended by only one teacher, who was impatient and short-tempered. "I suppose I shouldn't blame her," Tanya said. "She's probably exhausted from dressing them to go outside and then bringing them in and taking their clothes off all over again." Still, her little daughter hated the day-care center and often had to be taken there forcefully.

Many women who work full time complain that after they add shopping and housework to their day, they have virtually no time to spend with their children. Tatyana Zaslavskaya, one of the Soviet Union's top sociologists, said in 1988 that working mothers spend less than thirty minutes each week playing with their children. Soviet fathers were found to be even less attentive, devoting only six minutes a week to their offspring. Zaslavskaya blamed this inattentiveness for the rise in juvenile delinquency in the Soviet Union.

MARITAL DIFFICULTIES AND NONTRADITIONAL LIFE-STYLES

So far, the state has had no success in altering the divorce rate. Among young women aged twenty-five to twenty-nine, six of every ten married in 1985 are now divorced. Three-quarters of the men in that age group are marrying for the second or third time. The majority of divorces occur among young couples—where both parties are under twenty—who have been married less than a year.

At the root of the high divorce rate may be young people's attitudes toward marriage. Soviet youth consider their first marriage to be a relationship more than a commitment, and they often do not agonize a great deal over ending these first marriages.

Maksim, a Muscovite in his thirties who had recently embarked on his third marriage, was philosophical about his marital history. "We Soviets have a lot of divorces because we can't live together and try out the relationship like you Americans do," he said. "We don't have that luxury—we have to get married."

Another reason for the high divorce rate is the tendency among Soviet women to leave a marriage when they become dissatisfied. An article published in *Literaturnaya gazeta* said it is women who file for seven out of ten divorces. Experts say women seek divorce more often than men do because the majority have careers that give them the confidence and financial security to support themselves and their children. Also, slightly more women have a higher education than men. So when their husbands refuse to share the housework and child care and take to drinking, many women simply decide that they would be better off without their husbands, and they file for divorce. Although women's salaries are on the average lower than those of men, they are able to pay for the basics, such as rent, food, and clothing.

Sexual incompatibility, alcoholism, and inadequate housing are some of the other problems that many young Soviet couples face. One Moscow therapist wrote in the Soviet press in 1986 that 40 percent of all people who filed for divorce had sexual problems; many couples say they have nowhere to turn for help when problems arise. And a Soviet sociologist reported in 1987 that heavy drinking among men was at least partly responsible for 90 percent of all divorces between young couples.

About 20 percent of divorces are caused by the tension that builds up between young couples and their parents when they have to share an apartment. Many people divorce precisely because they want a bigger and better apartment. It is a measure of the housing shortage and the intricacies of Soviet housing laws that people will go through a divorce, if only on paper, to receive a new apartment. When couples file for divorce, they can place their names on the waiting list. Although they sometimes have to wait years, in the end they are given a second flat. Their next step is to remarry and trade the two one-room flats for a larger two-room apartment.

If couples encounter problems in marriage, they have limited opportunities to get help; there are very few marital counseling centers. One newspaper reported that the first centers designed to deal with marital and family problems in Moscow were set up only as recently as 1980. In many rural areas, such facilities are nonexistent.

✭ Infidelity, too, contributes to the high divorce rate. Couples who work in separate places often spend hours commuting between home and the office and end up seeing little of each other. Like couples anywhere, spouses who spend a lot of time apart have more opportunities to become involved with other people.

Many husbands and wives take separate vacations. They receive a *putyovka*, "vacation pass," from their workplace and go on holidays with their colleagues rather than with their spouses. Extramarital affairs during vacations are considered normal by many people. A young translator once said that she looked forward to the month-long separation from her spouse on her annual vacation. "Why should I care that I don't see my husband for one month out of the year? I see him as much as I want the rest of the time," she said.

And yet, when statistics on infidelity were released for the first time in the Soviet press in 1987, infidelity was found to be the cause of almost a third of the nation's divorces. According to the report, 55 percent of married men and 25 percent of married women have had extramarital affairs. So while it seems that young Soviets take a more casual approach to infidelity than do Westerners, this may be true only among the so-called intelligentsia—artists, writers, actors, and musicians. Extramarital sex is probably less common among workers. Unfortunately, no survey released in the Soviet press has listed the professions of those who admitted to having had extramarital affairs.

Many people say the biggest obstacle to having affairs is the same as that with premarital sex: lack of places to go for a little privacy. Married couples often try to borrow the apartment of a relative or friend. Others tell their spouses they are going on a *kommandirovka*, or "business trip," so that they can disappear for three or four days and spend time with their lover in a friend's apartment.

Masha once told an hilarious story about a married man who was having a passionate affair with a younger, single woman. His wife was becoming suspicious about his frequent absences, and he was running out of excuses. One day, he showed up unexpectedly at 5:00 A.M. on his lover's doorstep, wearing a raincoat and plastic hip boots and carrying a fishing pole. He had told his wife that he was going on a fishing expedition. "My friend and her lover had a very pleasant time. But at the end of the day, the man returned to his wife wearing clean clothes," Masha mused. "He hadn't caught a single fish, yet he was in a cheerful mood. His wife found it very strange that he seemed not to care he hadn't caught anything."

☆ In 1988, the press published figures on yet another previously taboo social issue: births to unmarried women. The weekly newspaper *Semya* (Family) reported that nearly 10 percent of all births in 1987 were babies born to single mothers—an increase of almost one-third over the figure for 1980.

The lack of dependable contraceptives is one reason for the large number of single-parent births. But as the newspaper *Nedelya* (Week) reported in 1984, a survey of single mothers found that four out of every five of these women had set out to become single mothers. According to the survey, the average age of these mothers was between thirty and forty.

One reason for the growing numbers of births among single women in this age group is loneliness and despair over their chances of finding a mate. The Soviet press said in 1986 that among single Soviets thirty to forty years old, there were ten women for every seven men. Many women say that alcoholism further reduces the number of eligible bachelors.

Another trend that has led to more single motherhood is the tendency among women to set high standards when it comes to men. The 1984 survey mentioned the example of a woman lawyer who had given birth. The father of the child, an unmarried man, was in love with her, loved their child, and wanted to marry. But since the lawyer knew that very few men share in the daily grind of shopping and housework, she pronounced him a burden and decided to remain single. Said the authors of the survey: "The new role of woman in society, and her growing economic independence, has given rise to a new, rather strange attitude toward sex and marriage."

☆ As in any society, homosexuality exists in the Soviet Union. But because it is a crime, punishable by up to five years in prison, Soviet gays tend to be more discreet than those in the West. There are said to be large numbers of gays in the world of fashion, dance, and theater, but unless they let it be widely known that they are homosexual, these men usually are not punished for their sexual preference. There is also an official reticence to acknowledge the existence of homosexuality. The criminal code does not even use the Russian word for homosexuality; instead it is referred to as *muzhelozhestvo*, a biblical term for "lying with men." There is nothing in the law against lesbianism.

Despite the illegality of homosexuality and the official reluctance to discuss it, there are many gays in the Soviet Union. A young gay man named Sasha, who was seated near a table of foreign correspondents at a

Moscow pizzeria, politely interrupted and said he had noticed that they were speaking English, and would they mind if he joined them. Despite a few unfriendly glances from one of the foreigners, who was immediately suspicious that he was a KGB plant, Sasha seated himself at the table. He was a small man in his early thirties, with sandy hair and large blue eyes. Sasha spoke excellent English; he later explained that his father had been a member of the American Socialist party and had moved to the Soviet Union during the 1930s and married a Jewish woman, Sasha's mother. The two had raised their son to speak both English and Russian.

Sasha had difficulty practicing a conventional Soviet life-style. He'd had his first sexual experience at age fifteen with a boy in his class. But he'd also had sex with girls. ''I enjoyed sex with boys and girls. I couldn't really decide which I preferred. But there was no pressure to make a decision,'' Sasha remembered.

He frequently got into trouble in school and was unable to enter an institute or a university. Because his father was a foreigner, Sasha could legally carry dollars, and he moved easily within the large community of diplomats and correspondents in Moscow. After high school, he became more involved with the black market, buying tape recorders and radios from foreigners and selling them to Russians at inflated prices. When he was in his mid-twenties, Sasha met and married a woman who worked as a secretary in the Embassy of Chile. The woman was a committed Communist and had come to the Soviet Union firmly believing the pro-Soviet propaganda she had heard in her own country.

She received a salary in foreign currency, which enabled Sasha to buy even more imported electronic equipment from the *Berioska* shops in Moscow that cater to foreigners. The size of his deals grew larger, and he became close to a group of small-time hoods, some of whom were homosexual. Sasha began hanging around the public toilets and other gathering spots where gays frequently meet.

Some of the gay pick-up spots that Sasha pointed out were a small park across from the Bolshoi theater in downtown Moscow, plus a cluster of public telephone booths across the street, where young men stood idly waiting, gazing intently at passersby. Another spot was a cafeteria that sold dumplings known as *pyelmenii*, the Russian version of ravioli. Located near the headquarters of the Communist party's Central Committee off of Nogin Square, the cafeteria seemed an unlikely place for gays to meet.

Once when Sasha was visiting with a foreign friend, it was winter and the cafeteria's windows were clouded over with steam. Hefty women with grease-stained aprons ladled out bowls of *pyelmenii* behind the counter. It was late in the evening; most of the customers were young men who demonstrated little interest in the food but stared curiously at each customer who entered. Everyone was either watching someone or being watched.

His friend was relieved to walk outside again. Across the street, Sasha pointed to the window of a brightly lighted government office. The curtains were drawn, and inside, beneath a large portrait of Lenin on the wall, sat a man in a gray suit, laboring away at a desk. The contrast was startling: the steamy cafe, so busy with intimate exchanges and underlying messages, and the bureaucrat in the neat, formal office with the officious portrait of Lenin. Which of the two images was the real Soviet Union?

Actually, both are real. Until very recently, the Soviet authorities refused to acknowledge the existence of this unofficial, or underground, reality. For many years, they hid behind platitudes, rarely touching on such problems as unemployment, sexual diseases, and prostitution. The most the official press did was to allude to homosexuality. Gays in the Soviet Union were forced to live a shadowy, paranoid life even more cautious than their counterparts' in the West.

In 1987, encouraged by Gorbachev's *glasnost* campaign, one of Moscow's newspapers for Communist youth printed a surprisingly frank story about the gay life-style. It began with a letter from a schoolboy, who signed only his initials, ''A. E.'' The author was so afraid of persecution that he wrote the letter with his left hand so that no one would be able to recognize his handwriting. He spoke of being beaten by other boys, while his teachers pretended not to notice. In the letter, he pleaded: ''Please help me, as I have nobody else in which I can place my faith.'' A sexologist interviewed for the article said the boy's experiences were a mere taste of the lifelong suffering that awaited him. The article acknowledged that the number of homosexuals was growing and concluded that it was the boy's upbringing that had caused him to become a homosexual.

Another boy mentioned in the article, Igor, was fourteen when his mother grew suspicious of his girlfriends and encouraged him to meet only with boys. When Igor talked about his problem with the boys in his class, ''the discussion turned into group masturbation and later into group sex,'' the article said.

No Westerner can fully understand the shock many Soviets must have felt in reading such statements. The article continued in a frank manner, saying there are more lesbians in the Soviet Union than gay men, partly because teachers encourage girls to be boyish, active, energetic, and independent. Girls find it even easier than boys to form same-sex relationships, the article said, because ''mutual caresses are natural for them.'' The story also revealed the existence of a small gay pride movement in the Soviet Union that ''expresses itself in the desire to justify abnormality.'' Its followers were said to consider themselves part of a superior race with white bones and blue blood—which may be the origin of the Russian slang term for homosexual, *goluboi*, or "blue."

Despite its openness, the tone of the article revealed the homophobic tendency common among the Soviet people. "From the point of view of a psychiatrist, we are dealing here with a real maniac. The homosexual way of life virtually always leads to psychological disturbances," the article stated. It argued against the legalization of homosexuality, for such a step "would almost automatically mean propagating it," resulting in a "homosexual epidemic." And encouraging a teenager to become a homosexual was considered tantamount to injecting someone with syphilis. "The main question of our discussion is: what should be done? The answer is: treat, punish, educate."

Emphasizing a punitive approach, the article advocated closer police supervision of homosexual haunts. Only a return to traditional values—a large family in which the father rules and the mother is loving and tender—would reduce the ranks of gays. The conclusion could have been written by a Christian fundamentalist in the United States, calling for a return to traditional family values. It is clear that while homosexuality is finally being discussed, Soviet society is still a long way from condoning a gay life-style.

POVERTY, PARENTS, AND PRESSURE

The picture painted here of sex, courtship, and marriage in the Soviet Union is a grim one. Not all Soviet couples grow unhappy with their spouses and seek divorce; millions of young Soviets fall in love, marry, and raise families. Nevertheless, remaining happily married and bringing up children is more difficult in the Soviet Union than in the West. The government, with its burdensome regulations and officially enforced prudishness, encroaches on people's private lives while its sloppily managed centralized economy creates hardships and deficits.

Poor living conditions keep young people dependent on their parents. Young Soviet couples find themselves living with relatives who, despite what may start out to be good intentions, end up dictating to the young. Many youth complain of feeling dominated and oppressed. These feelings are compounded when they have to postpone moving out on their own because getting an apartment may take years.

Until recently, Soviet newspapers went no further than to allude to the sensitive subjects of sex and marriage. Instead of a thorough examination of problems, along with their causes and consequences, there was silence. It did not matter whether the disagreeable subject was premarital sex or illegal abortion, the official reaction was to turn away and remain silent. Meanwhile, Soviet people discussed the problems of love, sex, and marriage in private and ridiculed the government's handling of the issues.

Glasnost has brought more open discussion of society's social ills, but the government programs needed to correct these problems will have to be far-reaching. That means they also will be very costly. At a time when resources are needed to retool aging factories to make *perestroika* a reality, people are clamoring for the basics: better housing, contraceptives, food, and consumer goods. The government faces the challenge of trying to pump up the productivity of workers already worn out by the daily struggle to meet their basic needs. It is a question not only of the Soviet Union's ability to resolve its social problems but also of its willingness to do so. The state must strike a delicate balance between trucks, tools, and rockets—or birth control pills, diapers, and comfortable apartments.

CHAPTER 3 THE MILITARY AND CAREERS

THE WAR IN AFGHANISTAN

 IN 1983, IT was difficult to believe that the Soviet Union was a superpower at war. For those American correspondents who had grown to adulthood in the years steeped in the anguish of Vietnam, the silence over the war in Afghanistan was shocking. The conflict across the nation's southern border was treated as a closely guarded state secret. Newspaper stories featured brave young Soviet soldiers who were fulfilling their internationalist duty "in the friendly country of Afghanistan," helping the Afghan people defend their homeland against the Western imperialist aggressors. Occasionally there were reports of battles, which the Soviet army always won and in which Russian soldiers rarely seemed to die. Unless their sons were of draft age and could be sent to Afghanistan, most Soviet people rarely discussed the war and knew little about it.

In the West, information about the war was scanty; the Soviet authorities rarely allowed reporters into that ancient and untamed land, and those who managed to get in through the high mountain passes separating Afghanistan from Pakistan risked being arrested as spies.

But the war dragged on inexorably, stretching twice as long as the Soviet effort in World War II. Casualties mounted and the signs of war became visible. The grave of a young soldier killed in Afghanistan appeared in the cemetery near the spot where the poet-author Boris Pasternak lay buried at Peredelkino, the small writers' colony outside of Moscow. One began to hear quiet grumbling about the war. Some said the Soviet army had no business being in Afghanistan. Others simply said that the Afghan people should be allowed to run their country without interference from the Soviet Union.

When a Western reporter took a train trip across Siberia in 1984 with a colleague, the two spent an evening in a cramped train compartment talking to two young Soviet construction workers. The two young men were on their way home to Murmansk, a remote city in the frozen Arctic circle. They were feeling jubilant, telling jokes and lifting their glasses of cognac and vodka in lengthy toasts. The mood suddenly turned sober, however, when the subject of Afghanistan was raised. One had been stationed there, and all he could talk about was his desire to avenge the death of a good friend who had died in the war. His buddy, a muscular blond with a good-natured grin, had been stationed at a post in the Ukraine that processed the bodies of men shipped home from the war. Shaking his head and averting his eyes, he said mournfully, "You can imagine what it was like to see a mother arrive to claim the body of her only son. It was terrible to see those women cry," he said.

Like the rest of Soviet society, both young men believed that the war would continue as long as the government wanted to send soldiers to fight it. After all, they had never seen their army withdrawn from any country it had invaded. There were no mass demonstrations and no one spoke publicly against the war. Few were willing to risk arrest or the loss of a job as punishment for criticizing government policy.

But the authorities gradually came to grips with the fact that the war could not be won. There was a growing awareness under the leadership of Mikhail Gorbachev that the conflict had become a costly drain on the nation's resources. In one speech, he described Soviet involvement in Afghanistan as "a bleeding wound." When Gorbachev met with foreign leaders, most made it clear that their countries' relations with the Soviet Union would never improve until the Soviet army withdrew from Afghanistan.

CRACKS IN THE WALL OF SECRECY

In 1987, the Soviet press began preparing people for the eventual pullout. Public opinion shifted against the war; almost all segments of the population now said that they disapproved of Soviet involvement in Afghanistan. Newspapers published letters from people complaining about the one-sided way the war was depicted. One Ukrainian woman whose two boys had been drafted wrote to a local newspaper to complain that while the sons of simple workers were sent to Afghanistan, the children of high-ranking party officials were awarded more comfortable assignments close to home.

Many other articles objected to the hostile treatment given to returning soldiers. For most Soviets, the veterans were not heroes, but a source of shame. Known as *Afghantsi*, the vets pleaded in vain that they needed psychological counseling programs to help them readapt to civilian life. One article said that about 100,000 veterans needed plastic surgery every year but that there was only one ward of thirty beds for such cases in the entire country. A veteran wrote that he had lost both legs in the war but was refused a ground-floor apartment. Another injured vet complained about how a doctor had dismissed him coldly, saying, "I did not send you to Afghanistan."

As the leadership moved to make the announcement that the Soviet army would withdraw, the popular weekly magazine *Ogonyok* (Little Flame) sent one of its young writers, Artyom Borovik, to Afghanistan. He had been the first Soviet journalist to report on the war as it was unfolding. Artyom Borovik was the son of the journalist Genrikh Borovik, a Kremlin hit man known for his especially vitriolic commentary on the United States. The younger Borovik had grown up in the United States and Cuba when his father was posted overseas. Fluent in English and Spanish, he had studied at the prestigious Institute for International Relations in Moscow. Borovik, raised on Ernest Hemingway, compared his articles about Afghanistan to Michael Herr's book, *Dispatches*, about the war in Vietnam.

But Borovik's writing fell far short of the moving and brutally honest depiction of the war that Herr had achieved—the literature that became part of the fabric of American society during the Vietnam War. Borovik wrote about the atrocities committed by the mujahedin, describing, for example, how they had sliced the skin around the waist of a Soviet fighter, pulled his skin over his head like a shirt, and thrown the poor victim onto the hot sand. And he wrote about how the resistance fighters would stick burning cigarettes into the skin of Soviet soldiers, or impale them on sharp poles, or tie their limbs to four camels and make the animals run in different directions. According to Borovik, the Soviet soldiers were much more humane and well behaved; the worst outrage committed by the Soviets was that they occasionally subjected their captured mujahedin to "severe beatings."

As a journalist, Borovik was an apologist, because his writings were slanted in favor of the Soviet soldiers. But they loved him for what he wrote; by becoming their mouthpiece and writing about the war from the perspective of the *Afghantsi*, he was a hero to many soldiers.

His articles were part of an at first carefully controlled public discussion of the Soviet role in Afghanistan. In the spring of 1988, as the Soviet withdrawal began, it became acceptable to peel back some of the layers of secrecy that had shrouded Soviet involvement in Afghanistan. For the first time, the press revealed casualty figures, reporting that fifteen thousand

Soviet men had died in the war. The government admitted that some Soviet soldiers had deserted their units, and it offered an amnesty for any soldiers who wanted to come home. The leadership of the Communist party even issued a secret circular calling the decision to send the army into Afghanistan an "error" and a "misjudgment."

A film entitled *Pain*, a documentary critical of the war, was released in 1988. In one of the film's most striking scenes, a veteran who lost his arm in the conflict says, "If the Afghan people came here to help us build socialism how would we react?" Answering his own question, he mutters, "They hated us." In early 1989, the newspaper *Znamya* serialized the short stories of Oleg Yermakov, a 28-year-old veteran of the Afghan war. His bitter and vivid portrait of the conflict was widely acclaimed.

Although the fighting began to find its way into literature and film, the examination of the origins of the war has not taken a deeply introspective turn. There has so far been no acknowledgment of Soviet influence over the bloody coups that Moscow used as an excuse to send its troops over the southern border into Afghanistan. There has not been adequate fault finding or finger pointing, no careful examination of exactly who was responsible for leading the Soviet Union into the war in the first place.

But the Soviets are not yet ready for that. After the government brings all of its soldiers home and the men and their families begin to heal, the self-scrutiny that is so necessary to put the war behind them may begin. Just as Americans waited a decade for their film industry to begin publicly agonizing over the Vietnam War, the Soviets, too, need time to recover before coming to terms with one of the most humiliating episodes in their history. Only real honesty about the war will guarantee that a military adventure like Afghanistan will not be repeated. One can only hope that when the nation is ready for a close analysis, the government will allow an open discussion to go on.

Even as the Soviets prepared to bring the last of their troops home in early 1989, the foreign press was discouraged from prying into the personal tragedies and losses suffered in the war. Although the Komsomol and the Foreign Ministry occasionally set up interviews between veterans and American correspondents, so far, these young men have stopped short of harshly criticizing their government's role in the war. They have expressed doubts and disillusionment and have spoken with some bitterness about the gap between their experiences and what the Soviet people were told about the war. Some of these veterans are invalids now walking on artificial limbs. But the interviews orchestrated by the Foreign Ministry and Komsomol are not with drug addicts, alcoholics, or psychologically disabled veterans; they are not the hopeless young men whose lives had been destroyed by the war in Afghanistan.

☆ There was a natural reluctance among the Soviet vets to talk to Western correspondents. To find *Afghantsi* and listen to them explain some of the searing pain they had endured in the war, it was necessary to work through acquaintances and friends, rather than official channels. One young Muscovite named Eddy agreed to an interview. He was a handsome young man, twenty-six years old, with bushy brown hair and a beard that covered his scars. He had the physique of a pole vaulter or a swimmer. Wearing a black sweater and jeans and a black leather jacket, he chain-smoked harsh Soviet cigarettes pungent with Asian tobacco. Eddy's most striking feature was his eyes; a pale shade of blue, there was something haunting, frightening, even animallike about them. It was disturbing to meet his glance.

Eddy said laconically that Afghanistan had made him crazy. He was not able to work or study and he had been in and out of mental hospitals for six years. He could not rid his mind of what he had seen in the war. Eddy had smoked a lot of hashish there, and when he returned home to Moscow, he began buying it illegally. He had been in trouble frequently with the police. Officially classified as a disabled veteran, Eddy laughed about his monthly pension of sixty rubles, or about one hundred dollars. "How is it possible for a person to live on two rubles a day?" he asked with a sneer.

A graduate of a PTU in Moscow, he was drafted in 1980 and sent to Uzbekistan, where he spent six months in training. His officers refused to tell him where he was to be sent, but then, as Eddy told it, "I got out of bed one beautiful spring day, and by evening I was headed for Afghanistan. When we arrived, there was fog everywhere. We didn't know where we were, but we figured we must be in Kabul." It was early 1981, when the press was still silent about what the Soviet army was actually doing there.

Eddy was sent to Osadabad, the capital of Kunar province, near the border of Pakistan. Narcotics were readily available in his base camp, and the hashish was "the best in the world." All of the men smoked. Some soldiers seemed to have a steady supply. The unit's truck drivers swapped gasoline with the locals for drugs; these soldiers were always the wealthiest in the unit. Others traded Kalashnikov rifles, army boots, or clothing for hashish. The only women allowed into his base camp were prostitutes brought in from Uzbekistan. Soviet soldiers were under watch by the Khad, Afghanistan's secret police squad, which was modeled after the KGB. Eddy said Khad agents were often cruel, informing on soldiers and seeing that they were given military prison sentences.

Like veterans of Vietnam and other wars, he was reluctant to talk about the death and suffering he had witnessed. With dejection and hopelessness in his voice, Eddy said, "I don't want to remember—but I remember." He said the constant fear of being attacked by the mujahedin had left him paranoid. But, he said, shaking his head, it was an accident involving a gas leak that "seared my mind and soul." The gas leak had caused a fiery explosion in Eddy's camp. He had looked on helplessly as dozens of soldiers burned to death. Eddy had suffered burns along his face and neck, but he was lucky to be alive. The tragedy had left him emotionally shattered, unable to cope, and helpless to forget about the war.

Most of his fellow soldiers had not wanted to serve in the military, but they had had no choice. Only young officers intending to make a career of the army volunteered for service in Afghanistan, because it offered quick advancement and many privileges, including special coupons that could be used to buy imported goods in foreign currency shops. "The majority in the army are just people—not intelligentsia, just simple guys from Russia, who never had anything and never will," Eddy said sympathetically. But he had mixed emotions about the soldiers who had served with him in Afghanistan. "Our guys are heroes, because they don't turn their backs on their country, but on themselves. They are forced to forget about themselves. On the other hand, they're murderers—occupiers," he said distastefully. It was clear that Eddy also felt both disgust and pride in his own involvement. The tragedy for him was that he really had no one with whom he could share his experiences and emotions.

After eighteen months in Afghanistan, Eddy returned home, arriving at Domodyedovo Airport, a sprawling complex of grimy waiting rooms filled with studiously indifferent or hostile Aeroflot personnel. The airport, located south of Moscow, serves flights to and from the Soviet Union's southern republics. His plane from Tashkent touched down at Domodyedovo on December 1. From there he took a bus into the capital and then rode the metro to Pushkin Square, where he had once spent so many pleasant hours sitting and talking to friends.

For months he had dreamed of coming home, but his return to Moscow brought him only estrangement and loneliness. "When I was among people, I thought I was among children," said Eddy. "I couldn't speak to them. I saw young women—chic women—and fashionably dressed guys, and I couldn't look at them and I still can't. I had lots of conflicts and I thought everyone here was dirt and they thought I was dirt." It was difficult for him to communicate to people what he had experienced in the war. "How can I forget it—but how can I explain it? They live with their family, they ride in cars, they go to stores, they can't understand what it was like in Afghanistan," he said.

Eddy shared a small apartment with his brother and mother in a Moscow suburb, but they were unable to help him readjust to civilian life. "At first, my brother was afraid to look in my eyes and my mother was frightened by me," he said. "Now, they try to help, but they can't understand. My mother doesn't want to know that I'm into drugs." Because of his drug use, he had been arrested several times. "And when I have trouble, it's even worse for me if the police know I'm sick. They're pretty cruel," he said.

After being given preference as a veteran to enter a history institute, Eddy found himself unable to study and was expelled because of some "unpleasantness," which he refused to explain but which probably had involved either drugs or low grades. Eddy went to work at a small book bindery, but he had problems there as well. "Something didn't work in my head," was the only explanation he was able to offer.

So he quit trying to work or go to school. Every few months, Eddy went to a mental hospital, where he met with a medical technician, who examined him and made a ruling on whether he was able to work. "Usually, the people in the hospital don't know what to say to me. They just say, 'See how you feel tomorrow,' " he said resentfully. "They should kill me. It would be better for everybody," he added, his voice filled with despair.

Eddy had not had a girlfriend since his return from the war. "No one can look into my eyes," he said, "especially women. They think I'm too evil or frightening. In fact, I don't have friends—I have no friends at all." There were no private counseling groups for *Afghantsi*, so Eddy had never attempted to share his problems with other vets. The Komsomol had formed some young veterans' organizations, but, as Eddy said, "the Komsomol is the party and I'm not interested in the party." He expressed similar disdain for the Soviet press, whose reporting he called "gibberish and delirium." Eddy believed that the Soviet media would never write honestly about the war in Afghanistan. But he also said that the Soviet people were not sincerely interested in discussing it. "They know what happened in Hungary and Czechoslovakia, but they don't know what's going on in Afghanistan and they don't want to know. In a year or two, no one will speak about the war—everyone will be absolutely quiet on the subject," he said bitterly.

For Eddy, however, leaving the war behind would be difficult—perhaps even impossible—without professional counseling or many hours in a veterans' support group. He had stopped trying to fit into Soviet society and seemed to have given up on ever finding a satisfying career. "I don't think of the future. I try not to, because it might be even worse. I know

I'll have to die sometime, but I don't know what I'll do until then,'' he said. "It's not possible to help me—it can't be done. Only I can help myself.''

With that, he ended the interview. As he was escorted past a Soviet policeman—one of many who are always posted outside foreigners' apartments, he fell silent. Turning to the reporter, he patted her on the shoulder, said good-bye, and quickly walked away.

How many young Soviet men continue to suffer like Eddy? During the eight-year conflict, at least 800,000 soldiers were stationed in Afghanistan; how many of them returned home emotionally crippled, tormented by memories, and unable to salvage what was left of their shattered lives? Until the government, or the veterans themselves, create widely available counseling programs to help men like Eddy, they will probably remain dropouts—unable to become productive members of society and unwilling to take part in Gorbachev's dream of restructuring the Soviet economy.

Western doctors who have experience with counseling programs for the *Afghantsi* have come away feeling guardedly optimistic that the vets will get the help they need. Dr. Charles Figley, an American psychologist and author of a book on the psychological trauma suffered by Vietnam vets, was invited to Moscow in 1988 to meet with Soviet army doctors. Figley also talked with fifty veterans of the Afghan war.

He found that government efforts to design treatment programs for Afghan vets have been stymied by the fact that there is no special department designated to take on their problems. Instead, there is only the party, and the party has been very slow to act. Mental health experts also have no experience with war-related stress, so they are unable to diagnose and treat it. Most important, they have no way of conducting the research they would need to develop proper diagnostic and treatment procedures, because the government won't back them up. As Dr. Figley said, many in the party and the military don't want to learn the extent of the suffering caused by the war. "They're afraid to know, because once they discover the human toll, there may be a public consensus that will make their society reluctant to get into a war again,'' he said.

The vets Figley met were bitterly disappointed by the government's lack of response to their plight. They contrast their treatment to that accorded World War II veterans, who remain tremendously revered in Soviet society, receive special housing and jobs, and are able to jump to the head of any queue. Afghan vets feel duped; they risked their lives, only to be ignored or hated.

Parents put pressure on the vets to slide quietly into civilian jobs.

Beauty pageants, once banned as bourgeois and capitalistic, are now allowed. The annual Miss Moscow pageant attracts hundreds of interested applicants.

Young pageant contestants wearing skimpy bathing suits once would not have been seen on television or in newspapers. Now, the media have become much more willing to show beauty pageants and partially clad models.

Soviet punks, once harassed by police and hauled into local stations for questioning, now feel more freedom to dress in nonconformist styles.

Because of the shortage of cafes and clubs, young Soviets find it difficult to entertain themselves after school. Many hang out in the doorways of buildings or gather with others at home.

Many parents take their children to Moscow's historic Red Square to see Lenin's tomb and the changing of the guard.

Young Moscovites, unable to find a place where they can be alone, often do their courting in the city's parks and squares.

The press once avoided any mention of motorcycle clubs, heavy metallists, or youth gangs. Now such groups are pictured in newspapers and on television and there is public debate about the social forces that lead young Soviets to join gangs.

A recent graduate from a polytechnical school takes his place in a factory alongside an older worker.

Young Soviets, emboldened by the increasing openness under Gorbachev, feel more free to question the rules.

When spring arrives, young Soviets eagerly take advantage of the welcome warm
weather.

Because of housing conditions and other problems, many young Soviets limit themselves to one child.

Girls in many parts of the country still wear a brown dress and starched white pinafore to school. Others have switched to a more modern dark blue polyester two-piece suit.

Outdoor concerts attract large crowds of young Soviets on weekends.

Most concerts are free of charge and open to anyone who has the time to stop and listen.

Soccer games between local teams are also a popular pastime for young Soviets.

Public swimming pools are a rarity in the Soviet Union, so most young people don their bathing suits and swim in lakes and rivers.

Most Soviet parents have only one son, and when their cherished only son is unable to conform and shows signs of mental illness, they desperately want him to be "cured." Soviets in their forties and fifties have been trained to look to the government for help, but in this situation, the government has had little to offer.

Like many of the Vietnam veterans who struggled with some of the same problems, Soviet soldiers believe that no one can help them but themselves. Most have given up on the government, believing that they must take their treatment into their own hands. Many vets have banded together in support groups of seven to ten men to meet regularly and help one another readjust to civilian life. The groups are not officially sanctioned and they have resisted efforts by the Komsomol to unite them into one national organization. They are very cautious about being affiliated with any group.

Acting on their own, one group of veterans has created a memorial for *Afghantsi* in Moscow's Friendship Park. The group meets every Wednesday evening in a veterans' hall to discuss problems and help each other. In many areas of the country, other groups have petitioned cemeteries to change the headstones of soldiers slain in Afghanistan. Instead of the inscription, "Died carrying out his international duty," they have asked that they read, "Died in Afghanistan." Private groups have founded a job counseling service for veterans in Moscow. Two cooperative apartment buildings have been constructed by *Afghantsi* and are open only to veterans.

Much as Gorbachev would want them to, some veterans are taking on more responsibility and not looking to the government to solve their problems. Their hostility toward those who started the war works in Gorbachev's favor, since he has distanced himself from the past by moving to withdraw troops from Afghanistan. But some vets have even gone beyond hating the Brezhnev leadership for making the war; they hate all government and even talk of insurrection. Although only a small minority, their talk of violence and retaliation can only spell danger for Gorbachev. Unless their anger is muted, it may spread among the population of veterans and turn them against Gorbachev's reforms.

The key to a full recovery for most vets, according to Dr. Figley, is getting close to their families and fellow veterans. "If they're able to educate themselves about their psychological needs and start their own support groups, they'll be fine," he said, adding that Afghan vets have the advantage of being able to build on the experience of American veterans of the Vietnam War. So far, the Kremlin has not stopped them from meeting with their American counterparts who visit Moscow. Under *glasnost*, this open dialogue will probably continue.

WAR GAMES FOR CHILDREN

In the spring of 1989, *"perestroika"* has found its way into the Soviet military. The armed forces had long been inviolate, receiving the best the nation has to offer: 20 percent of the gross national product and two years out of the lives of most young men.

There were hints in the Soviet press that the Kremlin was toying with the idea of diverting some of the nation's resources to the civilian economy. Military spending was hotly debated during the March 1989 elections to the Congress of Peoples' Deputies, when even conservative candidates frequently cited military spending as an area where cutbacks could be made. One 44-year-old officer even ran on a platform calling for the end of the student draft.

Then in April 1989, the Soviet press published a decree announcing the abolition of the draft for all students at institutes and universities. The decree said young men would be exempt from military service until they completed their studies, and, once they graduated, they would be required to serve only one year as junior officers. Soviet officials said the decision to exempt students from military conscription was made possible by the cutback of 500,000 men in the size of the armed forces, which Gorbachev announced a few months earlier when he went to New York for a summit with Ronald Reagan and George Bush.

The move was significant; Western intelligence places the size of the Soviet military at 5.2 million. Cutting into that fighting force—one of the largest in the world—will put millions of young men to work rebuilding the nation's economy rather than digging ditches, cleaning rifles, and marching in step. It will also free Soviet teenagers and their parents from having to invent medical exemptions and other schemes that will keep them out of the military. If the Soviet Union moves to an all-professional army, Soviet young men will not have to worry about the military until they graduate from their institutes or universities.

But generations of young Soviets who spent their first two years after high school in the army carry strong memories of the Soviet military. These two years are the formalization of the service they begin to prepare for with kindergarten. In every kindergarten classroom, civil defense corners are set up and children undergo drills on what to do in case of a nuclear attack, just as Americans did in the 1950s and 1960s. They learn the alphabet from readers illustrated with tanks, rockets, and heavily armed soldiers. Little four and five year olds are led on hikes to World War II battle sites and cemeteries. During the early grades, girls also receive heavy doses of military indoctrination.

Later, when they enter school, students are encouraged to set up exhibits of "combat glory" and to tend the graves of soldiers. Veterans of the war regularly visit schools to tell tales of heroism and glory.

Children learn to use gas masks and become familiar with them through games and drills. Two western reporters walking past a school in the southern republic of Georgia once came upon a playground with children wearing gas masks—a scene that was both ludicrous and disturbing. Dressed in their blue and white school uniforms, these children were playing a noisy game of basketball. Jumping up for baskets and throwing the ball to their teammates, they were behaving like children anywhere, except that each one was wearing a grotesque gray gas mask.

This emphasis on military subjects in schools and in the media often grates on Westerners' sensibilities. Correspondents in the Soviet Union complain to their Soviet friends about the society's preoccupation with war. But Soviets generally reply that the emphasis on war could prevent the possibility of another one. Often, even the most sophisticated among them cannot recognize that they are being manipulated by their country's propaganda organs.

The leadership dwells on Hitler's invasion of the Soviet Union and the dangers of Western imperialism to foster a belief in the necessity of preparedness for war. Children are trotted out to war monuments and frightened by graphic films about the war to instill a fear of being attacked. Such war lessons prepare them for their military duty.

At the age of ten, Soviet schoolchildren begin learning the skills a soldier needs to defend his country. They join the Young Pioneers, the Communist party's children's organization, and participate in the military sports games known as *Zarnitsa*, or summer lightning. For five days in May, millions of Young Pioneers, all wearing their red scarves, can be seen taking part in the games in fields and playgrounds around the nation. Each child joins a "youth army" and is taught to march, shoot, fight fires, read maps, pitch camp, keep physically fit, and master lessons in civil defense. They learn rifle marksmanship, the best marksmen among them competing in city and regional contests.

Another military organization that has a vast membership among children is the Volunteer Society for Cooperation with the Army, Aviation and Fleet, known by the acronym DOSAAF. Soviet children join the group at the age of ten. At least eleven million take part every year in its program of physical exercises called GTO—"Ready for labor and defense."

Students sixteen to eighteen years old compete in the *Orlenok*, or "Eaglet," games, which are conducted under the slogan, "Eaglet today, a fighting man of the Soviet army tomorrow." Once a year, they take a hike with a map and compass, learn first aid, and build a simple shelter. They are taught how to identify and avoid contaminated areas, follow safety rules and civil defense measures, and undergo more advanced military exercises, including nuclear attack drills. Winners of the *Orlenok* contests are given awards at ceremonies which are covered by newspapers and television.

In their last two years of school, boys attend two hours of military training classes every week. The classes are conducted by the Ministry of Defense and usually taught by reserve officers. Students learn to handle Kalashnikov rifles and compete to see who can take one apart and put it back together the fastest.

Live ammunition is handed out in these classes and safety precautions are not always followed. One Soviet now in his mid-thirties recalled that when he was in school, some of the boys had gone to their military training class drunk and had taken target practice. Although the teacher knew that some of the boys had been drinking, he did not stop them from using the rifles. Shaking his head, the Soviet remembered the scene with shock and disbelief: "We were shooting at trees and straight up in the air, just for the fun of it. I remember shooting into the dirt around my feet, because I liked the way it exploded in little puffs. It's amazing no one was hurt."

Not all are fortunate enough to escape injury in their military training classes; the Soviet press regularly carries articles about teenagers who are injured or even killed. In 1984, a Latvian paper reported that a sixteen year old in a Riga high school had died of a gunshot wound during his military training class. And the following year, a *Komsomolskaya pravda* article told of an instructor in a Ukrainian school who was killed while demonstrating how to use a hand grenade.

The military training classes are unpopular and many young men skip them or try to find excuses to avoid attending them. The military newspaper *Krasnaya Zvezda* acknowledged for the first time in December 1988 that students were boycotting military instruction classes in many large cities, including Moscow, Leningrad, Tashkent, and Riga. Other Soviet newspapers suggested abolishing the military courses or making them voluntary.

✷ The Soviet draft, and the ploys used to avoid it, in some ways resemble the situation faced by young Americans as the war in Vietnam began. When the Soviet Union first invaded Afghanistan, students who attended courses full time were exempt from military service until they completed their studies, when they usually entered the military as noncommissioned officers. But because of the plunging birthrate in the European portion of the nation and the pressing need for new recruits to serve in Afghanistan, the rules were changed in 1982. After that, except for those who attended certain schools, students were no longer allowed to postpone their two years in the army. The student deferment was reinstated once again in 1989.

Before the end of the war in Afghanistan, medical deferments became more difficult to obtain; the armed forces even began accepting boys with poor eyesight and serious ailments. One young Soviet told about an acquaintance with a bad heart who had managed to avoid the draft until he was twenty-four years old. He was called up in 1982, when the war in Afghanistan put new pressure on boys of his generation to serve. Although his mother, a doctor, produced documents attesting to his physical frailty, he was drafted and sent to a construction battalion near Baikonur, the Soviet Union's space launch site in central Asia. Two months after being posted there, he experienced heart murmurs. Even that did not win him an exemption. Following his recovery, he was transferred to a post in Russia to serve out the remainder of his tour.

For the children of the privileged elite, medical deferments were easier to win. For instance, one young man suffered from mild arthritis in his hands, so his family's sympathetic doctor had the boy hospitalized repeatedly. When it came time for the boy to report for active duty, he produced a document saying that his arthritis would prevent him from holding a rifle. He received a medical exemption and went on to study law at Moscow State University.

Certain professionals are also excused from military service. One young man avoided the army by getting a work certificate saying that he taught in a village school, when he actually only worked there part time. There was such a shortage of teachers in the area that the military authorities did not investigate his case and granted him a deferment.

Many parents would pay bribes to keep their sons out of areas where they were more likely to be injured or killed. The Soviet press reported in 1987 that a commissar in Estonia was caught accepting bribes from the parents of conscripts who were to be sent to Afghanistan. They had bought their freedom for one thousand rubles—about one thousand six hundred dollars at the official exchange rate. Others slated to help in the cleanup work at the stricken Chernobyl nuclear power plant had paid the commissar five hundred rubles, or about eight hundred dollars, to avoid being sent there. Draft dodging was reported to be widespread in Uzbekistan, where, in 1987, hundreds of Komsomol members were prosecuted for illegally avoiding the military.

But getting a deferment had been relatively easy in the 1970s. Many young men in their thirties today readily tell about the strategies they'd used years before to avoid military service. One said his parents had helped him obtain a medical deferment by claiming that he had psychological problems. His mother had found a document signed by a doctor that said that as a boy, he was afraid of the dark—"juvenile psychosis" was the diagnosis. When he reported to the local conscription office, he carried another certificate, signed by a doctor sympathetic to his plight, saying he still suffered from a form of the psychosis.

Like young Americans who used similar ruses to escape the Vietnam War, he had to pay a price. Although he had managed to avoid military service by being judged psychologically unfit, he was ordered to undergo treatment in a mental hospital for one month. During his stay there, he did not have the right to leave and had no privacy. The food was inedible and he was permitted to shower only once a week. He spent his time creating posters with patriotic slogans for the hospital walls. A doctor came to talk to him once about his supposed illness, but after he realized that he had been hospitalized as a result of avoiding the draft, the doctor never bothered him again.

Upon his release, this young man was marked for life. His military documents stated that he had received a medical deferment for "psychological reasons," which made him ineligible to travel abroad or to get a driver's license (under Soviet law, mentally ill people are prohibited from driving cars). But he was philosophical about these hardships: "I never expected to own a car or to travel abroad. It seemed a small price to pay to stay out of the army."

LIFE IN THE ARMY

What could have been so awful about the Soviet army that a bright young man would be willing to spend a month in a mental hospital, be marked for life as mentally ill, and forfeit all opportunities for foreign travel? At that time, he would not even have been sent to Afghanistan, since the Soviet invasion had come later. There were several reasons. He didn't want to spend two years of his life far from home in a dirty barrack with a hundred other noisy conscripts; he didn't want to eat bad food; and he didn't want to be subject to the rude orders of hostile, indifferent officers.

Soldiers in almost every army in the world voice similar complaints, but conditions in the Soviet army are especially rigorous. As one young army veteran said, "I grew up being told the rest of the world respected the Soviet army. Then I found myself a soldier. I discovered that the Soviet army was just a bunch of underfed, badly dressed, poorly disciplined kids." He said that his two years of service began with call-up day, which falls every March and September. On this day, notices are posted around the country summoning boys into the local draft office. Before the Soviet army began cutting its troop strength, about one million were called up every six months.

Recalling his first impressions of army life, he said that he and about thirty other recruits were first hustled into a large room. One at a time, each was seated in a chair, had a sheet tied around his neck, and got shaved with an electric cutter. All shades and textures of hair—red, blond, dark, curly—piled up on the floor around the chair. Dozens of men were left bald under the sergeant's touch.

After being deprived of their hair, the new soldiers were led into an adjacent room, where they were ordered to strip. They bundled their clothes and all personal belongings together and handed them to a clerk, who labeled and marked them for storage. Naked, empty-handed, and hairless, the fresh recruits were marched into yet another room, where they were issued shirts, underwear, nightshirts, belts, uniforms, and foot wrappings to go inside the tall black boots worn by all Soviet soldiers.

New conscripts are then transported by train or in olive drab army trucks to the nearest airport, where they are allowed one telephone call to their parents to tell them where they are being posted. These new conscripts, in their baggy, ill-fitting uniforms and prison-style haircuts, can often be seen sitting in open trucks, staring enviously at motorists and pedestrians on the streets of Moscow. Most of them look unprepared, even afraid; all of them appear terribly young.

Their apprehension comes in part from being sent far away from parents and friends for the first time in their lives. In the Soviet Union, soldiers are not allowed to serve near their hometowns. Muscovites are sent to Siberia, boys from the Baltic republics go to Uzbekistan, and Uzbeks are posted in the Ukraine. The policy makes it difficult for soldiers to desert and return home. Also, soldiers who are thrust into an unfamiliar climate and culture will feel more drawn to their unit and, thus, feel more unified. Most important, the authorities do not want soldiers serving near large nationality groups to whom they might feel loyal, because when nationalist protests break out among the local population, soldiers might be tempted to join in. And, because the soldiers are armed, it would be impossible for the officers to control them. If soldiers are ordered to quell an angry protest, they would be more willing to fire on members of another ethnic group than on their own people. But the practice of sending conscripts to serve far from home has come under attack. In the Baltics, large demonstrations have been staged to demand that local boys be allowed to serve in their own republics.

After arriving at their posts, the new draftees find themselves in crowded living quarters. One hundred soldiers are assigned to a single room furnished with three levels of bunk beds. The room is poorly heated in winter and has neither hot water nor indoor toilets. Soldiers are taken to the local bathhouse once a week, where they are issued a sliver of soap and given half an hour to bathe. Those who grew up in villages, where they haul their water from the local well and use outhouses, are accustomed to such conditions. But those raised in cities often complain bitterly about the rustic living conditions.

New recruits spend their first six months in the army serving the older soldiers, known as *dedii*, or "grandfathers." The younger men are made to clean toilets and barracks and wash clothes. They serve on guard duty while the more experienced soldiers sleep. Humiliated and used as slaves, the younger men are often forced to give their food to the older men. As they progress through their months of service, they become *dedii* and submit newcomers to the same humiliations they suffered.

In 1987, the Soviet press began to discuss the brutality of everyday life for draftees, although it claimed that bullying under the *dedii* system was an aberration that the military could not control. Many young men say otherwise—that the officers encouraged it, in order to turn recruits against one another instead of against the officers. Among soldiers, the tradition is strong. Most draftees enjoy finally being able to inflict the same tortures upon the new guys that they had been made to undergo.

There is little in the army to break up the monotony of daily life. A soldier's day is planned out for him from 6:00 A.M., when he is awakened by a recruit shouting *poidyom*, "get up," until late evening, when he is given an hour of free time. Most spend these fleeting moments washing their clothes or watching the nightly television news program *Vremya*.

Along with their physical and military training, soldiers attend political education classes three times a week in a study hall known as the Lenin Room. There, they study Marxist-Leninist theory, read newspapers, and discuss Gorbachev's speeches. Each works out of a textbook and completes exercises, which an officer checks once a week. According to one young Soviet, "The political classes are so boring that some soldiers even fall asleep. The officers are bored too, but they have to get through them."

As in Soviet schools, the *kollektiv* is strongly reinforced in the army; rewards and punishment are doled out to the group, not the individual. Army officers use peer pressure by blaming a whole group for the actions of one ill-behaved soldier. One young man recalled how his entire unit had been punished when a soldier tried to escape. He said that all the men had been looking forward to a one-day leave, when it was discovered that a soldier was missing. Instead of having the day off, they were required to search until they found the escapee. He was punished with a ten-day term in the local jail, where he was fed nothing but bread and water. But even worse, his fellow soldiers would never let him forget that he had deprived them of their day of drinking and girls in the nearby town. The incident kept other soldiers from even thinking about trying to flee.

Army food is very bad, and many men complain of being hungry and undernourished during their two years in the service. Breakfast consists of white bread, mashed potatoes, kasha, sweet tea, and a small pat of butter. For lunch and dinner, they receive gray bread, thin soup, and potatoes with pork fat. The cuisine improves only on military holidays, such as Tank Day or Missile Day, when they are given coffee and rice and perhaps a small, tough piece of meat.

Since the salary is only seven rubles, or about twelve dollars, a month, it is almost impossible for soldiers to supplement their diet by shopping in local stores, which offer only milk, candy, cookies, and cigarettes. One former soldier said the store near his base sold apples only twice a year. Many soldiers rely on their parents to send them money, fruit, and cakes.

The Soviet army raises its own livestock to supplement its meager rations. Typically, each unit of soldiers buys a pig from a local collective farm and raises it in the fields outside their barracks. They feed the animal leftovers from the kitchens. Soldiers usually butcher their pigs on a major holiday.

Theft in the Soviet army is common. One Soviet called the army ''a community of thieves'' and said that even when there is nothing worth stealing, the soldiers steal. He explained that while all of the soldiers want to have some personal belongings, they are forbidden to own anything, so they steal anything they can find—for example, government-issued fur hats, soap, and boots. Since items such as boots are not reissued, the victim then has to steal someone else's boots. Whenever a soldier manages to steal something valuable, such as a radio, he sells it in the nearest town or gives it to an officer in exchange for better treatment.

Another pastime for soldiers is improving their uniforms. Each young man is issued two uniforms—one for everyday use and one to use as a dress uniform while on leave. Soldiers usually devote a great deal of their spare time finding scraps of fabric to sew onto their dress uniforms in ways that will distinguish them from other soldiers. Many change the style and even the cut of their uniforms.

They also make albums of keepsakes, including letters from their mothers and girlfriends and photos of themselves and fellow soldiers. Traditionally, the book is covered with red velvet, which is difficult to buy; it often has to be stolen from banners around the military base. Soldiers like to place a photo of the Soviet minister of defense on the first page of their albums. In many remote areas, such photos are in short supply, so they end up being stolen from the Lenin Room. One Soviet said that all of his political classes were conducted under a poster with a gaping hole in it, where a recruit had removed a portrait to adorn the album he had made to remember his years in the army.

✻ Despite all of the official propaganda about friendship among the Soviet people, the Soviet army is rigidly segregated by ethnicity. Uzbeks serve in units with other Uzbeks, Ukrainians with Ukrainians, and the dominant Russians with fellow Russians. The soldiers are segregated because many non-Russians speak the language poorly and have difficulty communicating with those of other ethnic groups. Also, non-Russians are considered to be less loyal than Russian soldiers. Many fair-skinned Slavs look down on the dark-skinned central Asians and do not want to serve side by side with them.

This ethnic hatred is used as a tool by the officers to keep soldiers in line. The soldiers' resentment toward one another is manipulated to prevent them from becoming unified against the officers. If, during his first year in the army, a Ukrainian suffers under an older Tajik, he is sure to find a Tajik during his second year to repay him for his brother's torments. Instead of turning their animosity toward the officers, Soviet soldiers are kept busy hating one another.

One Russian said that the central Asians on his base were called *churkii*, the small chips of wood that are fed into ovens. The word is a slang expression for any non-Russian who speaks the language poorly, and is therefore considered as dumb as a piece of wood. He also said that the central Asian soldiers did not learn weapons training; instead, they spent most of their time digging ditches. None of them had a good command of Russian, and their officers, also central Asians, spoke to them in their native languages.

The discrimination this young man witnessed is part of a nationwide policy toward central Asians, many of whom are Muslims. Little effort is made to integrate them into the more demanding high-tech services of the military. Instead, they are assigned the army's dirty work. They are relegated to kitchen and warehouse duty or to construction battalions, where they labor with shovels or build truck garages and bridges. They may have the opportunity to learn a skill, and if they come into contact with Russians, they also might be able to pick up bits of the Russian language. But it is much more difficult for them to move into the officer corps, and there are no central Asians in the military's high command.

Eventually, these discriminatory policies are bound to backfire. The central Asians' soaring birthrates make them a growing force; Soviet newspapers reported in 1988 that the number of recruits from central Asia and Caucasia have grown to make up 37 percent of the draft.

There has been some effort to teach them better language skills and to enroll more of them in the Soviet Union's seventy-four military training academies, from which the officer corps is drawn. These four-year academies have begun to allow applicants to take their entrance exams in languages other than Russian; it was hoped that this would encourage more applicants from the Baltic republics, central Asia, and the Ukraine. Military students are still required to study in Russian, however.

Until they gain more fluency in the dominant language and overcome the system's built-in discrimination, members of minority groups will not be allowed into the military leadership. As their ranks grow to make up a larger force within the army, this can only mean that more of the military will be disaffected and dissatisfied, leaving the Soviet army weakened or even crippled as a fighting force.

★ Completion of two years' service in the army is cause for celebration; many soldiers stay drunk during the days they spend on trains on their way back home. Proudly wearing their uniforms and carrying attaché cases fashioned for them by the younger men in their units, they look relieved and happy. One such group of soldiers were on their way home when they were spotted by a couple of Western women correspondents aboard the Trans-Siberian Railroad. The young men were in the dining car, where they were drinking cognac at a nearby table. Louise Branson, a correspondent then working for UPI, began talking to two of them, who said they had just finished their tours of duty and were heading for Novosibirsk, a large city in Siberia.

Mesmerized by Marlboro cigarettes, as representative a symbol of *kife* as any, a bottle of Italian wine, and two Western women, one of the men moved to the reporters' table as his buddies looked on, jealously. Introducing himself as Boris, the young soldier said he hoped to find a good job and marry his girlfriend, who had been waiting for two years for him to return. He asked a few questions about life in the West and, after a brief chat, the reporters returned to their compartment. Boris headed back to the *platzkartny* car, which holds seventy-two people in bunk beds stacked three-high.

The next night, the reporters saw Boris in the *platzkartny* car, but this time his behavior was strange. Rather than friendly and curious, Boris had turned stiff and fearful. He just stared into a book of speeches about Marxism-Leninism and refused to speak. Not wishing to make him even more uncomfortable, the reporters quickly moved away.

After arriving in Novosibirsk the next day, the two correspondents were summoned from their hotel room by the manager. He said he had received a report from the local military base that the two women had been trying to persuade young Boris to reveal Soviet military secrets, that they had demanded to know what kinds of rifles he had used and what missiles the Soviet army possessed. The hotel manager even had a handwritten complaint on his desk filled out by the young soldier on the train. Obviously, Boris had been forced to write it.

The reporters were asked to sign a statement confessing that they had violated Soviet law by trying to learn state secrets. Louise refused, and she demanded to know why, if he was not a policeman or a KGB officer, a hotel manager was telling them what to do. The conversation with the young soldier aboard the train had continued only a few minutes and never touched on the Soviet military, Louise told him angrily.

Defeated, the hotel manager agreed to let the two reporters return to their room. But as they stood to leave, he fixed them with a cold stare and said, "Let me give you some advice, girls. Remember, you're foreigners, traveling in the Soviet Union. During the rest of your trip, don't go talking to Soviet soldiers, understand?"

It must have been his buddies who had put Boris up to the deed. They had looked on jealously as Boris talked with the two Western women, and they must have threatened to tell on him. Until later, the two reporters were unaware that Soviet soldiers are forbidden to speak to foreigners; poor Boris had defied the regulation as well as the *kollektiv*. So, faced with possible punishment, he concocted a story to protect himself. He lied to the local authorities that two devious Westerners had tried to coax military secrets out of him. The incident served as a lesson, both in the strength of the *kollektiv* and the strict secrecy surrounding the Soviet military.

OFFICIAL AND UNOFFICIAL WORK

The concept of a career in the Soviet Union differs from the Western approach. It is not easy for Westerners to understand the Soviet style of labor, which often involves the art of avoiding work without appearing to do so. Soviet people are required by law to have a job, but that doesn't mean they have to work. In the Soviet Union, it is possible to work yet still be free from work.

Many people divide work into two categories. The first is "official" work performed for the state, which pays a salary in rubles and is recorded in each person's work book. For many people, this official job is just a cover—a comfortable, warm place for them to spend part of each day, where the demands are few. They are much more attentive to the second category of work—the pursuit of goods or services that actually improve their lives. In this category, competition is fierce and the risks are sometimes considerable. It may require a lot of scheming, but in this line of work they can get a tender cut of meat, hard-to-find car parts, or a rare theater ticket, often through an acquaintance.

A young Soviet woman once recounted a typical day at her official workplace. Her tale was hilariously absurd but tragically poignant. Like millions of other Soviet workers, she spent a good deal of time trying to hoodwink her supervisor and do as little work as possible for her miserably small salary. Her story illustrates that quintessential Soviet proverb: "They pretend to pay us, and we pretend to work."

The young woman, a nineteen-year-old named Olya, lived in a distant suburb of Moscow and traveled an hour and a half every morning by train and trolley bus to reach her job in the library of a large institute in the center of the capital. The workday began at 8:00 A.M., and every morning there was a mad rush to arrive on time. Olya said her supervisor stood watching in a room where she worked with a dozen other women, making note of any employees who arrived even a few minutes late. Latecomers straggled in flushed and perspiring, armed with excuses about broken down buses, sick children, or traffic jams. Despite their pleas for leniency, the supervisor ordered each late arrival to complete a form explaining why they were tardy. The form was then stamped, signed, and placed in the employee's personnel file. Anyone who came late more than three times a month suffered a pay cut.

Olya laughed as she told the story of an obese woman who was late because the elevator in the institute was out of order and she was forced to climb the stairs. She wrote a copious explanation that continued for several pages, explaining how often and on which floors she had been forced to stop for a rest. The woman's approach was successful: her supervisor was overwhelmed by her torrent of excuses, and granted her a pardon.

But Olya said that all pretense of order ended once the boss had dispensed with the morning roll call; after that, there was chaos. The women usually spent the rest of the morning drinking tea, gossiping, and complaining about how their husbands had treated them the night before. Others put on their makeup and recovered from their rush to the office. Of course, whenever the supervisor entered the room, they pretended to be busy. The office was overstaffed, with eight women doing what could have been done by four. But they were not allowed to read books, sleep, or openly goof off. The system forced them to make a science out of looking busy.

At lunchtime, they shopped in local stores for food or deficit items. Anyone who found something to buy was excused from work if she bought something for all of her colleagues. In the afternoon, one young woman was sent off to buy patriotic posters at the government store on the Arbat, a street with a rich history that has been converted into the nation's first pedestrian mall. Before leaving, she made a list of purchases and took money from all of the other women, noting dress sizes and color preferences. Instead of going to the poster store, she spent most of the afternoon shopping for her fellow workers at GUM, the huge old government department store in Red Square. When she returned, her purchases were distributed and the women spent the remainder of their day examining one another's new lipsticks, putting on new clothes or trying on their new bras over their dresses.

Their work was mindlessly dull. It was Olya's job to make cards for all of the new books that arrived. She recalled once having to make one thousand identical cards, each one handwritten, for the latest collection of speeches by former party leader Konstantin Chernenko. A sympathetic colleague tried to ease her task by making five hundred cards for her on the institute's copying machine. But when the illegal use of the machine was discovered, the worker was punished and Olya was forced to write the cards out by hand. Olya's salary was only 80 rubles a month, or about $130, a sum so small that she could not dream of moving away from her parents' apartment, even if it would have been possible to find her own place.

Every three months, at the end of what was known as a *kvartal*, or quarter, the work pace picked up. Afternoon shopping trips to GUM ceased. Thousands of books were hurriedly processed and placed on the library shelves as the women struggled to meet the production targets set for their office by the state. No one cared whether the books were properly catalogued or placed in the correct section, so long as the target was met.

Olya's office was typical of many Soviet workplaces. In factories and offices around the nation, often only a semblance of work gets done everyday. Absenteeism is high. The management is sympathetic with the difficulties of finding food and clothing, often sending employees on shopping expeditions for an entire department of eager buyers. Salaries are so low and the economy so inefficient that workers spend much of their time in illegal schemes to find scarce goods. Few workplaces are computerized, which makes for many boring and repetitive jobs.

The nationwide labor shortage keeps bosses constantly on the lookout for new employees; often, workers are fired for only the most serious offenses, such as drunkenness or repeated absenteeism. Some young people dream of leaving their dreary, dead-end jobs, but they have no choice: failure to work may result in a prison term. There are a small number of challenging, prestigious jobs, but these go to the exceptionally talented few, to those with connections, or to others with Komsomol or Communist party credentials. For the average Soviet worker, a career that offers regular promotions and prestige is hard to find. This is especially the case for women. Many young Soviets grow up believing that work is something to be endured. Their first job often comes as a shock; when they get a glimpse of what lies ahead, many see their careers as hopeless.

But the natural exuberance of youth is on their side. If the established career path seems hopeless, many jump outside of it. They beat the system with black-market schemes which are illegal but at least improve their standard of living. *Perestroika* has given many Soviets new reason to hope. Under the new law that allows them to form cooperatives, young entrepreneurs are going into business for themselves. For the first time in years, they can channel their youthful energies into making themselves rich—by Soviet standards—without risking arrest.

Despite the promise of *perestroika*, the combination of entry-level wages and high prices makes their dream of *kife* practically unreachable for young Soviets. Even buying life's basics is difficult. An expensive meal in a cooperative restaurant is an unheard of luxury. One young man calculated that without the help of his parents, he would not have a fully furnished apartment and a car until he reached his fifties, and only then by the most stringent savings. Sneering, he referred to his small wage as "ice-cream money."

When most young Westerners get married, they assume that they will be economically independent and turn to their parents for loans only in an emergency or to make a major purchase, such as a new home. Young people in the Soviet Union often have to count on their parents' help in buying the most basic items. Their dependence is the subject of many rueful jokes. One Soviet once laughed about a colleague whose daughter got married and soon afterward had a baby. Asked about his daughter, the man joked that his family had grown. "Before, I only had a daughter. Now I have three kids"—his daughter, his new son-in-law, and a grand-daughter.

This kind of financial squeeze forces many people out of white-collar jobs and into menial, less demanding work that allows more time for lucrative black-market schemes. In 1988, a Soviet newspaper published a letter from a woman who said that her salary of 115 rubles (about $180) was eaten up every month on just the basics: food, rent, commuting to work, laundry, repairs, and income tax. She had nothing left over to buy clothing or furniture. But she had found her solution: in the kindergarten next door, there was an opening for a night watchman that would pay 180 rubles a month plus free meals, and it required her to work only every other night. She figured that her days would be free to take in sewing from friends. Although she held a diploma as the director of an amateur theater group, she said sarcastically, "Let that be my hobby. It's cheaper."

A young man from Kharkov, a large city in the Ukraine, wrote to the weekly youth magazine *Sobesednik* in 1986 about his struggle to provide for his wife and their two-year-old daughter. An economist with a higher education, he earned 160 rubles a month, while his wife earned 120 rubles. They could not afford to buy new clothing, which made it impossible for them to go out in the evening, and they lived in a communal flat, so they could not invite guests home for dinner. His aim, he said, was "to live an honest, orderly life," meaning that he was unwilling to get involved in black-market deals to supplement his income. But he said the "constant shortage of money made life depressing," and he suggested that the average wage was lagging far behind prices. An editor at the magazine snidely asked what the young man had done to help the Soviet economy, adding that every citizen should work harder instead of complaining.

Many people are not as scrupulous as the young man from Kharkov and they recognize that the only way to boost their income is through theft. Soviet people steal because their wages are so low that they feel they are entitled to whatever they can carry out from their workplace. They are raised on the adage, "He who works honestly won't build himself a house," meaning that workers who don't steal will have nothing to show for their labor. Another pithy saying goes like this: "Tell me what you steal and I'll tell you who you are." Office workers carry away carbon paper, a deficit item needed for typing projects they do in their spare time. Construction workers steal paint, tile, and other building materials to sell to friends who are remodeling their apartments.

CAREER DECISIONS

Some young Soviets believe that jobs which provide access to scarce products, such as meat and alcohol, or to imports, such as East German sewing machines, are the only jobs worth having. They yearn to become food handlers or truck drivers, because such jobs can lead to quick wealth and status. A group of Leningrad psychologists found in a 1986 survey that teenagers most wanted to become car mechanics so that they could service cars on the side. Others wanted to become shop assistants so that they could set aside desirable merchandise to sell to their friends.

A 1986 study of four thousand schoolchildren by the magazine *Smyena* showed that becoming a doctor, engineer, teacher, or physicist was no longer considered prestigious. Among boys, the most popular profession was journalism, in part because of the possibility of foreign travel. Crossing their country's closed borders is the dream of many Soviet people, but they have other motives besides just wanting to see the world. One Soviet who worked on a monthly magazine and occasionally received travel vouchers to go abroad said that the trips meant everything to him because he used his small foreign currency allowance to buy tape recorders, then came home and sold them for a big profit. Eventually, he was able to afford a cooperative apartment.

Service jobs have become desirable, too. Although the monthly salaries in this field start as low as 90 rubles ($145), supplementing such a small income is easy: just grab a few items from every shipment of goods that arrives and sell them later to friends. Access to deficit goods is so important that when young people begin to get acquainted, they don't discuss what profession they are in or where they work, they ask, "What do you sit on?"—in other words, What goods do you have access to? Bolshoi theater tickets? Gasoline? Ladies clothing?

Young people also look for jobs that provide access to the *nuzhnik*, which literally means "outhouse" but is slang for "useful person." A guard at a store who can help you into the front of a queue or a saleswoman who will sell you deficit items are very popular *nuzhnikii*.

There is also stiff competition for jobs in bartending or waiting tables. A two-year technical school for barmen in Moscow quickly became popular after Gorbachev's antialcohol regulations were introduced in 1985. The school, which trains bartenders to work in restaurants and hotels, began receiving three hundred applications for every opening. People quickly recognized that any job related to vodka would offer instant profits. They knew it would be possible to dilute the alcohol they sold legally, then sell the remainder on the side at high prices to people who preferred to avoid the long lines outside the state liquor stores.

In the southern republics, where the nation's fruits and vegetables are grown, many people earn more money in their spare time farming private gardens than they do in their official jobs. Many fly into the capital for a week at a time, loaded down with melons that cost the equivalent of forty dollars apiece in the summer, or tomatoes that sell for fifteen dollars a pound in the winter. They stay in rooms above the market for about two dollars a night and rent a booth to sell their wares for less than a dollar a day. An article in a Soviet newspaper estimated in 1986 that the nation's fruit and vegetable sellers earn up to three billion rubles in profits each year but are taxed only 260 million rubles a year, or less than ten rubles a family.

Some young people opt for Siberia or the Far East, where they earn what is known as the "long ruble." Working on projects like the Baikal-Amur Railroad, they receive two or three times the salaries they would be paid in the European part of the Soviet Union. Their jobs often include an apartment and other benefits. Workers who live in northern villages on the Sea of Okhotsk, for example, get double wages and longer vacations. Every three years, the government pays their airfare to any part of the country. Such jobs promise quick independence from parents, higher salaries, and better housing; despite all of these pluses, most young Soviets avoid these jobs because the living conditions in Siberia are so harsh.

✶ Anyone who wants to enter a career considered prestigious must make the decision by no later than age fifteen. Entry into a special school is often essential, but competition for entry requires an early commitment, often long before the student is ready to make the decision on his own. Aptitude tests are rarely given. Instead of allowing the student an opportunity to decide for himself what field interests him, career decisions are often made by parents.

The drawback to this system is that if young Soviets end up in the wrong profession, they have little opportunity to select a new one. Soviets rarely go back to school at the age of thirty-five to begin a second career, as Americans increasingly do. For many, entering an institute is so difficult and expensive that they would be ashamed to admit that they had chosen the wrong field. Also, credits cannot be transferred from one institute to another, so if they decide to switch fields, they must start over again with the basic classes.

The tragedy is that some Soviets end up spending their entire lives hating their work. One woman suffered this fate because her father had insisted that she enter the Moscow Aviation Institute, considered one of the city's top five institutions of higher education. She was a quiet, introverted girl who loved to read and collect rare books. Her job as a designer in a noisy airplane assembly plant paid a good salary and she and her husband had been given a small apartment to go with it. But she dreamed instead of working with books in a quiet library.

Young Soviets who have not received a higher education may change jobs repeatedly. Labor turnover among youth in blue-collar jobs is extremely high. A study in Alma-Ata, the capital of the southern republic of Kazakhstan, showed that people under the age of twenty-nine made up 64 percent of the employees who quit their jobs frequently. The study said that 54 percent of the young people who left explained that they had chosen the wrong career. Many added that they were not sure which line of work they wanted to pursue. Another study conducted in Soviet Georgia showed that more than a third of the workers who changed jobs two or more times a year were thirty years of age or younger. Many left their jobs in search of more money or to hunt for a cushier position. Both studies called for job counseling programs to help young people make more informed decisions about their careers.

Some young people become dissatisfied with their jobs because they are unprepared to work. Lenin's wife, Nadezhda Krupskaya, decreed that young people should be kept out of the workplace. She thought that money was a corrupting influence and that children should not be allowed to earn it. As a result of her theory, most Soviet teenagers are not encouraged to work. Soviet boys and girls do not earn extra money delivering newspapers or babysitting. They do not take part-time jobs during school, nor do they work during summer breaks from classes. Soviet teenagers occasionally tutor younger children and redecorate their schools, but these jobs are unpaid. If they want to work as a receptionist or janitor to earn extra money while attending a university, they need their dean's written permission. Only students in the upper grades are allowed to work, and only then if they are very good students. Soviets often enter their first jobs after college with no experience in any working environment.

Only the Baltic republics stress a work ethic among their youngsters. Estonian teenagers often take jobs during summer breaks selling ice cream on city streets. They are paid a percentage of their profits. In Pärnu, a resort town on the Baltic coast, teens as young as fourteen are hired by the municipal government to wash dishes in restaurants and do other simple work. By the time they are adults, people in the Baltics have already learned to work hard. The tradition has proven itself in the area's labor productivity rates, which top the rest of the nation.

★   When a student graduates, he leaves friends and the relative freedom of his institute or university and is sent into the working world. The transition is not easy in any society, but it is made more traumatic in the Soviet Union by distribution—the system in which graduates are assigned to their first jobs by a commission. They may have to work with people they don't know and don't feel comfortable with. Worst of all, the workplace may be in Siberia or the Far East, where the life-style is rigorous, stores are poorly stocked, and diversions are few.

During his last year of study, each young specialist signs a contract with the state that requires him to do three years of work in the job selected for him. A student's destination is supposed to be selected by carefully matching his skills with the area that has the greatest need. In reality, many young graduates are sent to areas where they are neither needed nor wanted, and where nothing has been prepared for their arrival.

Many young people dread distribution and do everything possible to avoid it. One young Soviet recounted the story of an acquaintance in Leningrad named Boris, who managed to win at the distribution game. He had studied for six years to become a surgeon in one of the city's most prestigious medical schools and, at twenty-four, had entered his final year of studies. A good-looking young man with blond hair and glasses, Boris was not a diligent student, but he was street smart. He drove a car, always had extra spending money, and easily managed to obtain much-coveted tickets on the Red Arrow, the train that runs between Leningrad and Moscow.

When Boris began contemplating life after medical school, he realized that he had to find a way to avoid begin sent to a small hospital in the provinces. Sure enough, as his fellow students began to prepare for graduation, Boris announced that he had been given one of very few spots open in a Leningrad hospital. His acquaintances speculated that Boris, whose father held a high position, had "pulled strings and paid some rubles here and there." When asked about it, he replied mysteriously that he had "gone through channels."

There are several legitimate ways to avoid distribution. Some with especially rare skills or talent manage to stay in the cities. Young women avoid being exiled to the provinces by marrying men who have managed to get assigned to a city job.

As unpleasant as this system of distribution may seem to Westerners, some Soviets find it comforting, because they are relieved of having to make difficult decisions about their lives. They do not have to scan the newspaper want ads for job openings or prove themselves in countless interviews with prospective employers or weigh the relative merits of one job offer over another. All of this is done for them by the state. They are given a job and they fill it.

Managers are often loathe to take on young graduates because so many of them have no practical experience. And even if they are poor workers, they cannot be fired. Appeals to the local party committee often are met with orders to "reeducate" the young worker. Many bosses simply wait until the worker's three years elapse, then write glowing references in his work book to get rid of him. Only insubordination and drunkenness are grounds for immediate dismissal.

✭ Once a young specialist has completed three years at his first job, in theory he is free to pursue any work he chooses. In practice, finding a good job is almost impossible without connections. Intelligence is not enough. A young Soviet also needs assistance from someone powerful— or as it said in Russian, someone "with a hairy arm"—to jump onto that first rung of the career ladder.

One young Soviet's struggle to find work in a prestigious institute ended unsuccessfully because he failed to enlist the aid of someone influential. Volodya, a Muscovite in his late twenties, had decided he wanted to work in the Scientific Research Institute of Fine Arts and Knowledge, a well-respected institute where scholars study the works of Shakespeare and write articles for literary journals. Even though salaries there are low, Volodya reasoned that the work would be stimulating, give him status, and provide occasional invitations to interesting parties. But Volodya found that the institute staff was "like a mafia"—a "closed and isolated circle." Said Volodya, "If someone special comes along, like the daughter of a party official, they arrange an opening for her. Otherwise, it's just impossible to enter their world." After a few months of struggling, Volodya gave up in bitter frustration.

Many Soviet people have learned to rely on connections to ease their way at work. Corruption and bribery also play roles in some Soviet workplaces. A bribe to a supervisor may secure a promotion or win a trip abroad. But bribes are risky, and many young people cannot pay them without cutting corners and stealing from the workplace to come up with the needed cash; often, bribes must be paid to several people.

Sima, who worked as a taxi driver, said that without paying bribes, he would not have been able to keep his taxi in working order. When he first started driving, Sima was assigned a car, but he found that it had no tires, no brakes, and no battery. His bosses looked the other way when he stole parts from other cabs. "Even after seven days of stealing, I still had to pay a bribe to the mechanics to make the car work," Sima said.

A typical day on the job was full of misadventures and gambles. He had to find a way to get gas illegally, as it was too expensive to buy legally and he was allotted too small a ration. He paid the mechanics a few rubles every night to make sure that his gas was not siphoned by the other drivers. Sima stored everything that could be stolen from his car in the trunk, which he locked with a chain and heavy padlock. Because he could not afford to bribe the mechanics every time his car broke down, Sima had to learn to make minor repairs himself. Often, by the time his taxi was ready for the road, it was late afternoon.

In addition, he was prevented from leaving the lot by a policeman who checked to see that each car had good tires, lights, windshield wipers, and exhaust pipes. It was not until the policeman went off duty that Sima could leave the lot and officially begin his workday. But he was paid only for the time he actually spent driving. At the end of his first month, his salary was only 120 rubles (about $190). Sima grudgingly paid his boss a bribe so that he would get a better car. "The system makes a scoundrel out of you," he said.

THE KOMSOMOL AND THE PARTY

During his time at the taxi park, Sima became friends with the chief supervisor, a man of only twenty-seven who already had a staff of 180 people answering to him. The boss obviously had followed the correct career path to the top. Named Fouat, he was born in Moscow into a family of Tatars. Fouat started working at the taxi park while studying part time at the Institute of Auto Transport, where he was a leader in the Komsomol and spent his leisure time in party activities. After receiving top grades, Fouat graduated with an engineering degree and was allowed to enter the Institute of Foreign Languages of Maurice Torrez, a tony college for the elite. Again he devoted much of his spare time to the Komsomol, and, two years after graduating, he joined the Communist party.

When he assumed his position as the manager of the taxi park, Fouat continued to be a party activist. "He was attentive, ambitious, self-confident, tyrannical, and vengeful," said Sima. "He spoke only in commands. Everyone was afraid of him—but everyone was nice to him."

His description of Fouat matches that of many young party members: intelligent, well dressed, relaxed, and comfortable with power. Many Soviets say it is easy to spot the students who will become party members and go on to successful careers. They are often the brightest, although being bright is not enough. They are also fiercely loyal.

A foreigner once asked a twenty-nine-year-old doctoral degree candidate at Moscow State University why he spent so much time organizing Komsomol events and had applied to join the party. He was dumbfounded that the foreigner did not already know the answer. "Why do you want to work in the job you have? Because you want a good career and everything that comes with it—an apartment, a car, trips abroad—because you want to live well," he said. "That's why I want to join the party—so I can have a better life." For him, the party was a career ticket.

The best jobs—and thus the best salaries and the most spacious apartments—are reserved for party members, which make up a tiny, elite segment of the nation's population. In every career, whether it is in science, music, or carpentry, the party is important. It is difficult to move into a top management position without being politically active.

One Soviet described the route to success via the party. He said a high school graduate should avoid going to an institute or university and instead work in a factory or on a collective farm. He should attend classes in higher education part time and become active in the Komsomol, then apply to join the party. "It's easier to get accepted if you're a soldier, worker, or farmer. Then you can move up to a career in the party and you can attend any college, without competition," he said.

Of course, Westerners also make concessions and endure hardships for their careers. They work long hours and take jobs in undesirable locations to win promotions. But in the Soviet system of advancement, the path to success is narrower. There is one route to the top, and that route is defined by the Communist party.

Many young people believe that the rewards are not great enough to compensate for the ideological baggage that must be shouldered to win them. Those who do not have a tradition of party activism in their families are typically not politically minded and are turned off by the party's structured system. Being a loyal Communist, both on and off the job, is simply too much. So they enter institutes and go on to join the work force, without seriously devoting themselves to building a career.

Others easily fall into dreaming of party membership and a high-powered career. Two of these young activists came to America in early 1989 on the first exchange of high school students between the United States and the Soviet Union. Slava Goryachev, sixteen, and Anya Petrova, seventeen, attended the Friends School in Baltimore and lived with a Baltimore family for two months. Then they traveled back to Moscow and hosted visiting American students from Baltimore. Both were in their last year of study at school Number 15, a specialized English school near the center of Moscow.

Interviewed a few days after their arrival in Baltimore, the two fresh-faced teenagers laughed when they were asked how their lives had changed under Gorbachev. Slava, a blond boy with steely blue eyes and a bit of adolescent fuzz sprouting from his upper lip, replied, "Without Gorbachev, we wouldn't be here. It's the trip of a lifetime." Anya, a pretty girl with long dark hair and an impish smile, was flustered by the intense curiosity Americans directed toward her. She shyly took questions. Slava was more confident; he fixed a questioner with his level gaze and spoke brashly, at times criticizing his country and at other times enthusiastically and hopefully talking of reform.

Both were from families considered wealthy by Soviet standards. To qualify for the exchange program, students had to be able to offer an extra room in their apartment to the visiting American; for most, such excess space is an unheard of luxury. Their family income had to be no less than 550 rubles, or about $880, which is above the average for two working adults. They also were required to take their American guests on excursions to the theater or ballet, which meant that their parents had to have the connections necessary to find tickets. Finally, they had to receive grades of 4 or 5 on all English tests.

Anya's father, grandfather, and grandmother were all doctors; she planned to carry on the family tradition and already knew which medical school she would attend in Moscow. Slava's father worked for the Ministry of Internal Affairs, which oversees the police force, and his mother had a job at the Rossia Hotel in Red Square. He had hopes of studying Chinese and becoming a specialist in Asia and Africa, then going to work in one of the nation's most prestigious think tanks.

Both teenagers were active members of the Komsomol, although they did offer some mild criticisms of the organization. Flushed with conviction, Anya said she had been eager to join the Komsomol; she had dreamed of helping with projects in her school, such as working with Young Pioneers and handicapped children. But when she joined the organization, she found herself frustrated and bored in the meetings. "We wanted to be active and change something and the school administration blocked us or the other pupils didn't support us," she said. "We sat in chairs for hours and listened, then voted for everything automatically."

But the organization began to reform itself in 1987, as formerly taboo subjects were opened up for examination by the press. Komsomol meetings turned into roundtable discussions instead of boring lectures. Anya talked excitedly about the group's work to set up a small cafeteria in their school. For her, Komsomol was no longer something to be endured. She looked forward to the meetings.

Slava was not so optimistic. He said forthrightly that the Komsomol had not drastically changed; there was still plenty of dead time spent in useless discussion. "Our school administrators raise both hands in favor of the changes we propose; then they do nothing," he said, rancor edging into his voice. Slava explained that they had tried to establish a disco to raise money for the school and give students a place to gather, but the principal and teachers had opposed the idea. Their teachers didn't want to spend extra hours after school supervising the disco, nor did they want outsiders from other schools coming into school Number 15. "The administration has been brought up in the old way; it's pretty hard to get them to see the new style of doing things,'' said Slava.

Anya wasn't interested in carrying her party activism past membership in the Komsomol; she said simply that she would not join the party. ''I think people should only join the party if they want to be a real member in spirit; it's wrong to join just so you can have a party card,'' she said. Countless generations of young Soviets had done just that to boost their careers, but Anya had too much integrity for that. She was infected with Gorbachev's urge to rid Soviet society of what had come to be known as ''formalism''—the practice of going through meaningless rituals to conform to the party's high ideals.

Slava bristled at the suggestion that joining the party was the key to success and that many people enter it only to build their careers. Pointing to the head of the Ministry of Culture in Lithuania, Slava said the man was not a party member but still had managed to rise to the top. He was willing to agree, however, that the man was a rare exception—one that was likely to occur only in the Baltics, where nonconformity is more readily tolerated than in the Russian republic.

Slava spoke eagerly of joining the party; his motive was not to further his career, he said, but to change society. He knew he would have a more powerful role if he were an active party member. ''Many people have good ideas about making change, but they can't do anything, because they're acting alone. The party will bring people together,'' he said brightly. He hoped to lead other young people toward taking responsibility for their own lives. Slava disapproved of young people who formed cooperatives to get rich quick, and said that young Soviets should instead go into business to help rebuild society. He was especially enthusiastic about a cooperative in Moscow that manufactured prosthetic devices for Afghan veterans. ''Most people support *perestroika*, but they've been brought up to sit back and just raise their hand. They're passive. That's the most important thing we need to change,'' he said.

COOPERATIVES

The government set out to make that change in 1987, by enacting a law that allowed people to form their own cooperative businesses. Workers were given permission to quit their state jobs, take out loans from banks to set up businesses, and hire other workers. Cooperatives were granted the right to engage in foreign trade and form joint ventures with state-run companies.

Of course, there were still restrictions. Small publishing houses and home video parlors were outlawed. People were prohibited from opening firms that offered legal counseling. And for some products, prices were fixed at 30 percent above the cost of production.

Although the state still accounted for 99 percent of all Soviet production, cooperatives began making inroads. By the end of 1988, cooperatives employed 1.4 million people. They offered an eclectic range of services and products, including lonely hearts clubs, medical clinics, silkscreen T-shirts, and car repairs. More than 2,000 cooperatives were owned by young people, and the services they offered were worth 40 million rubles.

In the Baltic republics, where there was a tradition of private initiative left over from twenty years of independence from Soviet rule, cooperatives skyrocketed. Estonians formed music cooperatives to provide entertainment for privately owned clubs. Farmers brought their horses and buggies to town, offering rides to tourists along Tallinn's cobblestone streets. In Riga, the capital of neighboring Latvia, it became possible to eat a meal in a cooperative restaurant, buy clothes in a cooperative boutique, and catch a ride with a driver who had replaced the state-owned taxis. In the Lithuanian capital of Vilnius, young people said that the talk of every party was how to form a cooperative.

Back in Moscow, many older people clung to the belief that private enterprise was a criminal form of parasitism. But the idea sparked the imagination of young Muscovites, who were eager to experiment with their newfound freedom. Many quickly realized that forming a cooperative offered them a way out of their boring, low-paying state jobs.

In 1988, a friend arranged for a Western reporter to visit a cooperative that manufactured women's clothing. The Dionn co-op was born in a renovated room on October Street. Marking the entrance was a silky black awning with *Dionn* printed in flowing gold script. It looked like something from an avenue in Paris rather than a dusty back street near Moscow's old Red Army Theater. Inside, a freshly painted room had been furnished with rows of tables, where women sat at sewing machines, busily stitching denim coats.

The two presidents of the cooperative, Nadia Novikova and Alexander Karganov, explained that they had decided to quit their state jobs when they heard about the new law on cooperatives. Unlike most of the other young people interviewed for this book, the two readily agreed to give their last names; they were proud of what they were doing, and their cooperative was sanctioned by the state. Nadia, a striking blond with luminous green eyes and a slender figure, had graduated from a design institute and worked at a factory, then joined the artists' union. She received a studio through the union and was sewing for friends. Many of her designs were shown in exhibits. Her partner, Alexander, or Sasha, as he was known by his friends, had been a journalist before forming the Dionn cooperative.

The local city council rented them an empty room in an old building and they took out a bank loan of twelve thousand rubles, or about nineteen thousand dollars, for the necessary remodeling. Forming the co-op had been full of hardships. Nadia and Sasha bought seven old sewing machines from a factory and learned how to repair and service the machines themselves. In the beginning, they worked so hard that they were able to steal only four hours of sleep a night.

It was difficult at first to coax seamstresses into joining, because no one was sure whether the co-op would succeed. "Only workers who figured they had nothing to lose at their state jobs would come work with us," Nadia explained. But those who were willing to take the chance found themselves well rewarded. The seamstresses earned four hundred rubles a month, a very high wage for a factory worker in the Soviet Union and almost four times what they would have been paid to sew in a state factory. But they had to work hard and, most important, get along with one another. "It's not crucial that they have a lot of experience, because I can teach them to sew. But they have to work well with other people. I want to have a good atmosphere here," Nadia said.

Finding high-quality fabrics was another challenge. Nadia or Sasha sometimes spent weeks traveling around the Soviet Union visiting textile mills. Some raincoat fabric hanging on a rack was bought while on a trip to Tashkent. They'd had to negotiate for several months to arrange for a factory there to ship it to Moscow. Plants in the Baltic area produced the best materials, but they refused to sell to Nadia and Sasha. Nationalist pride prevented manufacturers there from exporting to the Russian republic.

The clothes they made were expensive by Soviet standards, but they were more fashionable than those manufactured by the state. Their line of designs included a shiny electric blue women's raincoat that sold for 150 rubles (about $240) and a black-and-gold evening dress decorated with elaborate beadwork that sold for 550 rubles (about $900). Finding stores to sell their clothing was not difficult. Their retailers ranged from GUM, the cavernous department store in Red Square, to a boutique that sold Pierre Cardin creations under an agreement with the French designer.

They would have liked their co-op to grow faster, but the state economy had thrown a number of obstacles in their path. For example, although a bank had given them a loan to buy a truck for deliveries, there were no vehicles available. All they could do was add their names to a long waiting list. In the meantime, the co-op rented a truck every time they needed to make a delivery. Also, they would have liked to add a showroom onto their factory, but so far, the city council had not acted on their application to expand into the empty room next door.

Prohibitively high taxes were a problem at first, since salaries of over fifteen hundred rubles could be taxed at 90 percent. The progressively steep taxes were designed to prevent get-rich-quick schemes; they also discouraged workers from starting cooperatives. Under a revised tax schedule, cooperative workers were allowed to pay the same as state workers —a maximum of 13 percent. The cooperatives had scored a victory, successfully defending themselves against conservative economic forces that had choked off private initiative in the past. After the lower tax rate was set, the Soviet press triumphantly announced that cooperatives were forming at a faster rate.

Seated in the factory's kitchen and sipping glasses of cool *kvas*, a fermented drink made from brown bread, Nadia and Sasha were optimistic, yet cautious, about the economic reforms that had allowed them to build their own co-op. "It's now possible, if a person has the will and desire and wants to work hard, to make something for himself here," she said. "Among older people, co-ops are not popular. They have worked all their lives and they want to go on pension. The simple workers don't want co-ops, but the intelligentsia understands the process."

Looking around the kitchen, Sasha added wistfully, "Many things have appeared with *glasnost*—films and interesting changes in the press. It's all a surprise, but who knows how it will end. We really want to hope that the co-ops will continue. In fact, we don't like to think about what will happen if we're not allowed to continue."

Nadia and Sasha had given up blossoming careers to create a small business they could be proud of. Their sacrifices were no greater than those made by small business owners in the capitalist world, but in some ways, the personal risks they had taken and the obstacles they faced were considerably greater. Although they were too young to remember, entrepreneurs who had set up their own businesses under Lenin's New Economic Plan soon after the Russian Revolution were among the first sent to Siberian labor camps when the freeze set in under Stalin. It seemed unlikely that a similar fate might befall the founders of the Dionn co-op. However, there was still a possibility, if only a remote one, that Gorbachev's reforms would be rolled back and the two would lose everything they had worked so hard to build.

Sasha and Nadia were unlike most other workers in the Soviet Union in that they had not allowed themselves to be drawn into the inefficiency that the Soviet workplace fosters. They had left behind complacency, corruption, and laziness. Rather than sew clothes at home, fix Western labels inside them, and sell the imitations at the local markets, they were working legally. The two were making stylish women's clothing—a consumer demand that the inept Soviet economy had proven itself incapable of satisfying.

If Gorbachev himself were to stroll into the Dionn cooperative, he would pronounce them *molodsi*—"great guys"—and hold them up as shining examples of what workers should be doing to rebuild society. Gorbachev's biggest problem is that the Nadias and Sashas are difficult to find in his society.

Soviet people have had very little experience with individual initiative, and the brief period in which entrepreneurship was allowed to thrive was quickly stifled by authoritarian crackdowns. Most Soviet workers have known only Stalinist tyranny or the widespread corruption, cynicism, and inertia of the Brezhnev era. If Gorbachev is to rebuild the economy, he will have to ease government restrictions and unleash the spirit of private enterprise. Without this, the Soviet people will never change their sheeplike ways. Reform will touch only small pockets of their economy, such as the Dionn cooperative, with its handful of workers busily sewing raincoats on Moscow's October Street.

Young Soviets are as yet unfamiliar with the process of making the countless decisions that are so crucial to setting up their own small businesses. Some are eager to start their own cooperatives, but lack the skills that are needed to make business decisions. When they look to the adults around them, few set a good example to follow. Instead of being their own bosses, they are accustomed to taking orders. As Slava, the young exchange student from Moscow said, Soviets are brought up to be passive rather than to take responsibility for their own lives. But this passivity is a particularly destructive attitude in the workplace; sitting around in monotonous jobs, drinking tea, and passing the time hardly inspires involvement in *perestroika*. The traditional Soviet approach to work, in which they have one foot in a dull official job and another foot in a passel of black-market schemes, is the only way they know of achieving *kife*. If these young workers refuse to tighten their belts and learn new work habits, they will never rebuild their country's economy. The Soviet Union will remain what it is today: a Third World country with an arsenal of powerful nuclear weapons and an economy that cannot begin to fulfill anyone's dream of *kife*.

CHAPTER 4 COMMUNISM AND NATIONALISM

 THE BIRTHDAY of Vladimir I. Lenin, an almost godlike figure in the Communist pantheon, falls on April 22. The day is a sort of Soviet thanksgiving. People take off from work or school, linger over dinner with family and friends, and drink late into the night.

For a couple of Western correspondents, it seemed somehow fitting, on Lenin's birthday, to visit the huge museum dedicated to his memory. The museum sits at one end of Red Square. It is a gaudy, red-brick, three-story building containing more than ten thousand pieces of Lenin memorabilia stored lovingly for posterity with great pomp in thirty-five exhibition halls. It is like the Washington Monument, the Lincoln Memorial, and Saint Patrick's Cathedral rolled into one, with a dash of Elvis Presley nostalgia thrown in. Millions of Soviets visit every year, gazing at the old printing presses used by the revolutionaries, Lenin's wigs and disguises, and his silver-handled cane. The museum contains some of the hand-painted, black-and-gold lacquer Palekh boxes prized by Westerners for their beautiful portrayals of Russian fairytales and wintry scenes. But the Palekh boxes in the Lenin Museum are painted with the traditional portrait of Lenin, his beard neatly trimmed, his eyes gazing stonily into the future.

Strolling through the exhibits made the correspondents feel dwarfed by the enormity of this monument to the long-dead hero, enshrouded by its tomblike silence. There were few Soviets around to examine the museum's vast displays; most people were off enjoying the holiday. The guards looked apathetic and weary, eager to head home from their jobs.

In an exhibition hall on the third floor, the silence was suddenly broken by the high-pitched voices of children. It was a mass induction ceremony for the little Muscovites who were joining the Young Pioneers. Ceremonies were being held simultaneously in a dozen rooms in the museum. Hundreds of children, all nine years old, were dressed identically: the girls in white blouses and navy blue skirts, the boys in white shirts with blue slacks. Many were carrying bouquets of flowers. The girls wore large, stiff white bows on their heads like gauzy wads of cotton candy. The children were singing patriotic hymns, their small faces flushed with excitement. Parents looked on, beaming proudly. The museum, a faceless symbol of Soviet adoration for its founding father, had become vigorously alive and filled with a burst of childish enthusiasm.

A handful of Komsomol members, teenagers of sixteen and seventeen, delivered lengthy speeches, their voices weighty with formality and custom. Then they walked down the rows of Young Pioneers, tying new bright red scarves around each child's neck. The children also received a new badge—a red star featuring the bust of Lenin laid over an eternal flame —to replace those that the children had worn as Little Octobrists.

Each child stood raptly, hand uplifted and slightly in front in the Communist salute. The Komsomol leaders intoned, "Will you be prepared to struggle for the cause of the Communist party of the Soviet Union?" Hundreds of childish voices responded, "Always prepared!"

Their voices echoed among the marble walls of the museum. After somberly taking the young Pioneer oath, the nine year olds turned happily toward their parents. They had made their first step toward becoming Communists.

The carefully scripted ceremony symbolizes the contradictions within the communist system: the children's guileless enthusiasm and the emptiness of the party cause. Millions of Young Pioneers are sworn in every year with plenty of pomp and flash, but underneath it all is a gray, decaying hulk, much like the Lenin Museum itself. The children, the lifeblood of the system, are swept along on the party's path, yet unless the party somehow regenerates itself, most will never truly embrace its beliefs. Many children, like many adults, have little use for party rituals. Growing numbers of young people have begun to resist the meaningless formalism and orchestration that are forced on them.

A striking example of their new rebelliousness came in 1987, when a group of elite children sent to Artek, the nation's premier summer camp for young Pioneers, refused to follow a format that had been crafted for them well in advance. Before the children had even arrived at the camp, a final resolution on the future of the Pioneers had been prepared. Some of the children's names had even been written into the statement. Journalists assigned to cover the canned event had already sent in their stories, secure in their presumption that it would take place as planned. The Black Sea resort, reserved for the children of party members and trade union officials, had even received a personal message of congratulations from Gorbachev.

But during an evening program, a rebel group of Pioneers stormed the stage, protesting that their suggestions had been ignored. They demanded, and won, a new resolution that incorporated their views. One of their criticisms of the Young Pioneers' congress was that there was too much "formalism"—the hollow regimentation that bears no resemblance to people's concerns. For too many years, they knew, the Young Pioneers had merely been going through the motions—taking part in rituals that had no meaning and making a show of patriotism and devotion to the party. The feelings of resentment had broken through to the surface, and children were no longer willing to act out the charade.

This brief act of rebellion must have been startling to the leadership, coming as it did among youngsters who would someday join the Communist party. In Soviet society, there is no more exalted building block than the party. The party protects the regime and provides stability and leadership. Membership is a privilege; only 17 million of the nation's 285 million people qualify to enter this elite organization that grants access to the very best the Soviet Union has to offer—the best housing, food, vacations, cars, and other luxuries. Party members are the top managers of industry, the ranking officers in the military, the heads of the most brilliant research institutes, and the government's most powerful figures. The party has millions of professionals—organizers, teachers, secretaries—who do nothing but full-time party work, carrying out orders and administering party affairs and organizations. All of these good Communists have to be carefully bred.

The Soviet Union's system of formal political indoctrination is set up to identify and cultivate its leaders while they are still young. Working in tandem with the schools, three youth groups—the Little Octobrists, the Young Pioneers, and the Komsomol—teach children to accept and support the dominant ideology and prepare them to become loyal, contented citizens.

Ideally, this is how the system works. But the children's party organizations have fallen on hard times. Young people complain that the groups, especially the Komsomol, are no longer relevant to their lives. They join only to ensure that they will get into their chosen university or institute, not out of loyalty to the system. They endure the dull meetings and study the nation's Five-Year Plan to further their careers, not because they feel devotion toward the party.

In the more open atmosphere under Gorbachev, Soviet youth have stopped complaining about the Komsomol and started acting against it. A large number has quit and others have refused their parents' and teachers' entreaties to join. For the first time, alternative clubs and movements are challenging the Komsomol's hold over Soviet youth. Groups as small as ten are gathering all over the nation to share their common interests. Some discuss subjects as innocuous as gardening or as explosive as political pluralism and democracy. Others have even called for new parties to defy the Communist party's monopoly on power.

Alongside these informal groups, nationalist movements have grown in strength, passion, and prominence. In 1988, nationalism emerged as the single greatest political crisis facing Gorbachev. Hundreds of thousands of people in the Baltic republics demonstrated openly in the streets, publicly discussing their grievances against Moscow. In Armenia, what was once a peaceful effort filled with the hope that Gorbachev would approve their demands for reunification with their homeland grew into militancy and violence. At a loss to control the situation without a show of force, the authorities sent tanks and armed internal security police into the region.

But one thing has become clear: the party has given no hint that it intends to open up its system to what it sees as destructive forces. Still, it must bring its young cynics and mavericks into the fold. The youth groups, especially the Komsomol, came under new pressure to remake themselves into lively, engaging organizations that young people would want to join. Their members, even down to the six-year-old beginners, had to be exposed to competition among differing viewpoints and then see communism emerging as the victor.

THE LITTLE OCTOBRISTS

On November 7, the anniversary of the Russian Revolution, millions of six-year-old boys and girls all over the Soviet Union become members of the Little Octobrists. Girls are told to wear starched white pinafores over their brown school dresses; boys are ordered to come to school in clean white shirts. Together with other members of their first-grade classes, the youngsters are taken to a local monument or museum for their induction ceremony. One friend recalled being driven by bus to the museum of Feliks Dzerzhinski, the founder of the precursor to the KGB. Another remembered walking along the streets of his small town to the Lenin monument in a nearby park.

During the ceremony, children sing patriotic anthems and hear speeches by their teachers and older students, as their parents and grand-parents look on. Each child is issued a small plastic pin—the ubiquitous five-pointed, ruby-colored star adorned with a portrait of Lenin as a little boy. For the next two years, they are required to wear the pins every day to school. The class is divided into small groups known as *zvezdochkii*, or "little stars," each consisting of five children, symbolizing the five-pointed pin. Even at this tender age, the children have already joined the basic unit of the Communist party organization—the cell. They have taken their places in the *kollektiv*.

Membership in the Little Octobrists is almost automatic, but children who do not properly mind their teachers are threatened with being barred. Most are excited about becoming part of a movement they are told is for grownups.

The group's activities are led by an adult and two older children from the Young Pioneers or the Komsomol. As in Cub Scouts and Brownies, the American equivalent of the Little Octobrists, most of the lessons are primarily games and play. But the Octobrists' program carries a much stronger overtone of propaganda; its purpose is not so much to socialize children as it is to politicize them. While the American scouting organizations emphasize patriotism and devotion to God and country, the Octobrists concentrate on communism.

The program is simplified so that very young children can understand it. Lenin is "Grandfather Lenin" and the Little Octobrists are his grandsons and granddaughters. They are given small books about Lenin and political posters, which they are instructed to hang on their walls at home.

Once a month, they see a film or take a field trip to a museum or monument. They also have a political information session. A typical lesson goes something like this:

> Children, you live in the Soviet Union, which is the best country in the world and where all people are equal. Before Grandfather Lenin came and changed our society, the bad people took from the good people. But Grandfather Lenin made the revolution, and every day since then, everyone in the Soviet Union has been happy.

The young woman who recited this simple lesson for a Western journalist had learned it at the age of seven; the memory was just as powerful in her mind as an American's recollection of the Pledge of Allegiance.

Little Octobrists are expected to live up to high standards. In many classrooms around the country, a pledge is posted that reads:

> Little Octobrists are future Pioneers. Little Octobrists are diligent children who love school and respect their elders. Only those who enjoy working are called Little Octobrists. Little Octobrists are brave and truthful, deft and skillful. Octobrists are friendly and merry children; they read and draw, play and sing.

YOUNG PIONEERS

When they enter the third grade at the age of nine, Soviet children graduate to the Young Pioneers, which was founded in 1924 to become "a school for communist education." The Young Pioneers is much more overtly political than the play and games of the Octobrists. Children repeat the same ideology they heard in Little Octobrists, but in a more adult way. "Grandfather Lenin" becomes Vladimir Ilich—an honorific reference to Lenin that they will use in formal settings for the rest of their lives. They study his life and activities, learn about the history of the Soviet Union (to the extent that is politically acceptable), hear about the evils of capitalism, and listen to speeches by the party leadership. Many of their lessons are about atheism.

Pioneers wear uniforms: blue slacks and white shirts for the boys and blue skirts and white blouses for the girls, both complemented by a red scarf knotted in front, which must be worn to school every day.

Virtually all Soviet children join the Young Pioneers. Exclusion from the organization is used as a weapon or threat by schoolteachers and principals. Being left out is a very heavy burden for a little girl or boy to bear and a disgrace to her or his family.

Once inducted into the organization, children participate in Pioneer activities several times a week. Young Pioneers is decidedly military as well as heavily political. During assemblies, one member carries a red banner, another hoists a flag, a third plays a bugle, and others bang on drums. Leaders wear the insignia of rank on their uniforms. Children are assigned to groups of five, which form to make up a larger group called a detachment, and an entire school forms a brigade. Each brigade is named after a Soviet hero, such as Mikhail Frunze, a general who led battles during the civil war and the revolution. They elect a governing council, which in turn chooses a secretary. An after-school gathering is not simply a meeting; it is known as a *sbor*, the military term for "assembly." They salute their leaders, march in formation, and assemble in ranks.

Every year on October 19, Young Pioneers all over the country join the Soviet Pioneer Line, when they flock to their gymnasiums to stand at attention in single file and reaffirm their oath of loyalty to the state and to the party. In the summer, millions of children go to the nation's forty thousand Pioneer camps, where they learn to put together Kalashnikov rifles and take lessons in civil defense.

In their school lessons, they use a Pioneer notebook printed with the words, "I solemnly pledge, before my comrades, to deeply love my country, work and study, as the great Lenin commanded and the Communist party of the Soviet Union teaches." Encouraged to demonstrate their devotion to communism by performing "social work," they are told to help the elderly and are summoned to the *Subbotnik*, a day of mandatory voluntary work. During the *Subbotnik*, which usually comes four times a year, Pioneers clean the grounds around their schools or plant flowers in city parks. Most children resent this voluntary social work, but some, especially those whose mothers and fathers are party members, already know the usefulness of becoming an activist. As one young Soviet said, "Even at nine or ten, you can see who's going to become a party member."

Pioneers are required to subscribe to the newspaper *Pionyerskaya pravda*, the children's edition of the Communist party organ, and one of the more than sixty publications for children. They are occasionally ordered by their teachers to bring the newspaper to school, as a check to see that they are receiving it at home, but rather than subscribing, many children simply run to the nearest kiosk and buy a copy. Those who fail to produce the paper in class have to listen as the teacher derides their parents for failing to bring up "good patriots."

As with Soviet newspapers for adults, the editorial content of *Pionyerskaya pravda* has changed to reflect the shift in the political winds under Gorbachev. Once it carried articles about heroic efforts to build the huge Baikal-Amur Railroad in Siberia and preachy stories about Pioneer boys and girls who helped others become better citizens. With *glasnost*, the paper began publishing mild criticism of Soviet society's shortcomings.

On the second page of an issue published in July 1988, the newspaper carried a story about the nationalist conflict in Armenia. Although the article concluded in an optimistic vein, much as the authorities would have liked the Armenians to give up their demands and be silent again, an attempt was made to discuss the issue honestly. Samvel, a little boy depicted in the article, asked why there were not enough schoolbooks in Armenian, the dominant language of the area. Why, he wanted to know, hadn't the Armenians been given enough money to build a clubhouse for their Pioneers? And why were meat and cooking oil impossible to buy, even with rationing coupons? His questions echoed those of many adult Armenians.

The newspaper's revamped approach made it more appealing to Soviet children, and it became difficult to buy copies in newsstands. Children began to complain that they could get it regularly only with a subscription or through their parents' connections.

✷ Many Soviets turn nostalgic when asked to recall the time they spent as Young Pioneers. While they remember the formal meetings and dull routine, they also look back affectionately on weekend excursions and games. Most recall a favorite Komsomol leader, usually a girl of sixteen or seventeen, who had made their years in the Young Pioneers exciting and interesting. Like American Boy Scouts and Girls Scouts, being a Young Pioneer meant field trips and camping. As Pioneers, they built fires in forests and lived in tents, leaving their parents behind in cramped city apartments. Being Pioneers allowed them to escape from the watchful eyes of their teachers and school authorities.

But young Soviets also remember their Pioneer groups with mixed emotions. Some of what they did in the organization was irrelevant. One young woman recalled that as part of her lessons about the Soviet role in World War II, her Young Pioneer group had been ordered to find a veteran and bring him to the school to speak about his wartime service. They went searching in the apartment buildings around their school, ringing doorbells until they came upon a veteran who grudgingly agreed to come. "We felt strange and we hated it," said the woman. "We didn't want to do it, but our teachers made us."

Every child was required to donate 20 kopecks, or about 35 cents, for a gift for the old soldier. After gathering 6 rubles, or about $7.50, a small group of Young Pioneers went to a store and bought a book about politics to present to him.

The young woman spoke derisively as she remembered the meeting that was organized to honor him: "The veteran was an old guy with no talent at all for speaking to kids, and he talked about his experiences in the war in very boring terms. He had had a tragic life, but it was impossible to talk to the kids about such tragedy." When children presented him with a pin and the book and applauded, they noticed that the veteran had tears in his eyes. "We saw he was moved, but everybody felt awkward," the young Soviet said. "The whole experience was done up for the adults— only our teacher felt good, because she had organized an event for which she would get credit."

As with so many situations in the Soviet Union, the meeting in honor of the veteran was carefully scripted, allowing for little spontaneity. When it was over, most of the children were left with the empty feeling of having done what was expected of them, with none of the satisfaction of having created something on their own. But the elderly vet was clearly moved. Honoring him was an effort to teach the children respect for the veteran and to make World War II a real war with real people, not just some ancient battle.

In addition to paying homage to their veteran elders, generations of Young Pioneers have honored the legend of little Pavlik Morozov. One of the saints of the Stalin era, the teenager was glorified as a model young Communist. Pavlik's father was the head of a local governing council, but he fell under the evil influence of relatives who were kulaks, or rich peasants. As the standard Soviet mythology goes, the Communists had sent troops to collect grain, but Pavlik's father lied to the authorities. The boy, true to Communist ideals, reported on his father and denounced him as a traitor. Pavlik's father was arrested by the secret police and executed. Pavlik was then murdered in retaliation by his grandfather and two uncles. The little boy was lionized in Soviet literature as a loyal patriot, which sent a clear message to generations of children: his loyalty to the state came before ties to his own family.

Monuments were built honoring Pavlik in his hometown and in Moscow, where a street was also named after him. Young Pioneer camps and schools all over the nation were dedicated to him, and his story was studied and recited over the years by countless young Soviets.

For outsiders, the ironies of this story and its fragile logic were obvious. It came as no surprise, then, that as many of the Stalin-era myths were exploded under *glasnost*, little Pavlik was officially denounced as well. In 1988, the Soviet press transformed him from a socialist hero into a victim of the 1930s Stalinist mentality. The journal *Yunost*, or "Youth," said Pavlik was "not a symbol of steadfastness and class consciousness, but of legalized and romanticized treachery." It elaborated on the "deep psychological and moral deformation" of the Stalin years, when millions of party members and government figures were executed as traitors and their families were encouraged to denounce them.

The magazine *Novoe vremya* (New Times) suggested that little Pavlik's denunciation of his own father was a shameful act. The magazine praised the Soviet leadership for finally agreeing that humanitarian values were more important than class consciousness, an admission that in the Soviet context carries enormous impact.

In 1989, the quest for a redefinition of little Pavlik grew into a raging controversy that was played out in the press. Conservatives objected to the defamation of what they considered a sacred symbol of communism. Liberal voices in the intelligentsia said that training children to betray their own father was immoral. New rumors about Pavlik swept the nation. One newspaper reported that Pavlik had been a little monster who was so ugly that the child depicted in posters and statues around the nation was actually another little boy and not the real Pavlik. Another newspaper tried to portray Pavlik as a Gorbachev-style hero. The paper said he was not a traitor, but an honest fellow who tried to oppose corruption and bureaucracy in his village for the sake of restructuring.

Finally, the central committee of the Komsomol launched a full-fledged investigation and found that the boy's father, who had been living separately from the family, was the chairman of the local government council. The man also drank heavily and accepted bribes. He fought bitterly with his sons, the oldest of whom was Pavlik. After the man was tried on a charge of corruption, he got drunk and killed Pavlik with a knife. When the committee issued its findings, it said Pavlik's story had been misrepresented to suit the propaganda needs of the time. The boy had been transformed into a hero, when actually he was merely the victim of domestic family violence.

Textbooks used by Soviet teenagers had to be altered to make them mesh with the new line on little Pavlik. Books that called Pavlik "honest and brave" were removed from schools and library shelves. Only the reminders of his earlier mythic heroism now remain. Two bronze statues of Pavlik still stand in Moscow, as do countless other monuments dedicated to him in cities all over the Soviet Union.

THE KOMSOMOL

The final step in the state's socialization of young people is the All-Union Lenin Communist Youth League, known by its acronym, the Komsomol. Formed in 1918 for youth from fourteen to twenty-eight, the Komsomol was to act as a sort of conveyor belt that would carry communist ideology to the masses and bring workers, farmers, and the intelligentsia into the party. The Komsomol was to help the party mold youth in the spirit of communism and direct them in building a new society.

In the 1920s, when the Soviet Union began trying to transform itself from a backward agrarian nation to a modern industrialized power, the Komsomol assisted in the collectivization of agriculture. "Komsomol member—to the tractor!" was one of the slogans that was common in Soviet villages. Later, the Komsomol rushed to help build some of the nation's biggest construction projects. In 1935, the young coal miner Aleksey Stakhanov and his comrades set production records in a movement that became known as the "Stakhanovites"—workers whose race to improve efficiency sometimes cost them their lives.

During World War II, even very young Komsomol members became guerrillas in the forests and plains of Byelorussia and the Ukraine, helping the Soviet army fight off the invading Nazis. Their heroism and sacrifices were recorded and made larger than life in war museums, which featured graphically frightening sepia-tone photographs of teenage Komsomol members, taken prisoner and hanging from the gallows of the German army. In the 1960s under Nikita Khrushchev, thousands of fresh-faced Komsomol volunteers suffered the privations of Siberia to construct mammoth power plants, railroads, and pipelines.

But once this era of heroic labor was past, the Komsomol, an organization of idealistic, utopia-minded young people with the fervent desire
to build communism, faded into an empty shell of what Lenin and his
fellow revolutionaries had dreamed it would be. During the slowdown of
the Brezhnev era, there were no towering dams to build or foreign invaders
to fight. Instead, Komsomol members attended uninspiring political information sessions in which their leaders droned on for hours, quoting
Brezhnev's speeches and party pronouncements. Revolutionary ardor faded
into cynicism. The Komsomol became an object of derision and scorn.
Some young people masqueraded as shining examples of Komsomol youth
during school hours and joined Fascist gangs after classes.

In the 1980s, young people became Komsomol members not because
they had faith in its lofty goals but because they knew membership would
help ease their way into universities and prestigious jobs. Komsomol members were no longer building power projects, they were too busy building
their own careers.

Young people complained bitterly about the tedious political sessions
they were required to attend in Komsomol. They tried to avoid the so-
called voluntary work in potato fields and school cafeterias—part of their
Komsomol duties. One young former member of the Komsomol said: "In
all my years in the organization, I never knew one person who enjoyed
being in it. I never knew anyone who sincerely believed all that stuff we
had to study in Komsomol." Most envied the ones who, with the support
of their parents, managed to avoid joining the Komsomol—often they were
either Jews waiting for permission to leave the country or artists and
musicians, whose parents encouraged their children to be mavericks.

Unlike the Little Octobrists and Young Pioneers, membership in Komsomol is not automatic. To enter, teenagers must take an exam on current
events and the history of the party and they must learn the Komsomol
charter. In many schools, students who wish to join get recommendations
from either two Komsomol members or one party member.

For one Moscow teenager, Maria, the induction process had been
difficult. Armed with her *karakteristika*, she first made an appointment
with the *Komsorg*, the Komsomol organizer in her school. He set a date
for her classmates to gather and debate her ideological suitability. On the
appointed day, Maria submitted herself to the group, all of whom had
already taken the big step of joining. "Each one had to say something—
that I was a good student and active in social work and that I deserved to
be in Komsomol, or that I didn't know math and was not a good Young
Pioneer," she recalled unhappily. "But it was hard on kids. Sometimes
it happens that a kid is questioned about his best friend, and of course he

says his friend is good and should be a member. But if his friend has some problems, the teacher can denounce a kid for being loyal.''

Before many students began to drop out of the organization in the late 1980s, teachers and school directors pressured students to join. They wanted their school to be on record with 100 percent membership. Teenagers were threatened with not being given a positive *karakteristika* and told they would have difficulty entering an institute if they refused to join. Just before high school graduation, the pressure would mount.

A young man who lived in the Black Sea resort town of Yalta resisted when the adults tried to coerce him to join, but he was punished for his nonconformity with a negative evaluation from his teachers. They wrote in his *karakteristika* that he was "ungrateful to the motherland, passive and had an immoral personality." The engineering institute he managed to enter was not considered a desirable place to study. His bitter resentment of the arm twisting used against him made the young man even more determined to stay outside the party.

Many young people were leary of the Komsomol because of the lengthy meetings they were required to endure. Once they had joined, they were required to meet after school for an hour and a half every two weeks. Longer sessions lasting up to three hours were held quarterly. Each Komsomol member was required to take on an area of responsibility. Most tried to select one that was interesting to him. For instance, one who enjoyed reading news about foreign countries might volunteer to be in charge of posting clippings from newspapers on bulletin boards. Others organized political education, sports events, musical education, or the school library.

The most powerful member of each Komsomol group records the academic progress of his classmates. Every week, he collects grade books from his fellow students and marks down their grades, which they must take home and show their parents. If students are afraid of receiving 2's or 3's, the equivalent of D's and C's in the American system, they may try to bribe him with chewing gum, candy, or toys. In return for these small bribes, he can agree to give them better grades. Thus, the system inadvertently can teach young people to use bribery to get ahead.

A separate record book is also kept for each Komsomol member by a secretary, who places a stamp in the book marking the monthly payment of dues. These are nominal, usually amounting to only ten kopecks, or about sixteen cents. Officially, when a member allows his dues to lapse for six months, he is expelled from the Komsomol. But many of the organization's leaders will pay the dues out of their own pockets to avoid having problems with membership records.

Before the organization began to change under Gorbachev, almost everyone who belonged to the Komsomol wanted to quit, but such an outright act of rebellion sometimes created a scandal. In 1986, the youth magazine *Sobesednik* reported that when a questionnaire was circulated among students in one Moscow institute, the majority said they would quit the Komsomol if promised that there would be no repercussions. "Leaving the Komsomol is worse than never joining," one of the students said. "Joining is passive and almost everyone joins, but quitting attracts a lot of attention. You can enter Komsomol without a lot of bother, but you can only leave with a huge scandal."

One way many Komsomol members managed to quit the organization without attracting too much attention was to change jobs and, when they appeared at their new factory or office, simply said that they had never been in the Komsomol. This tactic worked so long as the supervisor or local leader did not decide to check. But this was an option taken only by young people who did not care to pursue any kind of official career. For others, such a defiant act was considered too risky.

In the atmosphere of greater openness under Gorbachev, young people began to feel more free to criticize the Komsomol for being stuffy and dogmatic. Even the children of the nation's elite, who automatically would have joined Komsomol in earlier times, began to publicly debate the merits of wasting time in its tedious meetings. Although the organization had been in decline since the early 1970s, under Gorbachev the Soviet press acknowledged for the first time the existence of a real problem. One newspaper said that in 1987, recruitment fell by 35 percent and membership dropped by 2.5 million. In some areas of the country, only half of the young people of Komsomol age made the decision to join. One in ten Komsomol members fell behind in his dues.

In a 1987 survey by a sociological journal of 1,260 Komsomol leaders, nearly a third said that everyone they knew had joined only to advance their careers. A poll of Moscow youth conducted by a Soviet radio program found that two-thirds of those who responded said they had negative attitudes toward the Komsomol; the higher the level of education, the more critical their evaluation of the Komsomol.

There were other signs that the Komsomol had lost its influence among young people. Soviet youth were clearly more interested in rock music than in Marx and Lenin. The press was full of stories bemoaning the nihilistic, bourgeois values of Soviet teenagers. Articles told of fifteen-year-old boys who dressed up in leather jackets and gloves and "frightened" people at bus stops. In Moscow, the police reported that juvenile delinquency in 1987 had jumped 20 percent above the 1986 level. The newspaper *Nedelya* or "Week" said that in 1988, more than half of all criminals were less than twenty-nine years old.

Neo-Nazi groups in Leningrad donned black uniforms tailored to replicate Nazi uniforms. They went far beyond just painting swastikas on walls. Some were charged with beating and killing other young people in gang attacks.

Stories about the *Lyubertsy*, a gang of teenage vigilantes whose members spent their time bodybuilding in a network of cellars in a Moscow suburb, were printed in the popular magazine *Ogonyok*. Parents were warned to keep their teenagers home at night so that they would not get caught up in gang wars between the *Lyubertsy*, the hippies, the punks, and the *metallisty*, who adopted the costumes and mannerisms of heavy metal musicians and turned their theatrical affectations into a way of life. Violence between rival gangs became more common; in Kazan, the capital of Tatarstan, police reported more than fifty gang battles in two years. Twelve people were killed and seventy-three others seriously injured in the street wars.

Motorcycle gangs of up to one hundred bikers raced along Leningradsky Prospekt in Moscow to Sheremyetevo Airport, breaking speed limits and scaring other motorists. The city government issued a ban on such group motorcycle rides from 11:00 P.M. to 7:00 A.M., but the edict was virtually ignored.

A group in the Azerbaijan capital, Baku, called themselves the "Don't give a damners," based on a notion reminiscent of the 1950s film *Rebel Without a Cause*. Said one member proudly: "We don't care about anything. We're on our own. We don't give a damn about the people around us, of the events and the problems. We never were able to do anything and we never will."

Many among the Soviet leadership began to hold the Komsomol responsible for the breakdown in Marxist values among Soviet youth. Boris Yeltsin, Moscow's former party chief who was forced out in 1987 after he made too many enemies in the politburo, had harsh words for the Komsomol. The erstwhile reformer appeared on Soviet television as he toured the Moscow factory that manufactured ZILs, those sleek black limousines that glided along the streets of the capital carrying party officials. Lashing out at the Komsomol, Yeltsin claimed that the organization had become "overgrown by bureaucratic moss, cobwebs, trite phrases and paperwork." He said that its Moscow branch had announced more than a thousand empty initiatives. Warming to his subject, Yeltsin's face reddened with anger. "That's where the real, double-dyed red tape is—the Komsomol," he said.

The Komsomol leadership swallowed a strong dose of self-criticism during its April 1987 congress. Stanislav Smirnov, first secretary of the Moscow City Komsomol Committee and a protégé of Yeltsin, was strikingly blunt in his speech to the congress, questioning even the wisdom of the Komsomol's existence. Cloaking himself in the poetic heritage of Shakespeare, Smirnov said, "With regard to the Komsomol, we now hear the question: to be or not to be?"

When it was his turn to speak to the congress, Gorbachev blamed the Komsomol for red tape and empty rhetoric and for slowing down his program of restructuring the economy: "The Komsomol leaders organize gaudy campaigns and give boastful reports. In analyzing the work of the Komsomol leaders, one gets the impression that the masses of young people are moving on one side of the street and their leaders are on the other side and moving in the opposite direction."

The party's newly installed Komsomol leader, Viktor Mironenko, promised reform. Mironenko, at thirty-four, the youngest man to lead the Komsomol in nearly twenty-five years, was brought in from the Ukraine in 1986 to shake up an organization led by middle-aged bureaucrats who had no way of communicating with its young members. In his speech to the congress, Mironenko said that compulsory membership at all Komsomol meetings should be "consigned to the scrap heap." Rather than mourning the loss of members, Mironenko said the Komsomol had begun a process of "self-cleansing." He called for an end to dogma, bureaucracy and demagoguery.

There were some changes made in the Komsomol following the congress, but not enough to revitalize it. The Komsomol announced plans to cut its staff of one hundred thousand by a third. One press report said that the number of compulsory meetings was cut eight times during 1987, but young people complained in letters to newspapers that their Komsomol group's political information sessions continued to be wearisome and dull.

A letter to the editor in the youth group's newspaper, *Komsomolskaya pravda*, recounted an incident in 1988 that dramatically illustrated the Komsomol's failure to make itself more vigorous and imaginative. The letter was written by students in Yerevan, the capital of Armenia and the site of what were then the nation's largest street protests. Students there decided that for the first time, they sincerely wanted to participate in the annual May Day parade, which in the past had been a mere formality for them.

All they needed were materials to create their own placards. They applied to the Communist party's supply office for paper and submitted their slogans for approval: "Leninism Without Excuses," "More Democracy, *Glasnost* and Light," "Lenin, Party, Gorbachev," "Down with

Modern Stalinists and Brezhnevites,'' and ''Honest Communists at Party Conferences.'' All of their slogans were rejected.

They decided to make their posters out of cheap paper and participate on their own. When they reached the city square, they were greeted by the police, party officials, and Komsomol leaders. Their posters were taken away without a word of explanation. Some of the students were attacked by ''well-dressed'' young men—a euphemism for the elite who had been sent to carry out the leadership's orders. At the end of the demonstration, the students' torn posters lay on the wet ground. The letter said that one of the attackers later was discovered to be a secretary of the regional Komsomol committee. It was no wonder that the young followers of Gorbachev turned their backs on the Komsomol. Their attempt to be innovative was rebuffed by officials spouting hackneyed phrases or by Komsomol punks.

It was another example of the Komsomol leadership lagging behind the young people it was supposed to lead. Young Soviets need to feel that the Komsomol is changing and growing with them. They need a youth group that is as demanding, as restless and as full of curiosity, as they are. Otherwise, they will only continue to shun it and, by extension, the communist system.

★ Because it is a bureaucracy that, like all bureaucracies, lumbers along slowly, the Komsomol has been unable to keep pace with the changes reshaping Soviet society. Many young people feel that the Komsomol has nothing to offer them, and they have begun to form their own clubs and organizations. For many, these activities have taken the place of the party organization.

During the Gorbachev era, more than thirty thousand of these unofficial organizations have sprung up, as the Soviet press said, ''as fast as mushrooms in the rain.'' They exist in almost every city and village of the Soviet Union. The groups are not officially sanctioned, but neither are they outlawed. Because of their undefined status, Soviets describe them as *nyeformalny*, ''informal.''

A poll conducted in Moscow in 1987 showed that more than half of the young engineers and technical workers surveyed said they were members of informal organizations. Among students, 72 percent said they had joined one or more organizations. The number was particularly high among students of PTUs where 90 percent said they were involved. Meanwhile, 60 percent of the young people surveyed said they were also members of the Komsomol.

The groups have names like Candle, Salvation, Crimson Sail, and

Che Guevara Club. Some are made up of only ten or fifteen members; they are often groups of soccer fans, nature enthusiasts, or poetry lovers. Others do charitable work.

But some dare to tread the more dangerous ground of political activism. Members of these informal groups are mainly young intelligentsia who live in large cities; many have white-collar jobs doing research or teaching in institutes. Some gather signatures on petitions calling for democracy and human rights. They publish 1970s-style *samizdat* newspapers, using typewriters and layers of flimsy carbon paper. Many regularly hold demonstrations and marches, a step that would have resulted in certain arrest and harassment under former Soviet leader Yuri Andropov. Several groups want to build a monument to the millions of people who perished under Stalin. Two ecology clubs, Epicenter and the Council for Ecology and Culture, formed in Leningrad and organized street protests to block the destruction of the Hotel Angleterre, a famous landmark and a favorite spot among writers and intellectuals.

Among the more radical groups is the Democratic Union, which declares itself an opposition party and challenges the authority of the one-party communist system. An ultra-Nationalist Russian organization called Pamyat, meaning "Memory," blames the Soviet Union's problems on what it sees as a conspiracy of Zionism and freemasonry.

The rise of such groups marks the first (albeit tentative) independent political activity in the Soviet Union outside the framework of the Communist party since Stalin crushed the last faint sounds of dissent fifty years ago. Soviet authorities tolerate the groups in the belief that their activities will help spur society toward *perestroika*. Gorbachev may be thinking that members of the clubs that relish the outburst of public debate will be more inclined to fall in step with his restructuring plan, if only to keep the debate open. Perhaps he also believes that the clubs' activism will help him fight his battle against the bureaucracy.

COMMUNITY CLUB

In the 1970s and early 1980s, there were two paths for nonbelievers in the Soviet Union: lifelong cynicism or emigration. Young people who had no faith in the system either paid lip service when it was necessary to get what they wanted or they left the country. Few thought they could change the Soviet Union through social activism.

Things are different now. Some young people are very busy forming clubs, staging demonstrations, drafting petitions, and printing newspapers. Encouraged by the promise of reform, they have become more outspoken and less fearful of a crackdown by the security organs. While they do believe that a conservative backlash might come, in the meantime, they push for as much freedom as the system will tolerate.

Volodya and Alexei, two such newfound activists, were as surprised as anyone to find themselves cast in the role of social reformer. On one sunny Sunday afternoon in the summer of 1988, the two had just finished marching in a noisy demonstration near the Bolshoi Theater. They had held up placards that read, "Socialism without freedom is slavery" and "Freedom, democracy, *glasnost*." Their fellow demonstrators were a mixed lot, including Armenian nationalists, human rights activists, and Muscovites pushing for a monument honoring the victims of Stalin's purges.

Police officers, yelling through bullhorns, warned demonstrators against blocking traffic. Only two years earlier, they all would have been arrested, but this demonstration was conducted under *glasnost*. Like nonviolent demonstrations in the West, the police and the protesters fulfilled their predefined roles. Protesters walked where they were told to walk, and the police kept a respectful distance.

It was just one of countless demonstrations that Volodya and Alexei had helped organize. The two were members of a club that called itself *Obshchina* (Community). When a Western correspondent contacted them by telephone, she expected the conversation to be brief and the subsequent meeting furtively arranged. That was how things had been done in the old days. But under *glasnost*, the new political activists conduct their business out in the open; they are taking Gorbachev at his word. Volodya and Alexei spoke openly on the telephone, and they were unconcerned when told that the agreed on meeting place might be bugged. In another switch from the fear and suspicion of the Soviet human rights movement of the 1970s and early 1980s, both insisted that their first and last names be used.

Volodya, age twenty-two, whose full name was Vladimir Gurbolikov, was intense, with curly black hair and doleful brown eyes. His shaggy haircut and fiery oratory were reminiscent of the protesters on American college campuses in the 1960s. A student at Moscow State Pedagogical Institute, Volodya's life was consumed by demonstrations and other forms of social activism. His friend, Alexei Vasilivetsky, also twenty-two, had recently graduated from the institute and was teaching history. He was small and bespectacled, with pale eyes, frizzy brown hair, and the air of a skeptic.

Volodya spoke with conviction, and at times even with passion, leaning forward in his chair and pounding his fist into his palm. Alexei was detached and nonchalant. Volodya talked on for hours, while Alexei sprawled out on a couch, flipping through Western magazines as he listened, occasionally interjecting a wry comment or criticizing the authorities.

They said they had known each other since they were teenagers, when they occasionally got together to discuss Trotskyism, Yugoslavian communism, and socialism. Their parents were Moscow intelligentsia and had encouraged an atmosphere of intellectual discussion at home. As teenagers, Volodya and Alexei had doubtless sat up late into the night around a cramped kitchen table arguing about Eurocommunism with their friends.

The two formed *Obshchina* after the official press published an article calling for a new draft law on the Komsomol in 1986. Volodya and Alexei opposed the idea of having any centralized youth organization and suggested that Komsomol be reformed into a loose federation of clubs. They weren't able to convince the group's leadership, but they discovered that hundreds of young people felt a similar aversion to the organization. As Volodya said, "We found our allies." They watched as the Komsomol's middle-aged leader Viktor Mishin was replaced in 1986, but decided that even with a change at the top, the organization would never become democratic enough to accommodate their concerns. A month later, they formed a dissenting group—*Obshchina*.

The philosophy of *Obshchina* placed its members squarely at odds with the Communist party establishment. They opposed a centralized government and the narrow Soviet definition of socialism. Volodya ran his hands through his hair and shifted restively in his seat as he tried to define the group's views. He explained that Soviet-style socialism could be made to work, but it had to be redefined. "No one knows what socialism should be. We want to develop other voices of socialism—not only Marx and Engels. But we don't believe the Western model is best. We're against capitalism, but we're in favor of self-government and an end to exploitation. Right now, there's very little democracy and self-government in the Soviet Union," he said.

Alexei added, "We don't want to order anyone around and we're against having only one party. We don't want to follow just one path. There isn't just one path." But both quickly added that *Obshchina* was not a party and that they had no intention of trying to overthrow the Communist party of the Soviet Union.

Their group opposed bureaucracy and did not have a leadership figure. The Soviet press had identified Boris Kagarlitsky, a thirty-five-year-old Muscovite who spoke excellent English and spent a lot of time with Western reporters, as the leader of all of the informal groups, but Volodya and Alexei dismissed this idea as "insulting to us." They spoke derisively of Kagarlitsky and said he had been mistakenly tagged as a leader only because "Radio Liberty" once issued a lengthy broadcast about him. It was clear that infighting and jealousy had already broken out among the informal clubs; it was the same destructive force that had left other Soviet dissident and émigré groups tragically weakened in the 1970s.

After Boris Yeltsin was demoted to a job in the construction ministry in 1987, *Obshchina* organized a demonstration near a metro station, where hundreds of people offered their signatures in support of Yeltsin. But the protest turned ugly when plainclothes police officers, probably KGB and undercover police, moved in to destroy a portrait of the former city party chief. Crowds of people, including innocent bystanders, were taken in buses to a local police station. Volodya and Alexei were among those arrested, but now they just laughed about the incident. "The police had been given orders to arrest us, but they weren't sure what to do next. They kept us three hours at the station and then let us go," said Alexei.

Many members of informal groups thought Yeltsin's removal signaled the end of *glasnost* and *perestroika*. Instead, they were allowed to continue their actions as before. *Obshchina* began publishing a small political journal, also called *Obshchina*, that featured articles about the Soviet invasion of Czechoslovakia in 1968, the Armenian nationalist movement, and factory strikes. Every two weeks, the group produced one hundred copies on old typewriters, using layers of carbon and tracing paper, and mailed them to thirty towns in the Soviet Union. Members around the country then reproduced them, violating state laws against the illegal use of copying machines. Volodya said proudly that the newspaper had correspondents in fifty cities.

In the tradition of Soviet dissent, the group's most important function was to maintain its network of members. When activists in small provincial towns were arrested, harassed by the KGB, or prevented from holding meetings, their allies in Moscow would call Western reporters. Even if the correspondents did not always write stories, Volodya reasoned, the authorities knew that *Obshchina* had connections with the press and could use those connections to protect its members.

Still, the group found itself occasionally harassed by the security organs. The KGB put drugs in the apartment of one activist in Kuibyshev, an industrial city on the Volga River. He was arrested and forbidden to make trips to Moscow.

For Volodya and Alexei there was pressure as well. Faculty members at their institute discussed what to do about the two young reformers. The director of the institute tried to expel Alexei, although he gave up when he found there were no laws to support him. The local Komsomol denounced them. "But so far, they don't act against us. They don't know what to do to make us stop our activities," said Alexei. "We're just working against tyranny," Volodya said earnestly, his voice rising with emotion. "We're constructive. We'd like to work officially with them and we want to have pluralism."

But both of these young men were skeptical that the Soviet Union would allow real pluralism to exist. When he looked toward the future, Volodya's voice took on a fatalistic note. "We believe our country is entering an economic crisis. The nation has reached a crossroads; it can take a great step toward reform or away," he said. "Perhaps the Stalinists will win and they'll beat us. We don't know what will happen—but we have to take part in the process."

Volodya and Alexei admitted that because of their social activism, certain paths in life were closed to them, perhaps forever. They knew they would never be accepted into graduate school or work in a prestigious institute. To reach such goals, they would have to renounce *Obshchina*. Clearly, the price was too high.

Alexei sneered at the dissidents left over from the Soviet human rights movement of the 1970s. His voice full of confidence, he said, "Theirs was a movement of leaders, but we're different. Because there are so many of us, the police can't possibly arrest us all." To Alexei, *dissident* was a dirty word. "They only wanted to build a Western model, and it's not right for this country" he said scornfully. "What's left of that movement is neither honest nor trustworthy. Those people don't participate in what we're doing now, because something was crushed in them and they're afraid. They talk, but they don't act. They are working to join the establishment—they want to be bosses."

He had to be reminded that the activists of the 1970s had made incredible sacrifices and had been sentenced to labor camps or forced into exile abroad. In their struggle for broader freedoms and more democracy, dissidents like Anatoly Shcharansky and Yuri Orlov shared the same principles as Alexei and Volodya, but at a time when the Kremlin was less permissive. Alexei could not imagine another crackdown like the one that had come before, perhaps because he hadn't been old enough to understand what was happening as the earlier movement was destroyed. He didn't feel fear because he had not seen the full force of the security organs flexing their muscles against dissent.

While today's young activists have not come under the heavy pressure that their predecessors faced, the state has moved to oversee and manipulate them. As informal political clubs became increasingly active in 1988, demonstrations on the streets of Moscow and other major cities became an almost daily occurence. The security organs began to look for ways to curtail the protests; a law was quietly passed enabling them to crack down. Under regulations approved by the Supreme Soviet in July 1988, all demonstrations were required to be registered with the police ten days in advance, local authorities were empowered to prohibit any demonstration, and the police were authorized to bear arms and suppress public protests. Anyone found in violation of the new law was subject to stiff fines. First-time offenders could be jailed for 15 days or charged up to 300 rubles (about $480), more than most young political activists earn in a month. A second offense was punishable by a fine of up to 1,000 rubles, or $1,600, or two months in a labor camp. People who organized more than one illegal demonstration a year could be imprisoned for up to six months or fined 2,000 rubles or $3,200.

The new regulations are a sign that the Soviet authorities want to be in the position of deciding who will be allowed to stage protests. The crackdown can only hurt activists like Volodya and Aleksei in *Obshchina*, who once planned at least one demonstration a week. For them, organizing a protest is more than an act of defiance; it is a way of educating the general public about their cause and drawing more people into their movement. Their right to free speech and assembly, considered so vital in a democracy, has been circumscribed. Evidently, someone in the Kremlin decided that democracy was becoming too noisy.

NATIONALISM

Traditionally, one of the Komsomol's missions has been to teach children "Leninist internationalism," the notion that Lenin had envisioned a society in which all national differences would melt away. According to Lenin's dream, the Soviet Union was that society. In the country's patchwork of more than one hundred ethnic groups, young people were supposed to be, first and foremost, Soviet. Their ethnicity, or nationality, was considered secondary. This was not simply the melting-pot notion that was also fundamental to American society, because in the Soviet Union, expressions of ethnicity are equated with nationalism, and that, in turn, is equated with separatism, a destructive force that breaks up the *kollektiv*. In speeches and in the press, the leadership condemned nationalism as "alien to the Soviet way of life." There were no movements among minority groups that worked to build self-respect for ethnic identity and differences, such as black pride or the American Indian struggles in the United States.

Komsomol leaders were instructed to organize lectures and discussion groups that encouraged young people to reject their national backgrounds and become more patriotically Soviet. They urged young members to turn their backs on local customs and traditions, especially ones based on religion.

As the Soviet press launched into honest discussion of the Komsomol's shortcomings, there was talk that the youth organization was losing its battle against nationalism. Komsomol leaders were not well schooled in Lenin's nationalist policies, it was decreed, and the Komsomol was urged to become more vigilant in combating "the growing disease of nationalism." In 1987, Viktor Chebrikov, then KGB chief, blamed the Komsomol and the nation's schools for neglecting the "internationalist education of youth." He called nationalism a "stagnant phenomenon" stirred up by Western propagandists.

The fact that the KGB chief, head of the nation's top security organization, felt compelled to address the issue spoke eloquently about how gravely the Soviet leadership viewed this problem. They seemed to be saying for the first time that it was an indigenous problem, not one imported by hostile "foreign elements," as the propaganda organs had always insisted. Young people, especially those living around the nation's periphery, already knew that the nationalist passions that were so irritating to the leadership were not stirred up by "Voice of America" broadcasts. Many of the one-hundred distinct ethnic groups living in the Soviet Union's fifteen constituent republics had been taken in against their will; as people began to feel more free to discuss social problems, their frustrations over Russian rule spilled out into the open. From the European-minded Estonians to the predominantly Muslim Kazakhs and the Orthodox Christian Armenians, minority groups became increasingly vocal. Nationalism broke out even in Soviet Georgia, long one of the nation's most well-integrated republics. They all clamored for greater freedom from Moscow's centralized control and relished a cultural renaissance. What started out as peaceful protests grew into riots, strikes, and killings.

In 1988, the movement loomed as the single greatest threat to Gorbachev's reforms. Many feared that the demands of the minority groups would be seen by the politburo as a threat to the country's unity, prompting the conservatives to call for a crackdown on any dissenting voices. They feared that reform would quickly halt and that *perestroika* and *glasnost* would become mere buzz words of a forgotten era.

The nationalist movements in Estonia and Armenia attracted large numbers of teenagers and young adults. In these two small republics, nationalist leaders called for greater independence from Moscow. These spokesmen were loud, bold, and at times even insolent in their attacks on the Kremlin and in their demands for broader freedoms. Young people had grown up watching the older generation humiliated in the face of Moscow's power; now the nationalists made it clear that they would no longer bow down before Kremlin control. Their cause had an immediacy that the Communist party, with all of its stagnant doctrine, could not hope to match. The spirit of rebellion and calls for a more equal partnership with Moscow found resonance among youth. Many were eager to join protests, attend lectures, and take part in meetings.

In Estonia, nationalism was especially alluring for young people because it offered another opportunity to achieve *kife*. Young Estonians were used to watching helplessly as their milk, meat, and consumer goods were shipped away to Russia. Their republic, one of the most productive in the nation, was being drained of its resources; the more food that was sent to Russia, the less that was left for Estonians. Nationalist leaders moved to stop the flow by requiring that all shoppers show their passports before buying clothes, footwear, or appliances. Only local people were allowed to buy Estonian-produced items. They wanted to sell Estonia's goods and food to Estonians—or to Western countries, for foreign currency. Finally, they sought to make it easier to set up cooperatives and joint ventures with Western companies, which promised better salaries and travel abroad and they established Western-style business schools to help young entrepreneurs become better managers. If the nationalists had their way, having it all would be easier in Estonia.

In Armenia, young people saw the nationalist movement as a way of correcting injustice. Under Russian rule, they had been made to forfeit pieces of land and live near dangerous factories that spilled pollution into their water and air. The nationalists captured the natural enthusiasm of youth by demanding the return of this territory and the closing of industries. They organized protests that drew hundreds of thousands of supporters. They shouted, made demands, shook their fists, even hurled insults at Moscow. Just like youth everywhere, young Armenians were eager to join in the noise and commotion of protest. The changes that began to stir in their country under Gorbachev offered them the hope that they could make changes. Many were imbued with a new sense of self-respect.

★ Armenia's relationship with Moscow has historically been a complex mixture of dependence and resentment. When bitter feuds with the Turks forced Armenia in 1827 to seek help from the Russian army, it became a vassal of Imperial Russia. After the Russian Revolution, Armenia was faced with a Hobson's choice: cooperate with the Kremlin or face certain annihilation by the Turks. The Soviet military provided them with security, but at a high cost; their economy was threatened by Stalin's collectivization and industrialization, as thousands of Armenians were jailed or executed. Stalin gave away chunks of Armenian land to Azerbaijan, a neighboring republic whose culture, language, and religion were similar to those of their enemies, the Turks. It made the division of their territory all the more difficult to swallow for the Armenians.

Under Stalin, a large rubber factory was built in Armenia's capital of Yerevan, threatening the health of workers and residents and polluting the nation's water and air. This act was to have major significance decades later, under Gorbachev, as Armenia's nationalist sentiments coalesced among environmental groups.

Other protests focused on a nuclear power plant built in the 1970s in the small village of Metzamor, about 25 miles outside of Yerevan. Many Armenians believe the plant polluted groundwater, pushed up the cancer rate and killed trees and plants. Armenians also demonstrated against the construction of a new chemical factory just outside of Yerevan.

As the newfound environmental awareness of the 1980s spread through the republic, the wave of liberal thinking that permeated Soviet society under Gorbachev made Armenian campuses the seats of unrest. The natural willingness among the Armenian students to question the decisions made in Moscow gave impetus to the movement. Because college students of the 1980s had not experienced the Stalinist terror, they were not so afraid to challenge authority.

One former activist named Derenik proudly recalled the first demonstrations in 1987, when students gathered on the university campus in Yerevan where he was studying. Hundreds of students participated in protests, carried posters, and attended mass rallies. Despite pleas for calm by the school's administrators, the students boycotted classes and tried to close the university. Classes were finally canceled.

The environmentalist movement later grew to include calls for the return of two territories that had been taken from Armenia during the Stalin era. The Armenians backed up their demands with strikes, closing down factories, offices, and schools. Economic losses totalled millions of rubles. *Pravda* and other central organs of the press appealed repeatedly for calm.

Events one night in February 1988 forced Moscow's hand. After word spread that two young people had been killed, the Azerbaijanis rose up in a murderous rage against Armenians. Sumgait, a small industrial city south of the Azerbaijani capital of Baku, erupted in rioting and ethnic violence. Angry mobs moved from house to house, beating and killing Armenians. Derenik's voice rose in anger as he recalled what many Armenians now believe was a pogrom directed against them. "The authorities approved it and they knew it was going to happen," he said. "They even helped plan it. How is it possible, in a country so strictly controlled, for people to commit acts of violence without the authorities knowing what was going on? Why didn't the police take steps to stop them?"

After the earthquake of December 1988 left tens of thousands in Armenia dead, the authorities behaved even more harshly against dissent. When Gorbachev visited the earthquake-stricken area, he harshly castigated

Armenians as "extremists." His words angered and alienated many young people in Armenia. Thirteen members of the Karabakh Committee, intellectuals who had guided the movement for reunification with Karabakh, were arrested and held without charges. Protests halted. Armored troop carriers driven by Russian soldiers patrolled the streets. After a year-long burst of nationalist energy, the Armenians had been silenced. Moscow was once again firmly in control.

The republic's young people looked on in frustration and cynicism. Their efforts to recapture their lost lands and define a new relationship with Moscow had been slapped down. Because they had started out with an optimism that was undimmed by the terror of Stalin or the corruption under Brezhnev, the disappointment among young people must have been even more acute than the sense of failure experienced by older people. When the fresh breeze of *glasnost* was stifled by ethnic violence and by Moscow's indifference to their injustices, the young people of Armenia were given the same lessons that their parents and grandparents had learned. They too had tried to change the system, but the system had proven inflexible.

Derenik, his voice full of frustration, said, "Under Gorbachev, we are allowed to say how we feel. We thought we could get justice, but now we know that these are just promises that will never be kept. Gorbachev had his chance. This was a test to show he really was in favor of democracy. He failed it."

Many young people like Derenik have become convinced that the Soviet system, with or without Gorbachev, is one that cannot be made to respond to the calls of the minority. Their newfound disappointment can only spell danger for Gorbachev and his reforms; young people who are cynical will hardly pitch in to help with *perestroika*. The Armenians of Derenik's age may be the first young dropouts under Gorbachev.

✭ Estonia has been a captive nation for much of its history. Once held by the Germans and Swedes, the tiny territory on the Baltic Sea enjoyed a brief spell of independence from 1918 to 1939, between the first and second world wars. Then Estonia became a victim in the contest between Hitler and Stalin to divide up eastern Europe. Soviet history books say that the Red Army rolled in to "liberate" the Estonians from their "bourgeois period" and that the Estonian people unanimously voted to install a communist government.

Estonians know that hundreds of thousands of their people were executed or sent to Siberian labor camps. Their home became an occupied territory, its government and economy managed from Moscow. Many

Western countries, including the United States, never recognized the incorporation of Estonia, as well as neighboring Lithuania and Latvia, into the Soviet Union. Despite the planned economy that was forced on it by Moscow, Estonia is one of the most productive and affluent republics in the Soviet Union. Its 1.5 million residents enjoy the highest per capita standard of living. To the first-time visitor, signs of relative wealth are abundant. Car ownership is higher there than in any other republic. Estonians live in single-family homes that resemble the bungalows found in American suburbs. Stores are better stocked. Estonians watch the American television series "Dallas" and foreign movies on Finnish television, picked up from Helsinki, only thirty miles away.

The Estonian capital of Tallinn is a jewellike city with cobblestone streets and red-tile roofs, encircled by an ancient wall. There are dozens of inviting cafes and cozy basement bars that serve appetizing dishes made from Baltic fish. The notion of prompt service has not been exercised from the waiters, as it has been in much of Russia. Tallinn's Viru, a foreign tourists' hotel built by a Finnish firm, is far superior to any in Russia.

Before nationalist protests became common in Estonia in 1987, the mood of the country was bleak. Animosity toward Russians was palpable. Estonians, who resemble Swedes and other Nordic people, refused to speak the language of their occupiers. Muscovites who visited Estonia complained of open hostility; when they asked directions on the street, for instance, they were purposely sent off in the wrong direction.

In the fall of 1986, a couple of Western reporters on a trip to Tallinn spent several hours strolling around the city, then ducked into cave-like wine bar built into the side of a hill. An Estonian walked up, introduced himself as Rolf and began relating the story of his life. In halting English, he recounted how, as a young man, he had once spoken too loudly against the Russian authorities. He was arrested, forced to move to the neighboring republic of Latvia, and give up his career as an engineer. Instead, he worked as a truck driver, and was paid a pitifully small salary. After 15 years, he was allowed to move back home, but he was prevented from holding a skilled job. As he drank more wine, he was overwhelmed by his memories. Tears slid down his cheeks.

While he stood in the bar, crying over his crushed hopes, a long-haired young Russian at a nearby table began mocking him. The young man, who carried a guitar and said he was a musician from Moscow, sneeringly called Rolf a silly drunkard. He ridiculed his nationalist pride and said Estonia could not survive independently. Rolf became angry and started to stutter out a response, then realized it was no use. He had been beaten a long time ago. The exchange could have been a metaphor of Estonia's occupation by its Russian captors; Estonians were a wounded people and Russians were an arrogant lot.

Monty, a young Estonian teacher and translator who lived in an apartment over a throbbing disco, elaborated on the tensions between Russians and Estonians. He said the authorities had failed to reach into the tiny nation on the northwest border and suppress all intellectual freedom. But that didn't keep Estonians from hating the Soviet system, he said, and they felt that a cultural gap separated them from Russians. "They are an Asian people, and we are European. We can't understand them and we never will," he said.

Monty relished the opportunity to refer to Russians as "them." The presence of two Westerners helped Monty feel a foreigner. Russians had moved into his country, but they were only a small part of his life. There were Russians outside, but as long as he stayed inside, he could avoid them. When he retreated into his nest, the sole reminder of the Russian-dominated Soviet Union outside came from the sounds of the disco below his apartment at night.

Despite their strong feelings about their occupiers, no Estonian spoke with hope of driving the Russians out. No one dared dream of an Estonia free of Moscow's rule. There were occasional riots in Tallinn, usually after soccer matches when people had been drinking, but there was no sustained independence movement in Estonia because the Soviet security organs were too overwhelming and any group would have been quickly crushed.

Before *glasnost* allowed them to speak more honestly, Estonians were forced to keep their resentment quiet. Still, Estonians sent their children to Estonian-language schools, where many of them never mastered the Russian language. Their teachers devoted less time to Soviet history than dictated by the Russian school system. Although they studied from textbooks that said the Estonian leadership had invited Soviet Communists in during the 1940s, Estonian teachers anticipated the scorn that such lies provoked and wisely skipped over these lessons. Many youngsters studied for eleven years, rather than ten, and received a better education than did those in the general schools of the Russian republic. And instead of the standard polyester blue skirts, slacks, and jackets worn year after year by Russian youngsters, Estonian children were given outfits of higher quality, and the uniform changed frequently.

Estonia's young people ridiculed the party organizations. One recalled that instead of the Young Pioneer salute, *Vsegda gotov*, or "Always ready," Estonian children poked fun at party loyalty by saying, *Alasti vannis*, which sounds similar but actually means "Naked in the bathroom."

They delighted in showing Westerners a monument to Vladimir Lenin on a back street in Tallinn. The statue showed Lenin extending his hand, palm downward, below his waist and slightly in front of him. Viewed from the back at a certain angle, Lenin appeared to have an erection. The statue's sculptor, and the government commission that approved it, had to have known that the outstretched hand produced this odd, hilarious assault on the legend of Lenin.

As teenagers, when they joined the Komsomol, Estonians rarely bothered to attend meetings. Komsomol leaders paid other members' dues, because they knew it would be easier to donate the small sums themselves than try to extract money from young people so openly resentful toward the organization.

But there was always a minority of young Estonians who became activists in the Komsomol, who learned Russian, and who later joined the Communist party. Some studied in Moscow and returned to Tallinn to run the party organizations or become managers in Estonia's factories, farms, and offices. They realized that if they wanted to become part of the power structure, they had to forego nationalist separatism and follow the party's path. Moving up the career ladder gave them a stake in preserving the system defined by Moscow.

A nineteen-year-old activist named Marta, who had grown up in Tallinn, was not one of these party loyalists. Marta was a grave woman with a furrowed brow, a husky, Lauren Bacall–like voice, and cropped hair. She had lived her entire life in the Soviet Union, but her Russian was worse than that of most American correspondents assigned to Moscow. She had isolated herself from Russian influence. In 1985, Marta dreamed only of emigrating to the West. Over the years, a change occurred in Marta that reflected shifts in the attitudes of her countrymen. In 1988, as a tide of nationalism swept over her country, Marta found a new goal: she wanted to remain in Estonia and take part in the struggle for independence from Moscow.

As in Armenia, the flowering of the nationalist movement in Estonia began with an environmentalist cause. In 1987, the planned excavation of a large phosphorus deposit sparked public opposition. Newspapers began printing critical articles revealing that the project would require vast amounts of water. Estonians objected that the project would turn some of their farmland into desert. The proposal drew a May Day demonstration of several thousand protesters. Eventually, Estonian officials announced that work on the mine had been canceled. As Marta said, "For the first time, we understood the power of public opinion in our country."

Instead of trying to throw up imaginary barriers against the growing onslaught of Russification, Estonians began for the first time to draw up proposals designed to force the Russians from their midst. In Tallinn, where Estonians made up only 60 percent of the population, people called for a law that would cut down on Russian immigration. Under the law, factories importing workers from other republics would have to pay a fee of $27,000 for each new employee. Marta, speaking confidently about the justice of the new draft law, said, "We realistically want all Russians to leave. They must leave—it's not their home."

Local party leaders demanded that all meetings be conducted in Estonian, rather than Russian. Shop assistants and waiters were required to speak Estonian. Estonians used only their native language at work and on the street. The most important demand made by the nationalist movement, and the one most threatening to Soviet rule, was the call for economic independence from Moscow and the right to have their own currency. Estonian factories and farms had always been more productive than the ones in Russia, but they were rewarded for their hard work by being forced to ship meat, milk, clothing, and other goods to Russia. Their exports were so high that Estonians were left without enough to eat. In return, Estonians received mostly shoddy merchandise from Russia.

Nationalists looked for other ways to assert their independence from Moscow. Their Estonian Popular Front, a group that was independent from the Communist party, organized demonstrations and lectures on Estonian history and culture. Estonia's experiment in political pluralism sent an important signal to people who were dreaming of forming independent parties in other areas of the country. The front claimed sixty thousand active members and many more sympathizers around Estonia.

Despite her guarded words of praise for the changes she witnessed under *glasnost*, Marta spoke acerbically about its shortcomings. Frowning darkly she said, "Moscow wants to keep silent about what is happening in Estonia—like it's a little storm in a teapot that can't spread to other parts of the country." She had watched as some of her young friends were arrested for their political activism and offered the choice of exile or a prison camp.

Another visible sign of growing nationalist pride in Estonia was the return of its national flag. The Estonian blue, black, and white banner had been stored away for fifty years and, under Andropov, showing the flag would have resulted in certain arrest. Under Gorbachev, it flapped from flagpoles and balconies and even found its way to Tall Herman, the highest tower in Tallinn. The Estonian flag was allowed to take the place of the Soviet Union's blazing red banner, with its golden hammer and sickle.

The political changes in Estonia were felt even among very young children, who were allowed to stop attending meetings of the Little Octobrists and the Young Pioneers. *Poiste Liit*, the Union of Boys, took the place of the Young Pioneers, and little girls were given their own organization. Instead of herding all young Estonians into these groups, membership was considered a privilege that children had to earn. Said Marta, "We try to keep the groups special, not just automatic like the Young Pioneers, which have come to be so meaningless for kids."

The Komsomol, which had fallen on hard times in the Russian republic, lost practically all of its membership in Estonia. Marta said she had not attended Komsomol meetings in more than three years. Echoing the views of many young Estonians, she said, "You can do anything to me, but I'm not going to the meetings and I'm not paying my dues."

The growing anti-Russian sentiment in Estonia angered and frightened many Russians who lived in a vast suburb of Tallinn. In retaliation, they formed their own nationalist group known as Intermovement. The organization staged rallies to protest the law that had made Estonian the official language of the republic, rather than Russian.

When Marta was asked to define what had changed in Estonia under *glasnost*, she carefully pondered her response. "Before, Estonians did nothing against the Russians. We had no hope. But then we started to become activists. What we have now is hope—although we fear." She acknowledged that many Estonians were apprehensive of being arrested and losing privileges; these were the risks that came with dissent in the Soviet Union. "But it's not as frightening now," she said. "The authorities can't arrest everyone, because everyone is active."

Marta said proudly that Estonian nationalism had become a broad-based movement that included workers, students, and even ranking party officials. In her own family, despair had given way to activism. Her father, a party member and journalist, was involved in the Popular Front. Her brother had risked arrest for his work with the Estonian Greens party, a group of environmentalists who had affiliated with Greens in West Germany.

Marta herself had given up her dream of marrying a Swede or a Finn and emigrating. She had taken a job teaching English to aspiring young entrepreneurs who wanted to form joint ventures with Western firms. In her spare time, she translated English books and plays into Estonian. "The whole system of having to hold a diploma and a good *karakteristika* has broken down. Now, getting a job is based on skill and experience and on how you work, not on whether you're in Komsomol or whether you've gone to the right institute."

She dreamed of attending a humanities institute—one of the first privately operated colleges in the country—that was founded by the Popular Front. Annual tuition was 500 rubles, or about $800—a lot of money for people accustomed to receiving a stipend to study. Applicants did not need to present a high school diploma or *karakteristika* and were not required to take an entrance exam. Instead, they were judged on an essay or translation. Once they were accepted into the institute, they could plan their own schedule of courses. There were no mandatory classes and none on communist ideology.

Estonia did not experience the same violence and death that had broken out in Armenia, but the political challenge it presented to the Kremlin was just as potent. Many people in Tallinn, including Marta, watched nervously. In a letter written to an American in 1988, she said:

> The political situation here is getting worse. After our extremely hot summer, the winter has got to be cold. There are lots of people who are trying to provoke enmity between Estonians and Russians. Everything happening in the Soviet Union is extremely interesting, but at the same time very dangerous, especially for Estonians. I'm worried for my country.

For young people, the nationalist struggle has grown into a fascinating game of give and take. Many are learning new rules of negotiating with Moscow. Some have invested heavily in the nationalist movements; when the establishment encouraged them to speak openly, they took the grownups at their word. When Moscow refuses their demands, there is the risk that the younger generation of Soviets could distance itself from Gorbachev's experiment. If the energy that young non-Russians put into their nationalist movements can instead be applied to *perestroika*, the result could be a cohesive union of republics in which the creativity of the fringe may yet revive the center.

But so far the Kremlin has not shown an ability to handle the nationalists' demands. In April 1989, a decree gave the authorities broad new power to act against nationalists. It provided for a three-year jail term and a fine for anyone found guilty of inciting racial hatred or ethnic unrest. Many feared it would be directed against nationalists, who have emerged as the new dissidents under Gorbachev's regime. In terms of his tolerance for national identity, Gorbachev has given young people little reason for hope.

CHAPTER 5 DIET, HEALTH CARE, ALCOHOL, DRUGS

 MOST WESTERNERS notice it soon after they arrive in the Soviet Union: Soviets look unhealthy. Their skin is pasty and lined. Their hair is dull and prematurely streaked with gray. Their teeth are stained from nicotine and capped with gold. Their eyes are bleary from too many bouts with the vodka bottle. Obesity seems to be a national disease, especially among middle-aged and older women. It is difficult to judge a Soviet's age; he always turns out to be younger than you think. When told that a chapter of this book would be dedicated to food and health care in the Soviet Union, one Soviet laughed bitterly and said, "That should be easy—we don't have any."

Soviets start life with a handicap. Even in the major cities, their diet is so poor that many children suffer from rickets and other deficiencies. As they grow older, they rely on bread, sweets, and potatoes to drive away hunger. Few of them exercise, and the combination of a starchy diet and a sedentary life-style has produced a nation of fatties.

Young people are more aware of their diets than are older generations of Soviets, but eating well in the Soviet Union is not easy. Having enough food is an important part of the good life; getting it is time consuming. Most young people want to avoid standing in line to buy food. They continue to live with their parents into their twenties or even early thirties because they can count on Mom to do the shopping and cooking.

The "right to free health care" is guaranteed in the Soviet constitution and is one of the country's proudest achievements. But, like so much in the idealized workers' state, ready access to quality care exists only in their propaganda. A handful of well-staffed clinics and hospitals cater to the elite, but when the average worker falls ill, he is faced with rude doctors, dirty hospitals, and shortages of the most vital medicines. Often, only a bribe will help him find a competent doctor or the necessary medication. As one Soviet said, "It's OK to be healthy in the Soviet Union, but it's a very bad place to be sick."

To add to their system's failings, Soviets are killing themselves with alcohol, drugs, and tobacco. Despite a draconian antialcohol campaign designed to force them to stop drinking, their consumption of hard liquor remains one of the highest in the world. Lines in the state liquor stores are lengthy and tiresome, so they brew fermented drinks in their kitchen sinks. Moonshining, once the province of grandmas on collective farms, has become a pastime among young city dwellers.

Drug abuse, for so long consigned by the Soviet press to the decadent West, has emerged into the glare of *glasnost*. The authorities have shifted from denying the existence of the problem to publishing lurid accounts of drug gangs whose leaders sleep with bodyguards nearby. In the meantime, drug addiction is taking root even in privileged families, and little has been done to provide treatment programs for young addicts.

While cigarette smokers in the United States have practically been rendered outcasts, no effective antismoking campaign has taken hold in the Soviet Union. Soviet boys typically start smoking at the age of twelve; by the time they reach twenty, at least 60 percent of males smoke.

The most poignant statistics are those on life expectancy and infant mortality. While people in most of the developed world are living longer, until very recently, the average Soviet lifespan was shrinking. In the 1960s, Soviet men lived to be sixty-six and women seventy-four. By the end of the 1970s, male life expectancy had dropped to sixty-two, female to seventy-three. The decrease was a serious indictment of the Soviet health care system. For an entire decade, these numbers were so embarrassing to the state that the authorities ordered medical journals and statistical yearbooks to stop publishing them. When they were revealed once again, under Gorbachev's *glasnost*, alcohol was identified as the number one culprit among reasons for the drop in the Soviet male lifespan.

The infant death rate in the Soviet Union is even more shocking. When infant mortality increased sharply in the early 1970s, the press, again, stopped publishing the numbers. The silence was lifted in 1986, and the statistics were comparable to those of some Third World nations. The national average was twenty-five deaths per one thousand live births, placing the Soviet Union in the same category as Barbados and the United Arab Emirates. Even more babies were dying in areas outside of Russia; in the central Asian republics, more than one hundred infants died per one thousand live births. These children perished for the same reasons that newborns in the poorest parts of Africa and South America do not survive: primitive, overcrowded hospitals, contaminated water supplies, and inadequate prenatal care.

Gorbachev ordered an overhaul of the Soviet health care system in 1987 and installed Dr. Yevgeni Chazov, a co-winner of the Nobel Peace

Prize and a physician to the Kremlin elite, as Minister of Health. Chazov began by berating the nation's health care professionals and giving speeches that revealed some startling statistics: 40 percent of the nation's medical school graduates could not read an electrocardiogram, and 15 percent of all requests for prescription drugs were not being met. He excoriated the rural health care system, saying that even as the Soviet press bragged that the disease had been eradicated, more than sixty thousand residents in the southern republic of Kazakhstan suffered from tuberculosis. He said that in Moscow, where health services should have been at their peak, a hospital for war veterans had been under construction for eleven long years.

But there are shortcomings that even crusaders inspired by the righteousness of *perestroika* will likely be powerless to change. A key problem remains the state-oriented approach toward health care. In the Soviet Union, health care is not patient-centered. Instead, doctors submit to the state's interests first and the patient's second. From the viewpoint of the state, good health is a simple economic resource. A citizen's good health is important so that he can become a more productive worker; the rights of the individual are given little attention.

✸ The French have a proverb: "The destiny of nations depends on what they eat." If that is true, the Soviet Union is in grave danger, for on the road to good health, the national diet is a towering roadblock. For Soviet people, reality is empty shelves in food stores, rationing of meat and butter in many cities, spoiled vegetables and fruits, and barely edible canned goods. Together, they add up to the single greatest challenge confronting Gorbachev. All of his talk of *glasnost*, democratization, and economic reform has stirred expectations of a better life; yet, when Soviets walk into their food stores, they see there is no change. Feeding themselves and providing for their families' basic needs still requires much of their energy and time.

Soviets begin a life of poor nutrition soon after birth. As in many developing nations, 70 percent of the women in the Soviet countryside breast-feed. In Moscow and the other major cities, only about half of the women nurse their babies, according to a Ministry of Health official in 1985. These women rely on state-produced infant formula with the brand names Baby, Little One, Health, and Detolakt, an amalgam of the words *children* and *lactation*.

Huge amounts of these formulas are produced, and many mothers say that store shelves are stacked high with boxes of them. But much of what they find in the stores is either out of date or unhealthy for their children. In some rural areas, supplies are so bad that formula-fed babies suffer from

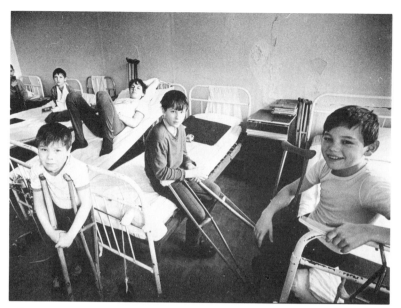

All health care and hospitalization is free of charge in the Soviet Union, but quality and cleanliness are frequently questionable.

Most young Soviets are married in state ceremonies at state wedding palaces. They later celebrate with friends and relatives in an apartment or restaurant.

Baptism of infants has become much more common under Gorbachev. Parents now take their children to church for the ceremony, rather than sending them off with grandmothers.

Young Soviets feel more free to worship openly and many are asking to be baptised for the first time.

When they report to their army induction center, young conscripts turn over their civilian clothes and prepare for a physical exam.

After being told where they will be sent, draftees are allowed to make one telephone call home.

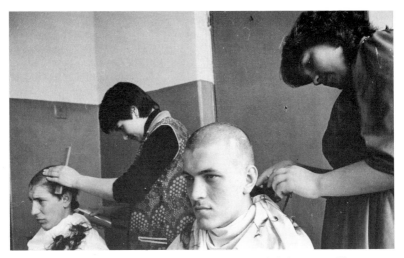

The new recruits are shaved bald and then issued their army uniform.

In a military funeral, young soldiers honor one of their comrades who was killed in the war in Afghanistan.

A first grader starts school near Ulan Ude, a city in the Soviet Far East.

Schoolchildren are made to sit with their hands neatly folded at their desks. But the Soviet classroom is not always so orderly; at times, chaos reigns.

Kindergarten students troop together after their teachers to the bathroom.

Like schoolchildren everywhere, Soviets stand at the blackboard to practice their penmanship as their classmates watch.

In some areas, young Soviets are among the strongest supporters of Mikhail Gorbachev and his policy of greater political freedom.

On Veteran's Day, men who fought in World War II don their medals and ribbons, and Young Pioneers and Komsomol members show their respect.

Hundreds of Young Pioneers join a line around the base of a World War II monument on All-Union Pioneer Assembly Day, which falls annually on October 4.

A Young Pioneer leader offers the standard response to a call for support for the motherland: "Always Prepared!"

rickets and anemia. Some infant formulas provide no instructions for mixing. When there are instructions, the writing on the packaging is dangerously imprecise. Parents complain in letters to newspapers that the formulas' composition is nowhere close to that of human milk, or that it is too sweet and leaves babies susceptible to disease. The problem arises not because Soviet scientists are unaware of what babies need; instead, the factories simply don't have the advanced equipment needed to make sensitive chemical analyses on the baby foods they produce.

The shortage of high-quality baby formula forces many women to use their *blat* to wangle a steady supply. Others turn to foreigners for help; formula manufactured in eastern Europe and sold in the foreign-currency stores in Moscow is highly prized among Soviets.

After Soviet babies stop consuming formula, they move on to canned food. Finding it presents a new dilemma for young parents, many of whom complain about shortages of fruit and vegetable purees. The state has yet to produce any canned meat or fish suitable for young children. The only solution for most parents is to make their children's food at home, adding to the already long hours devoted to searching for fresh produce and meat and then standing in line to buy it. As in most other aspects of Soviet domestic life, since men can rarely be counted on to help in the care and feeding of children, this burden falls mainly on the shoulders of Soviet women.

Finding edible food is a full-time job to which few Soviets can devote themselves. Usually only a housewife is able to stand in line for the hours required every day to maintain any semblance of a balanced diet. Young, single people would rather spend their leisure hours listening to music or visiting with friends than standing in lines outside of food shops.

As long as they live with their parents, most young Soviets at least eat regular meals. When they move away from home and cut themselves off from their parents' refrigerator, their diets usually suffer. Of course, the same is true of young Americans, but at least they can turn to fast food or the nearest convenience store.

Soviets don't enjoy such luxury. The food they find in state-operated cafeterias is often unappetizing, while the farmers' markets, where small producers sell food they have raised in private plots, cater mainly to foreigners and the well-to-do. Most young people survive on student grants or small salaries, and their first priorities are often clothes and entertainment. Many young Soviets say they would like to eat at least one piece of fresh fruit every day but find this daily purchase impossible to afford.

A Western reporter got a taste of the average Soviet student's diet during trips to Tallinn, where she stayed with friends. She shopped with them and shared their meals, and for four or five days every visit, she ate whatever they ate. Their diet consisted largely of bread and sweets. One young woman brought over a bunch of small, bruised apples and a cake made of cream, butter, and sugar; that was dinner. Another night, the meal was brown bread and applesauce made by a friend's mother. As the group sat eating chunks of bread dipped into the sauce, one young man talked longingly of the chickens his mother regularly sent by bus from neighboring Lithuania. The bus driver evidently thought nothing of being asked to deliver a bag with a cooked chicken inside; he knew that such a prize was expensive and difficult to find in the state stores.

Another Soviet confided that as a student, she had survived on handouts from friends; she dropped in on a different one every night. Each offered her bread, sweets, and tea. Once she set out to visit a friend in the hospital and decided to buy a small bunch of flowers at a local market. To reach the flower stands, she made her way past fragrant cheeses and pickles, tantalizing cuts of meat, and fresh vegetables. "The sights and the smells were torture," she said. "I was so hungry, I almost passed out."

A reporter once asked some young Soviet friends to record what they ate every day. Breakfast usually consisted of tea with sugar, cheese, and bread or perhaps an egg. Lunch was the main meal of the day. They ate in their factory or school cafeteria, which sold sweet rolls, bread, cheese, hard-boiled eggs, and, on a good day, hot dogs. The cafeteria at Moscow State University was known for its alluring cuisine: hotdogs and breaded cutlets.

The factory workers sometimes ate fried potatoes three times a day. But the white-collar workers fared far worse, because their offices had no cafeteria. Many brought food from home, usually bread and cheese or jam. For most workers, their long commute added two or three hours onto their already long workday, and they had to supplement their skimpy diets with food from nearby restaurants and cafes, which typically serve greasy dumpling soup, hard-boiled eggs, and doughy, deep-fried rolls stuffed with cabbage. All day long, they brewed strong tea on the little hotplates found in every office and ate bread, sweet rolls, candy, and cakes. Dinner was simple, often consisting of bread, cheese, and pickles.

⭑   As the long winter arrives and the temperature descends to forty degrees below zero or lower, most fruits and vegetables disappear from the shelves of the state stores. Only beets, onions, cabbage, and potatoes are available, and even these occasionally run short. The farmers' markets are more bountiful, but the produce there sells for exorbitant prices. Soft, sourtasting tomatoes go for more than thirteen dollars a pound in the winter, and cucumbers fetch eleven dollars a pound.

One Russian woman, asked if she could afford to pay such prices, snapped, "Certainly not. We don't expect to eat fruit and vegetables in the winter. When we go to the market, we don't even go near these things." Another Soviet said he had once approached a Georgian vendor who was selling cucumbers in the middle of winter in a Moscow market. When he asked him the prices, the Georgian shooed him away, saying, "These are for foreigners."

Dietary deficiencies affect most of the population. Soviets consume only one-third as much meat as Americans do and only half as much fruit and vegetables. One Soviet economist said in 1988 that Russians eat worse today than they did in 1913 under the czars. *Literaturnaya gazeta* reported in 1987 that in winter and spring, 25 percent of the population in some parts of the country suffer from a shortage of vitamin C. In the north, this number grows to 75 percent.

Deficits vary among republics. Only the Baltics have levels of meat consumption close to the recommended norms, while Caucasia and central Asia lag far behind. Milk and egg consumption is inadequate in nearly all of the republics, but it is especially low in central Asia.

The study by *Literaturnaya gazeta* also found that Soviets eat 116 percent of the recommended amount of bread and that their sugar consumption is very high. They average more than thirty-three hundred calories a day—a figure higher than the world average and much more than the typical Soviet factory or office worker needs. Much of the population is overweight; the press estimated in 1985 that half of the women, a third of the men, and 10 percent of the children in the Soviet Union are fat. The reason: too much white bread, sugar, candy, cakes, pies, and jams.

DINING OUT

Eating in a restaurant is difficult. Prices at state restaurants are high—25 rubles (about $40) for a meal. Such prices are prohibitive for young Soviets, whose monthly incomes average 100 to 120 rubles. A meal in a restaurant is a rare treat that is saved for a birthday, a graduation, or some other special event. Many young Soviets agree that a fancy meal in a restaurant, with caviar, smoked salmon, vodka, and other delicacies is real *kife*.

The government opened fifteen pizza parlors in Moscow and its suburbs in 1983 to appeal to youth and offer them places to dine that are less expensive than other restaurants. Some of the pizza parlors are built into basements, giving them a subterranean atmosphere that is cozy and enticing. They are furnished with red-and-white checked tablecloths, and the waiters wear high-heeled Italian boots. The pizza parlors occasionally serve imported Italian wine and play music by Culture Club, Michael Jackson, and Pink Floyd.

But these restaurants are also plagued by the ubiquitous shortages and long lines. Mozzarella cheese is not available. Red wine is frequently out of stock; mango juice is sometimes offered instead. Pizza toppings often include pickled herring, smoked salmon, and boiled eggs. Tomato sauce is frequently a deficit, so some pizza parlors substitute a single stewed tomato in the middle of the pizza crust. Sometimes pizza itself even slips off the menu. Large doughy popovers stuffed with cheese and bits of chicken take its place.

The only other cheap eating place that young people frequent is the state-run *stolovaya*, a sort of proletarian cafeteria in which customers stand around tall tables. The *stolovayas* in Moscow serve borscht, *blini*, or *pelmenii*, which are Siberian-style meat dumplings in soup. Some offer *pirozhki*, small doughy pies stuffed with cabbage or, occasionally, slivers of meat. The *stolovayas* serve foods that are heavy on fat and grease. Fresh slices of tomatoes and cabbage are sometimes sold there, but fresh fruit is virtually unheard of.

If a young Soviet manages to put some money aside, he may be able to leave the pizza parlors and the local *stolovaya* and go to one of the formal state restaurants. Money is not the only obstacle; connections are also needed to get inside. Most such restaurants keep their doors locked at all times to prevent unwanted people—in other words, almost everyone—from even entering.

In state restaurants, intimate conversation is out of the question. Restaurant musicians cater to patrons who like their music loud. Every year, one Western hit becomes popular in Soviet restaurants, and the melody is played over and over in eateries from Minsk to far eastern Siberia. One year it was Stevie Wonder's "I Just Called to Say I Love You," and the next it was the Italian hit "Suzannah."

The dreary dining experience in Moscow was transformed in 1987 by the introduction of a new law allowing citizens to open their own cooperative cafes. Surly waiters, long queues, and fistfights among patrons hoping to get in the door are not found in these new experiments with capitalism. In Moscow's bustling food scene under *perestroika*, it has become possible to get an appetizing meal made of fresh ingredients and be served by a polite waiter.

But these co-ops are beyond the financial reach of most young Soviets. Prices are unlikely to fall, and co-ops will probably remain the preserve of Westerners and wealthy Georgian tomato growers. For most Soviet young people, the co-ops represent little more than a dream—a place they can imagine entering only if an adult, and a wealthy one at that, pays for their meal.

EXERCISE

Generations of Russians have struggled to put on weight, considering plumpness a sign of wealth. Even their language reflects the idea that fat is good: the root of the verb for becoming slim means "to get worse," and the word for gaining weight originates from "to correct oneself."

Now Soviet youth are trying to shed extra kilos. Many say they would like to exercise and eat a healthy diet, but food shortages and the state-run system of health centers make it difficult to get and stay slim. Another problem is that few have time for keeping in shape. The Soviet press reported in 1987 that women stopped exercising when they left high school and men stopped when they reached the age of twenty-five.

Opportunities for exercise are limited by state-imposed regimentation. Unlike Western health centers which offer extended hours for working people, Soviet recreational facilities operate on the séance system, which requires people to line up to buy a pass for a specific session. They are allowed to enter for an hour and a half. At the end of that time, the locker rooms, pool, and gym are emptied and the next séance begins.

The *kollektiv* is the foundation of the Soviet approach to exercise. Physical activity is organized for groups and clubs; recreational facilities are made available to them first. At the Olympic-size pool built before Moscow hosted the 1980 games, individual passes are sold once a month. Purchasing one of these tickets requires a lengthy wait in line. Called an *abonement*, the pass can be used on three select evenings a week during rigidly controlled hours. The rest of the time, the pool is reserved for swim teams and Olympic competitors.

Gymnasiums are in short supply. The youth newspaper *Moskovskii Komsomolyets* published a story in 1987 about young women who wanted to get into bodybuilding but could not find gymnasiums or classes in Moscow. The paper suggested that they try to persuade men to allow them to join theirs, but added there were so few bodybuilding clubs for men that many had converted the basements of their apartment buildings into gyms, where there was hardly enough room for the men themselves. Women also complained that there was no do-it-yourself literature for bodybuilding in the Soviet Union.

The newspaper said that most women do not have the time to travel back and forth to a gym and prefer to work out at home or in their neighborhood. To help women stay fit, a television station in Moscow runs a fifteen-minute program called "Morning Gymnastics" at eight o'clock each day. Jogging is not the fad that it is in the West, although young men can be seen running in Lenin Hills or, occasionally, along the streets of Moscow. Women joggers are extremely rare; a Western reporter and a Soviet friend who regularly went running in the parks of Moscow drew curious stares.

The Soviet Union may not make it easy for the average young man or woman to stay physically fit, but it has one of the best systems in the world for identifying and training star athletes. Trainers have developed an efficient cradle-to-gold-medal production line that regularly produces new generations of Olympians. Physical education teachers in schools all over the country start the system by searching their classes for young talent. A youngster with potential is placed in one of the nation's five thousand special sports schools, which are similar to the general schools except that they offer sports clubs after regular classes.

These schools run advertisements in local newspapers encouraging children to try out for a place in their club. In Riga, the capital of Latvia, there is even a special day set aside for the schools to try to win new students. Every year on August 8, known as "Physical culture day," sports schools all over the republic set up displays and bring in their best coaches and athletes to talk to visiting students. The day ends with a concert and show at Riga's Palace of Sport.

The Spartakiad, a sort of miniature Olympics held all over the nation on one day every spring, also helps coaches spot future athletes. Students compete in their schools, then move to district, city, regional, and republic finals. The cost of travel to the competitions, hotel rooms, and food are all funded by the state.

CHILD HEALTH CARE

Soviet children are poorly nourished. Some are also underfed. The medical care they receive further endangers their health. The Soviet press reported in 1987 that only half of all Soviet babies are completely healthy at birth. Doctors blame their health problems on their mothers' smoking, alcoholism, poor diets, and inadequate prenatal care. At least one-fourth of all Soviet women do not see a doctor even once during pregnancy.

Parents all over the country are at a loss to provide the food, health care, and housing needed to raise healthy children. A 1985 survey of three hundred preschoolers in Gorky, an industrial city three hundred miles east of Moscow that might be compared to Cleveland, described the nightmarish existence of some Soviet youngsters. Many of the children there did not receive hot meals every day. Their families' apartments were small and damp. They did not get enough sleep, probably because of these cramped, noisy communal flats or one-room apartments. These children were taken outdoors to play and exercise only infrequently; like their counterparts in America, many spent too much of their time watching television. Their parents were ignorant about health care issues and diet. What they did know came from television rather than from doctors or other health care professionals. The survey's findings were clear: a Soviet child's life-style is likely to leave him sickly.

Soviet children are more exposed than Western youngsters are to a variety of childhood illnesses, including scarlet fever, measles, and influenza. The trade union newspaper *Trud* reported in 1985 that every year, flu outbreaks affected 20 percent of the Soviet population, at least 40 million people, many of them children. And the flu often became more serious among Soviet youngsters than among Americans.

The Soviet leadership has studied the problem of children's poor health. One medical newspaper reported in 1988 that only three to four percent of all students in Leningrad were in good health. Before he was thrown out of the politburo, former Moscow party Chief Boris Yeltsin lashed out at the city's medical establishment, saying that by the time they reach the eighth grade, 55 percent of the children in Moscow are ailing. He said that every third child has health problems of some type and that at least 10 percent are chronically ill.

The situation for children born in rural areas is far worse. In the Soviet Union, almost every part of life outside the major cities is more of a struggle; finding good health care and clean water is no exception. Primitive methods of sanitation poses one of the gravest threats to public health.

Soviet women know that the lack of modern facilities makes it risky to give birth in a country hospital. When their due date approaches, they try to be in a city so that they can rush to the nearest hospital. Many tell about having a baby on the run, much like the Mexican women who rush across the Texas border into American hospitals, where they will be given U.S. citizenship. But Soviet mothers are not concerned about citizenship, they want a better chance of survival for their children. A 1987 study showed that the flight of women to Moscow in search of a safer place to have their babies had grown so much over the years that it amounted to ten percent of the women who delivered in the city. Although these women had the advantage of the higher level of care offered in the capital, they still had a serious handicap: they were twice as likely as Muscovites to have had no prenatal care.

After their babies are born, rural mothers do not regularly take their children to see doctors. Often this is because the assigned clinic is located many miles away and public transportation is uncomfortable and unreliable. The long lines of mothers and their children, waiting for hours outside of clinics, must be daunting.

✦ The local clinic is the basic starting point for Soviet medical care. Citizens are assigned to a clinic based on their place of residence. If they dislike the doctors there, that is simply too bad. They are allowed to seek state health care outside their local clinic only in an emergency. Despite their limitations, these state clinics do have one distinct advantage over health care in the West: all exams, tests, and prescriptions are free of charge.

Still, the clinics also are staffed by doctors who are often rude or insensitive. Many accept bribes. Medicines are sometimes hard to find. Instead of looking toward their doctors with respect and trust, Soviet young people are so turned off by what they find in their clinics that many begin a lifelong habit of neglecting their health. Many grow up feeling cynical about their nation's system of free health care.

One young woman from a Moscow suburb described a typical visit to her local clinic, where she began going at the age of fourteen. The clinic was a three-story, prestressed concrete building with neatly attended grounds. Inside, the building was clean, its floors swept, its walls white-washed. On the first floor, there was a central hallway with signs over the doors for the clinic's eye specialist, gynecologist, laboratory, and general practitioners. Patients sat on benches along the corridor, waiting to see the doctors. The wait in these lines sometimes lasted up to three hours, especially in the winter, when flu outbreaks touched so many people.

The young Soviet said she usually found her doctor harried and cross after already having seen dozens of patients. Once, she recalled, "when she saw me walk through the door, she just said to take the pills that were available in the stores. She didn't even examine me."

On the rare occasions when her doctor bothered to perform a thorough checkup, she seemed more interested in hearing the local gossip than in examining her patient. Not exactly a staunch defender of doctor–patient confidentiality, she was always delighted to offer information about who had been in for an abortion, who was pregnant, and who had a venereal disease. If a man was brought to the clinic with alcohol poisoning, this doctor would pass along the story to her patients the following day. She had strong opinions on how to dress and on what kind of man made a good husband, and she was quick to dispense unsolicited advice on these topics to her patients.

The doctor thought every good worker should put in an honest day's work. She was loathe to fill out a sick leave pass, although she could be persuaded to do so for a small bribe. A larger present, such as a hand-knit sweater, might prompt her to issue enough three-day sick leave passes to get through an entire winter of colds.

The young Soviet's experiences at her neighborhood clinic are typical. Many learn early in life that the only reason to visit a clinic is to get a doctor's certificate excusing them from work or school. They also realize that they will be treated more attentively if they bring along a small present for the doctor. By the time they reach their late teens, they have grown to resist the idea of seeing a physician; many consider it a waste of time.

Most Soviet people also have little respect for their dentists. There is a common belief, especially among intellectuals, that dentistry is a dirty business—a world of black marketeers who make their living illegally. Many people complain that their dentists are willing to work on their teeth only if they are bribed with cash or presented with a gift.

Soviet dentists have their work cut out for them. Most of their patients seek dental care only rarely. Drinking water in almost all areas is unfluoridated. Toothpaste is sometimes unavailable in state stores. There is no dental floss; people instead use matches to clean their teeth. Most children have deficiencies in calcium, phosphorous, and other vitamins, which leaves their teeth weak and susceptible to decay. The national diet, so laden with sugar and sweets, carves holes in the children's teeth. Very young children do not undergo dental care; most see a dentist for the first time when they begin the first grade, at the age of six. A Soviet health journal published a story in 1986 about dental checkups among vocational students in Leningrad that found that more than three-fourths of them had cavities. Each student had at least eight teeth that were either filled, missing, or decayed.

The insensitive treatment that youngsters often receive at the hands of their dentists can create a lifelong fear of dentistry. One young Soviet recalled that the first time he was taken to have his teeth examined, the dentist pulled out a large bib caked with the blood of previous patients. He watched in horror as the dentist wrapped the blood-spattered bib around his neck. Then the dentist stood over him for an hour, poking and prodding and making the little boy's mouth bleed. The experience left him with a phobia about dentists, a fear that could only be reinforced as he grew older, since pain-killers are rarely used. Only patients willing to pay extra receive anesthesia; others suffer through extractions and even surgery without it.

When they suffer with a toothache or other malady, young people often turn to homegrown cures handed down to them from past generations. They resort to folk medicine and herbal cures instead of seeing a doctor or dentist. Soviets grow up hearing about the concoctions brewed by their grandmothers and often have more faith in these methods than in the pills sold in pharmacies.

They constantly swap cures among themselves and there is a home-grown treatment for every ailment. For toothache, one young woman said she drank a small amount of sunflower oil, held it in her mouth for ten minutes and allowed it to mix fully with her saliva. She claimed the oil stopped the infection in the tooth. When she scratched her leg, she took earwax and rubbed it into the wound; she claimed it made the injury heal faster.

One young Muscovite named Lyuda told a story of a home cure she learned from her grandmother. As a teenager, she had been painfully embarassed by warts that sprouted all over her hands. She tried for two years to get rid of them with different types of ointments. One doctor suggested she even try X-ray treatment, but her parents, fearing that the radiation would be dangerous, refused to allow it. Another physician offered to cut them off of her hands one by one, but cautioned that the surgery would be painful and the warts might reappear.

As she cast about for cures, her grandmother insisted she knew a treatment that was foolproof. The old lady's approach to the problem was simple: take a thread from an old sack, count the warts, and tie as many knots in the thread as you have warts. Let someone older than you dig a hole and bury the thread in the ground. The warts would gradually disappear. In desperation, Lyuda decided to follow her grandmother's advice and within a few months, the warts were gone.

Most home remedies involve a combination of vodka and grasses, berries or herbs picked in the forest. One young Moscow office worker, suffering from tonsilitis, turned to friends for a cure. They advised him to wrap his neck in a cold compress of vodka-soaked muslin, inhale the steam from boiling potatoes, place mustard plasters on his chest and gargle a mixture of iodine, salt, and soda. He was still sick after a week, so he relented and went to a clinic. The doctor's advice: stay in bed and drink lots of hot milk with honey.

SMOKING

The differences between the various brands of Soviet cigarettes hardly go deeper than their wrappers. There is *Yava*, which is sold in a white packet with a red circle on the front. Then there are the packs of cigarettes made up for every holiday and printed with cheery greetings, such as Happy

New Year or May Day. They all taste and cost the same as *Yava*, since that is just what they are, only packaged differently. Another popular cigarette is *Dimok*, which means "Little smoke." These cost only twenty kopecks a pack, which makes them a favorite among schoolchildren. And then there are the expensive brands: *Stolichniye*, in a package with red stars, which cost sixty kopecks, and *Kosmos*, in a blue-and-white box with a Soviet spaceship, which go for seventy kopecks.

The most distinctive Soviet cigarette is the papirosa, a pungent brand made in Russia since the time of the czars. The papirosa is very strong and is popular among young men. At one end, it has an empty tube, which takes the place of a filter, and at the other end there is an inch of tobacco. Soviet papirosa smokers go through a little ritual each time they smoke one, pinching the tube at the end and adding another pinch a little farther up. This gives the smoker a jaunty, dashing air and serves as a crude smoke trap that keeps the tobacco from flying through the tube and into the smoker's mouth. At twenty-five kopecks, it is one of the cheapest Soviet cigarettes available, and its price has not gone up in fifty years.

The papirosa is useful for young Soviets who smoke marijuana. They simply remove the tobacco, refill the empty cigarette, and enjoy the freedom of smoking marijuana in public. Most people simply assume that they are puffing on a papirosa, since the aroma of this particular cigarette is said to be similar to some kinds of marijuana.

All Soviet cigarettes are made with heavy, black Asiatic tobacco that is much stronger than the blended Western brands. There are no "light" cigarettes and no menthols, and there are no additives, such as sugar or chocolate, to vary the taste. Soviet tobacco is still wet when it is rolled; as it dries, it expands to pack the cigarette paper tightly. A Soviet smoker learns to hold a fresh cigarette between his thumb and forefinger, twiddling it back and forth slowly for a few minutes to loosen the tobacco and make it easier to smoke. When he lights up, he has to take several deep drags to force air through the tobacco and keep it burning—a little ritual that makes smoking in the Soviet Union especially harmful to one's health.

Among young Soviets, smoking is an alluring, fashionable habit. With only a few exceptions, most Soviet youth smoke. They say that taking up cigarettes as teenagers is almost automatic. Their parents smoke, their friends smoke, and, naturally, so do they. Unlike Westerners, they rarely torture themselves by trying to quit.

Smoking is as popular among young people in the Soviet Union today as it was with American youth thirty years ago. Smokers still enjoy a dashing, captivating image in the media; charismatic television and film stars puff away, unmindful that the message they are sending undermines the public's health. Cigarettes are widely available to the young, since most elderly women who work in kiosks have no objection to selling them to teenagers or even children.

Soviets begin smoking early in life. At least 17 percent of all Soviet children try their first cigarette by the age of eight; one-third of all boys are hooked by the time they turn seventeen. The largest group of smokers is men between ages twenty and thirty-nine; among this group, 70 percent smoke. Girls are beginning to catch up with boys. One study showed that in 1969, one out of ten girls smoked, but by 1977, the number had jumped to four out of ten. At least one-fourth of all Soviet women in the twenty to thirty-nine age group smoke.

There have been a few government edicts issued in an effort to cut down on cigarettes. Smoking has been banned on all internal Aeroflot flights, and many office buildings prohibit smoking except in corridors and courtyards. Smoking is illegal in restaurants, although waiters often look the other way when their customers light up. Packages of Soviet cigarettes carry a health warning, but it is small and largely ignored.

The antismoking drive has not taken on the mantle of a moral crusade as it has in the United States. Newspapers carry articles appealing to women's sense of vanity; they are told that smoking will make their voices coarse, their teeth discolored, and their skin sallow. The articles stress that pregnant women who smoke are twice as likely to have miscarriages or stillbirths. Under *glasnost*, the Soviet media gradually began to treat smoking with more candor; Soviet television now shows graphic photos of smokers' lungs blackened by tar from cigarettes.

One effort made by the media to steer young people away from smoking came in the form of a grim television spot that aired in 1988. In this brief cartoon, the ruggedly handsome face of a marksman appeared. He aimed a gun and fired. The marksman's double then took his place in front of a target, and the marksman fired into the double's mouth. The bullet turned into a cigarette. As more and more cigarettes were shot into the double's mouth, a harsh voice warned: "With each cigarette, you are killing yourself; there is no escaping it."

But the state's pronouncements on smoking remain contradictory and confusing. Smoking creates a kind of dilemma for the state that is peculiarly Soviet. Economic planners argue that cutting back on cigarette sales will mean a loss of government revenues; in response, the centralized planning agency calls for boosts in the production of cigarettes every five years. More and more farmland is set aside for tobacco, making the Soviet tobacco industry the third largest in the world. Workers in tobacco plants who fulfill government targets are rewarded with vacations at health spas and better apartments. Meanwhile, doctors warn that the cost of treating and hospitalizing smokers far exceeds the profits earned from sales.

So far, the government's halfhearted antismoking campaign has been a failure. Studies show that smoking has continued to grow in popularity; cigarette sales in 1986 were up 23 percent over 1970 sales.

LEARNING TO DRINK

Drinking is part of Soviet culture. Children watch their parents drink and they learn that alcohol is great fun. One Soviet recalled that the children in her kindergarten class used to sit around their little tables, clinking their glasses of juice together and repeating the traditional Soviet toast, *Na zdoroviye!* (To your health!), a scene they had witnessed countless times at home.

Most Soviet children get their first taste of alcohol from their parents. Some mothers drink a glass of wine before they breast-feed, so that their babies will fall asleep quickly and not wake during the night. Parents may give their children pieces of bread soaked in wine.

The Soviet press estimated in 1985 that three-fourths of all Soviet children get their first drink from their parents; most have already tried alcoholic beverages by the age of five. In an attempt to counter this parental influence, Soviet schools began antialcohol courses for seven year olds. In these classes, students are shown films of drunks run over by trucks, and they see the effects of alcohol on plants and animals. Parents are encouraged to attend these lessons too, but it is the rare adult who actually does so. Instead, they tend to allow their sons to drink at home, where they believe they can better teach them to control their consumption of liquor. Parents may invite their children to join them at parties and, referring to champagne as "lemonade," leave the bottle on the table within reach. Other parents allow their children to get sick on vodka, hoping they will stay away from it in the future.

Such methods of "teaching" sobriety have failed; a 1985 study found that at least 30 percent of all Soviet teenagers drink regularly. The average drinking age has fallen and the percentage of people who begin drinking under the age of eighteen has risen from 16 percent in 1925 to around 93 percent today. Alcohol leads many teens to trouble with the law; every third teenager who commits a crime has been drinking.

Many teenagers' favorite drink is similar to port wine. It is not the prized after-dinner drink produced in Portugal, but a Russian version of Ripple, cheap and strong. Its low price—less than a dollar a bottle—

appeals to young drinkers. The government stopped selling port wine under Gorbachev's antialcohol campaign, but many people started making a substitute version at home.

Beer mixed with vodka, usually in portions of three to one, is another preferred drink among teenagers. Before Gorbachev's antialcohol program closed many of the bars, young drinkers frequented them in Moscow. With their colorful histories and distinctive personalities, these were the local variant of the neighborhood pub. The beer was cheap and plentiful; it was served from an automatic spigot for only twenty kopecks, or about thirty-five cents, a glass. The glasses were washed out by the customers themselves before each use or, more often, simply passed from customer to customer without any cleaning. Conditions in the bars were, charitably speaking, rustic. They were furnished with tall tables, which people would crowd around instead of sitting in chairs. The floors were smeared with mud and the bathrooms were vile. Many beer lovers did not dare to drink there; instead, they brought in jugs or bottles and hauled their beer home.

Each beer bar had a name given to it by its loyal clientele. There was the Pentagon, named for its five-sided shape. Located near Gorky Park, the Pentagon was little more than a tent, with walls made of iron, formica, and plastic. In the winter, it was terribly cold, but that did not discourage customers from dropping by for a few glasses. Then there was a bar called *Yama*, which means "pit." It was a long, narrow basement room not far from the Bolshoi Theater, and it served foamy glasses of brew, fried shrimp, and small sandwiches.

Another, known fondly by its patrons as Charlie and his brother, was near the construction site of a museum dedicated to Charles Darwin. The museum was being built on a street named for Dmitri Ulyanov, the brother of V. I. Lenin; Charlie and his brother was a sardonic swipe at the Soviet hero. Work on the museum had been under way for more than ten years, and its slow progress was the subject of many barbed jokes among Muscovites. Another beer bar located near Kiev Railway Station had a large golden pheasant mounted on one wall. After the local authorities discovered that a Fascist organization in Italy had based its name on this bird, the decoration was quickly removed, but patrons continued to call their favorite bar by this name.

The bars served as hangouts for young people who had nowhere else to go. In the Soviet Union, there are no bowling alleys or hamburger joints to go to after school and on weekends. A 1985 survey by the youth newspaper *Komsomolskaya pravda* found that teenagers in the Soviet Union spend 60 to 80 percent of their free time sitting in their apartments. The situation is especially bad in small towns, where most of the stadiums and the volleyball and basketball courts are closed in the evenings because there are no employees to staff them. Cafes and discos for teenagers are scarce and close at 9:00 P.M. Restaurants and cinemas shut down at 11:00, so young people take to the streets. With nowhere to go and nothing to do, teenagers often pool their money and buy a bottle of liquor. The high divorce rate and large number of two-career families make for many absentee mothers and fathers. Some young people turn to drinking because they lack parental authority.

Because they have more leisure time, men drink more than women do. Young wives, overburdened by housework and child care, usually stay home while their husbands go out looking for entertainment, which often means drinking.

There are other reasons behind the heavy drinking that is so popular among young people in the Soviet Union. The press once referred to it only obliquely, but today the subject is being treated more honestly: young people have lost many of their values and feel a spiritual emptiness. They take a cynical view toward the beliefs shared by their parents and grandparents; few have any interest in the lofty goal of building communism. Until recently, religion has not been there to help fill the void.

A small Moscow theater staged a play in 1986 that explored the reasons for alcoholism among the young. Written by a young playwright named Mark Rozovskii, the play was called *The Red Corner*. The action was set in a Moscow dormitory for *limitchikii*, the provincial people who take menial jobs so that they can live legally in the capital. In the play, the main character is a young woman named Sarukhanova, who returns to her room every night, drinks half a bottle of vodka, and falls asleep. A female warden in the dormitory doesn't approve and summons her to the Red Corner, an area once reserved in Russian homes for icons and homemade altars but now set aside in every building for a bust of Lenin and the blazing red regalia of the Communist party. It quickly becomes clear that drinking is the only escape for Sarukhanova; she has no other interests.

The warden delivers a formal lecture about her responsibility to the motherland, but Sarukhanova dismisses this high-flung scolding and goes on another binge. When the warden finally begins to talk honestly about her own personal disappointments—her divorces, many abortions, boring job—the two women find some sympathy for each other. But the play does not end on the uplifting, optimistic note that once was so common in Soviet theater. Sarukhanova says defiantly that until she finds a substitute for the vodka bottle, she will keep on drinking. She symbolizes the breakdown in values among Soviet youth; with little to hope for in life, many see little reason to stop drinking.

✷ By the mid 1980s, drunkenness affected every aspect of life. The damage to the public health was enormous. One-fifth of all deaths were alcohol related. Life expectancy for men dropped by five years. The number of deaths from alcohol poisoning was 20 times higher than in any other nation.

Perhaps the most tragic effect of widespread drinking was the large number of mentally retarded children born to alcoholic women. Nearly ten percent of all Soviet children had birth defects; Western experts said alcohol was mostly to blame. Premature and stillborn children were twice as likely to be born into drinking families.

It was the damage to labor productivity that led Gorbachev to declare alcoholism domestic enemy number one in 1985. Under his antialcohol program, the legal drinking age was raised from eighteen to twenty-one and the price of a bottle of vodka was hiked to the equivalent of two days' wages for an average worker. A variety of new penalties were introduced to control alcohol abuse. Many hard-liquor stores were closed and the shops that remained open sold liquor only from 2:00 to 7:00 P.M. A strict two-bottle limit was enforced.

Young Soviets apologized that they had no vodka or wine to serve friends. They cursed the government's antialcohol campaign and complained that it was unreasonable to stand in line for hours to buy a bottle of liquor. Gorbachev became the butt of their derisive jokes. He quickly earned the sobriquet "Mineral Secretary," for his advocacy of mineral water over booze. Another nickname was *Gensok*, or "General Juice," for his calls on Soviet citizens to drink more fruit juices.

Home brew became the biggest threat to Gorbachev's much-heralded antialcohol campaign. Making moonshine, known in Russian as *samogon* or self-fired, grew into a popular pastime for millions and a highly profitable underground business for others. People who refused to join the interminable wait in lines outside the state liquor stores turned instead to brewing hooch in their kitchen sinks, or buying it from moonshiners who operated their own stills.

Moonshining was no longer the preserve of elderly women in rural villages; it spread to the cities and among all layers of society, including university graduates and industry managers. The average age of the *samogon* brewer dropped: more than half of those arrested and sentenced were less than twenty-nine years old.

Slowly, the government's strict program began to crumble under the constant assault of disgruntled drinkers. Young Soviets dismissed questions about the sobriety effort; they said Gorbachev's program was no longer taken seriously. Rumors swept Moscow that the state liquor stores would reopen any day.

The authorities started the official slide back to pre-Gorbachev days by extending liquor store hours and permitting two hundred vodka shops to reopen in late 1988. Beer, wine, champagne and cognac—but not vodka—returned to grocery stores. Orders were issued to factories to increase the production of all types of alcoholic beverages. Some of the popular beer bars in Moscow began to reopen.

Among young people, the announcement was greeted with a mixture of jubilation and relief. As one young woman exclaimed happily, "Great—back to *kife*. Back to buying what we want and not having to stand in lines all the time."

DRUGS UNDER *GLASNOST*

Until recently, the Soviet press maintained that drug abuse was a problem only in the decadent West. Soviets read lurid stories in their newspapers about heroin pushers roaming the streets of Harlem and addicts shooting up in Times Square. Despair over unemployment and homelessness turned Americans to drugs, the stories said. Officially, there was no drug plague in the Soviet Union.

After Gorbachev became leader, Soviet newspapers were awash with accounts of widespread drug abuse. There were stories of drug dens, drug mafias, and desperate addicts who robbed and murdered to support their habits. A television program that usually focused on tame subjects like diet and exercise shocked viewers with scenes from a drug treatment center, including an addict in the throes of withdrawal, cringing in pain, clutching his stomach, and staggering around the room.

The newspaper stories and television shows were all part of a nation-wide scare campaign to steer young people away from drugs. Concerned over an increase in drug use, particularly in the central Asian republics and Caucasia, health authorities hoped to frighten young people with the irreversibility of addiction. Supposedly, anyone who dared to experiment with drugs, even one puff of hashish or one mouthful of poppy seeds, would find the monkey of addiction on his back.

The frequency of these accounts and the urgency of their tone are misleading; drugs are much less popular among young Muscovites than among Westerners. The odor of marijuana that sometimes drifts along the streets in American cities is not found in the Soviet Union. At parties, vodka and champagne are still the preferred highs; it is unheard of for a young Soviet to casually pull a joint from his pocket, light it, and pass it on, or to share a line or two of cocaine in a bar. When young Soviets do drugs, they do them behind closed doors, with a very few trusted friends.

Stiff penalties against drug use and sales make such caution necessary. Under Soviet law, anyone caught with even a small amount of marijuana or opium can receive a three-year prison term; a drug sale draws a ten-year sentence. Anyone who loads up a papirosa with hashish and passes it to a friend may be sentenced to five years in prison for encouraging others to use drugs. So young people are extremely secretive and careful about drugs.

This secrecy makes it impossible to measure the actual dimensions of drug use. The government has added to the problem by providing few credible statistics. Sociologists have not released any comprehensive national—or even regional—statistics on drug use. While the press reported in 1988 that there were fifty-two hundred officially registered drug addicts in the Soviet Union, this estimate focused only on users who were hospitalized for addiction.

But what about the twenty year old from Yaroslavl who does drugs sporadically with friends? One law enforcement official reported in 1987 that another 123,000 Soviets use drugs but are not addicted. Among this group, hashish and marijuana are the drugs of choice. While the official's comments shed some light on casual drug use, they are hardly believable. For if the numbers are correct, it means that only a tiny fraction of the Soviet population uses drugs—so why the suddenly hysterical media campaign?

The answer may be that the authorities want to make up for all of those years they spent with their heads thrust into the sand, denying the existence of any drug problem. Thousands of young veterans got used to having their drugs readily available in Afghanistan; giving up a daily drug habit is not easy. Perhaps the noisy antidrug program is also inspired by a realization that drug use is indeed spreading; no longer the preserve of criminals and ex-convicts, drugs are becoming more popular among the young, the well educated, and the affluent.

Two studies completed in Soviet Georgia reveal that the profile of the average drug user has shifted. In the 1970s, more young people began using drugs while in prison; today, users are more likely to try drugs for the first time with friends, either at home or in school. The typical Soviet drug user of the 1980s is younger, better educated, and more affluent, and has been raised in a family with both parents living at home. Also, drug use has become more popular among women.

✦ Because official statistics on drug use are sparse, Western correspondents who write about the subject must gather information from Soviet drug users themselves. On the other hand, investigating the drug subculture too closely is dangerous. Many reporters instead talk to Soviets who have kicked serious drug habits or know others who use drugs.

One young woman named Lena had many friends who were opium addicts. She was from Yalta, a resort on the Black Sea whose harbor is surrounded by steep hills. Famous for being the site of the 1945 Big Three Conference, Yalta's warm, dry climate and white sandy beaches resemble any Mediterranean vacation spot. Its empty store shelves and long lines outside vodka stores are what give it away as Soviet. Millions of tourists travel by cruise ship and by train to Lena's hometown every year, carrying opium and hashish from the central Asian republics in the south to Moscow and Leningrad in the north.

Lena worked part time making government posters, but painting was her true passion. Her love of painting led her to move in a circle of artists and intellectuals, many of whom used drugs. She was a blue-eyed blond with a gravelly voice; her hard-edged look made her appear older than her twenty-eight years. She had seen a lot of tragedy unfold in Yalta's drug crowd. "I've known people who have died from injecting drugs in Yalta—at least twenty of them," she said, wincing at the memory of her dead companions.

Lena said she had three friends who began using drugs when they were sent to Afghanistan to serve in the Soviet army. "Before they went to Afghanistan," she said, "they were just normal guys. They drank, like everybody else, but that was all. They learned that in Afghanistan, life was impossible without drugs. They needed them there, because of the heat and because they had to carry forty kilos up and down hills. Then there was the fear—drugs helped with that. So they ate poppy seeds."

The poppy seeds were cut from the head of the plant, dried, and ground up. They were usually eaten with tea. Opium was easy to find in Afghanistan; Lena's three friends had simply traded cigarettes and clothing with the locals, who brought them drugs. Back home in Yalta, finding opium was more difficult. One of them went to work in a pharmacy, where he had access to hard-to-find medicines. He would steal medicines from work and trade them for poppy seeds. Their drugs habit was expensive; one cup of seeds cost 80 rubles, or about $130, and they ate two cups a day.

Injecting opium intravenously was dangerous. They would have preferred to use acetone to clean the seeds, but it had been removed from stores as part of the government's struggle against drug use. Instead, they used paint thinner and other bizarre substitutes, such as vinegar and douche powder, but these were risky. The three also discovered that they could get high by snorting ground poppy seeds with ephedrine, an antihistamine. The drug, given the nickname *Fyoder*, (Fred) was hugely popular among students in Leningrad and Moscow. They snapped up hundreds of bottles, until the authorities got wise and removed the drug from pharmacies. Lena's friends also planted small stands of hashish and poppy plants in the forests outside of Yalta, tending them carefully and using their small harvests to supply their own needs. Occasionally, they made a profit by selling drugs to other users.

As in any drug culture, these men had their own language. *Dur*, "stupidity," was their word for hashish. They also called it *plan*, from the word *plant*, or *shalash*, from the Russian word for pollen. Opium was known as "straw"; poppy seeds cleaned for injection were called *khimiya* (chemistry). Morphine was known by the woman's name *Marfa* and heroin was given the man's name *Gera*. As in other segments of the youth culture, they had their own understanding of *kife*. To them, "catching *kife*" meant getting high.

Drug use was considered sophisticated, cosmopolitan, and Western. Doing drugs was "punk" and "cool." Asking "Do you have an American cigarette?" was their code for, "Do you have any drugs?" Lena said that many of her friends dreamed of trying heroin on the streets of New York. "The young ones don't know enough to quit," Lena said sorrowfully.

But the older, more experienced drug users wanted help with their habits. "All the addicts I knew who were old—I mean the ones in their thirties—wanted out. But they couldn't do it without help," Lena said. "They knew it would be almost impossible without going to a hospital." It was the government's punitive approach to drug abuse that kept them from turning to hospitals for help. They were afraid that they would be placed under surveillance by the local police. "I know addicts are sick, but the authorities think they're criminals and want to punish them," Lena said. "People are afraid they won't be put in hospitals, but in jail. They are afraid they'll be beaten."

✷ Other young Soviets don't fall so deeply into drugs. Grisha, a young man who lived in a small ski resort in the Caucasus Mountains, was a casual drug user. He had never injected drugs into his veins, nor had he experimented with narcotics that were physically addictive. He preferred marijuana; it supplied a variation of the high he got from vodka.

Grisha worked in the discotheque at the local youth center. The disco was like a journey back to the 1960s: strobe lights flashing, colored oils swirling in a pool of light projected onto a wall. Grisha, the disc jockey, arranging a nightly program of music that ranged from Estonian folk songs to Bruce Springsteen's "Born in the U.S.A." and supplying a light patter between melodies. Like many young Soviets living in provincial cities, Grisha was fascinated by the prospect of talking to an American. When he heard that one was among his audience, he introduced himself during a break.

Grisha was a dropout. He skied in the winter and taught tennis every summer. Like any good ski bum, Grisha had insulated himself from the rest of society, moving only within a small circle of ski instructors and rock music enthusiasts. Grisha was less alienated from Soviet society than he was detached; he looked with cynical eyes at the rest of the country, understanding fully how the system worked and entering into the mainstream only when he needed something it had to offer. Most of the time, he was preoccupied with preserving his own *kife*.

A tall, good-looking man in his late twenties, Grisha skied every day in a bright orange ski suit and blue arm patch with the words *Vancouver Baseball* printed on it. He kept himself entertained with ski bunnies from Moscow and Leningrad.

While other young Soviets watched with interest as changes began to occur under Gorbachev, Grisha's thoughts never strayed to politics. "Young people in this country aren't interested in the government—I think it's the same everywhere. The people at the top make decisions and things drift down to us," he said. Grisha was contemptuous toward Andrey Sakharov, the human rights activist and Nobel laureate then exiled to Gorky. "Who cares about Sakharov?" he said dismissively. "Sakharov isn't doing anything for anyone—he's just helping himself. Besides, I hear he lives better than all of us."

Grisha's official salary was only 100 rubles a month (about $160), but he supplemented this by purchasing Western ski equipment from foreign skiers and selling it to tourists from Moscow. He never involved himself in the struggle to buy food at the pitiful local stores. Instead, he took all of his meals at the youth center. Grisha lived in a communal apartment with two other young men; each had his own room and they shared a small kitchen and bath. His room was dominated by a floor-to-ceiling photograph of his wife, a pretty brunette provocatively posed in a tiny bikini. She was living with her parents in Voronezh, a major industrial city in the Ukraine. He avoided talking about her.

His small room also held a stereo and a large collection of tapes and records. He owned many tapes with music by Akvarium, then an underground rock group that later became official under the more tolerant atmosphere of *glasnost*. He was particularly fond of one tape, by another underground group he didn't identify, that carried a song entitled "Hunters." Its lyrics: "Boys, guard your penis / Certain girls are hunters / They just want dresses, shoes / They're dressed in furs and diamonds."

The best thing about his apartment, according to Grisha, was his balcony. In the winter, he used it to store his ski equipment. In the summer, he cleared it off and relaxed there in the few short months of warm weather that come to the Caucasus each year.

Underneath the balcony, protected from the prying eyes of his neighbors, he cultivated his annual crop of marijuana. He was able to hide the small patch by placing boxes and barrels around the perimeter and growing a few plants in the narrow gaps that caught the sun's rays. To any casual passerby, it looked like the storage space outside any cramped communal apartment.

He had first gathered seeds for his crop from a friend who had brought a few joints from Moscow. The growing period was short and the soil poor, but over the years, Grisha had refined his yield into what he called, in English, "killer weed." He knew the exact spot to plant his seeds, the right amount of water to give them, and the fertilizer they required. He tended them only at night, so as not to arouse the suspicion of neighbors. Every September, he pulled his few small plants out of the ground and dried them in his closet.

Whenever he wanted to roll a joint, Grisha removed the tobacco from a Soviet cigarette and carefully packed a few marijuana leaves into the empty roll of paper. He rationed himself carefully, so that his supply would last through the long ski season.

Grisha seemed unconcerned about getting caught with a marijuana patch under his porch, but he was very cautious; only two of his friends knew that he cultivated it. Why, then, did he tell a Western correspondent? Because, he replied, the correspondent was American, and anyway, didn't all Americans do drugs?

He had never been caught with drugs; in fact, he had not even had any close calls. But there were signs that his idyllic existence was about to come to an end. His wife had grown tired of surviving on his discotheque salary. Grisha was about to be forced out of his ski bum world and into a city apartment shared with in-laws and a "normal" job. The transition was not going to be easy, and it wasn't clear whether Grisha would make it. Perhaps he did take a factory job and began putting in an eight-hour day. But Grisha didn't seem the type. Under Gorbachev, he's probably formed his own small ski-school cooperative, and he's probably still growing marijuana in the summer and smoking it every winter.

✮   As the Soviet media began to examine social problems more candidly, medical experts looked for the reasons behind drug use. For the first time, the press speculated about the social conditions that lead young people to use drugs. Could it be that Soviet youth are seeking thrills? Or is it a problem of hopelessness? In the 1987 hit film *Is it Easy to be Young?* a teenager asks his friend why he has turned to heroin. "Why *haven't* you?" asks the friend, sounding the bitter chord of a generation of young people who feel they have little to look forward to in life.

Sociologists point to the high rate of divorce and alcoholism in Soviet society; a young boy or girl who lives with an alcoholic parent may turn to drugs as a source of comfort and escape. As for the use of drugs among central Asians, smoking hashish and eating poppies is part of the traditional culture in the southern republics.

Psychologists will debate the reasons behind drug abuse for years; in the meantime, the government needs to prove its commitment to fighting the problem by opening centers all over the country to treat addicts. The government at first classified drug use as a criminal problem rather than a medical one. Drug addicts and even casual users were sent to prisons instead of hospitals.

The government has only recently begun taking a more enlightened approach to treatment. A Moscow newspaper published a story in 1986 about a hotline for people with drug problems. The newspaper promised anonymity. Law enforcement authorities stopped filing charges against people caught with small quantities of illegal drugs and against those who voluntarily turned themselves in for treatment. But the punitive policies remain; local police stations continue to register drug users, which makes many people hesitate to seek help. Once drug users have identified themselves, they are required to undergo treatment. Those who refuse are sentenced to work-rehabilitation centers run by the police; these hard-labor facilities treat addicts as prisoners, not patients.

The number of Western-style drug counseling centers falls far short of the need. While Moscow boasts ten clinics and two hospitals and Leningrad has established a hospital with minibuses that transport doctors to emergencies, the director of the Russian republic's health department said in 1986 that only one-fourth of the known drug addicts were receiving treatment. The others "remain outside medical control." In Turkmenistan, a southern republic thought to have the largest number of addicts in the country, only one drug clinic existed in 1986.

Most treatment programs are too short. Press reports in 1987 indicated that addicts received only seven to eight days of inpatient care and then were allowed to check out. An estimated 90 percent of all patients turn back to drugs.

Even if the Soviet Union had more treatment centers, there would not be enough doctors to staff them. The head of the drug abuse department of the Ministry of Health said in 1986 that few drug clinics were staffed with qualified doctors. Medical schools offer no classes in drug counseling. The country has set the goal of having four thousand trained drug specialists by the early 1990s—but that is only four thousand in a nation of 280 million people.

Government efforts to educate Soviet people about the dangers of drug abuse have been heavy-handed. Documentaries with such titles as "Business trip to Hell" and "Pain" have appeared on television. The national newspaper for teachers issued three million cut-out leaflets in 1987 that carried the headline, "Beware the white clouds." The leaflet included a gruesome description of a young drug addict suffering from withdrawal symptoms and convulsions, hallucinating that he was being eaten alive by white worms. Schoolchildren were warned not to take cigarettes from another person, as they could contain narcotics, leading to certain addiction. "If just one gram of narcotics is found in your home, or just a packet in your pocket, it means arrest, a trial and prison," the leaflet said. "There will be no escape."

Are such scare tactics really effective? Young people who read lurid accounts of the dangers of drugs and then experiment with marijuana and find that they are not immediately addicted will mistrust everything else adults tell them about drugs. The experience may lead them to question the risks of trying opium and heroin.

As with alcohol, the problem is that drugs are a way of fighting boredom, especially in small towns. If the authorities want to see drug use drop, they must build cafes, gymnasiums, and cinemas for young people to turn to as alternatives. Law enforcement officials should stop registering addicts who ask for treatment, because the stigma of addiction only creates problems for them later when they try to find jobs. Until such changes are made, the Soviet authorities will find themselves struggling with a growing drug problem among the young.

CHAPTER 6   RELIGION AND ATHEISM

RUSSIAN ORTHODOX EASTER

ABOUT FIVE miles outside of Moscow, just beyond the city's outer beltway, where the grime of the capital starts to give way to the birch forests of the Russian countryside, there is a tiny Russian Orthodox church, encircled by trees and nestled beside a small lake where it is barely visible from the roadway. A reporter drove out to this secluded spot one spring to see the Easter service. Seeking the relative seclusion of a provincial church, the journalist wanted to avoid the ornate cathedrals of the capital, which attracted hordes of diplomats, correspondents, and tourists every year. A young friend from Moscow had led the reporter to the church, so that they could quietly enjoy the ceremony as millions of Russians did, without the special treatment accorded to foreigners.

They parked the car on a nearby road and walked down a dirt path lined with tall bushes. It was midnight—the hour that Easter services traditionally begin in the Russian Orthodox Church. There was no moon and they could not see the church's gilded onion domes, but they could sense its hulking mass rising up at the end of the path. As the two rounded a corner, three uniformed policemen suddenly stepped toward them, blocking their way. They were polite, but firm. "Good evening. Young people are forbidden to enter the church tonight," one said.

The reporter kept silent, not wanting the police to know they were dealing with a foreigner. Volodya, the reporter's friend, immediately began to argue with the officers, asking why they could not go in when they had driven there all the way from downtown Moscow. "Are you believers?" one officer asked. Volodya assured them that they were. The policeman, his voice full of sarcasm and ridicule, said, "Yeah, sure, you're believers."

The police were not accustomed to having their authority questioned, and as Volodya persisted, they turned rude and dismissive. "No young people are allowed. Go home and watch TV. Can't you see—this is not for you," one of them said. Volodya tried a different tack. He told the policemen that he and his friend were in their thirties—not so young after all. But the officers were unimpressed. "The local Komsomol committee voted last week that no young people should be allowed into the church on Easter," they said. "Go home." One pointed at the slacks the journalist was wearing and said, "She's got jeans on. Jeans are not allowed in church." Volodya again argued with the officer. He insisted that there were no words about clothing in the laws of the church or the state. The officers stood in sullen silence.

Volodya and the journalist had exhausted all of their appeals. If they had defied the police and tried to force their way past, they would have faced arrest and possibly a few hours in the local militia station. Instead, they turned away from the police; Volodya whispered to his friend that she should identify herself as a foreign correspondent. They both knew it was the only way they were going to get inside the church. After the plastic-laminated ID card was pulled out, one of the policemen fixed the foreigner with a look of resentment, as if to say, Why didn't you show us that in the first place—we could have avoided all this fuss and bother. But the three quickly stepped out of the way. "*Pozhaluista*," one said deferentially—"please." Using the long, white stick that all Soviet police officers carry, he pointed the way to the church.

Although the reporter had not intended to misrepresent herself and masquerade as a Russian, by keeping silent and allowing Volodya to dicker with the policemen, she had been treated just as any young Soviet would have been treated. The experience pointed up the double standard that exists in the Soviet Union when it comes to religion. While older people are officially discouraged from attending church, they are not prevented from going on the major religious holidays. For the young, church is specifically forbidden.

At the church that Easter Sunday, services were off limits for youth. This was reinforced by a vote by the local Komsomol committee which had decided that young people were not to be allowed inside the church that night. Police officers were posted at the doors for the evening to carry out these orders.

Inside, scores of old women were waiting for the Mass. There were a few middle-aged worshipers but no young people. As the reporter and her friend stood there, she laughed about their tense confrontation with the policemen. An elderly woman turned and said angrily, "What's so funny? Did you come here to have a good time or to worship?"

The two quickly fell silent and listened to the choir singing in the balcony overhead. They gazed at the golden icons on the walls and pillars of the church and the lavishly painted frescoes on its domed ceiling. The iconostasis, a floor-to-ceiling holy wall decorated with the faces of saints, the Virgin Mary and Jesus, and the flowery script of the old cyrillic alphabet, stood behind the altar. In the Russian Orthodox Church, much of the service takes place behind the iconostasis, which symbolizes a wall through which one must pass to reach heaven. But it also separates the congregation from the priests and enshrouds much of what they do in mystery, allowing only a chosen few to have access to the full measure of the service.

Two elderly priests with flowing gray beards and gold-inlaid robes stepped through a door in the iconostasis. They began the Mass, swinging incense burners and chanting the liturgy. There were no pews; crowds of worshipers stood for hours, intoning the responses, bowing, and crossing themselves dozens of times. Fragile brown candles, sold by a wizened little woman in a kiosk at the door, burned low in churchgoers' hands. Witnessing the pomp and ceremony of the Russian Orthodox service in this small church, so far from the spectacles staged in the showcase churches of the capital, made it seem even more consecrated and mystical. As the service continued, the church filled with the smoke of the incense, the odor of tallow from the dripping candles, and the body heat of a hundred worshipers crammed together inside.

Finally, Volodya and his foreign friend, exhausted from hours of standing, squeezed through the crowd to the door. Several teenagers stood at the back, looking on with curiosity. Perhaps they had managed to enter with written invitations from the priest, or maybe the policemen had abandoned their watch as the hour grew late. On the path outside, the officers were gone. It was nearly four o'clock in the morning.

The journalist drove back to Moscow, her eyes burning from the incense and candle smoke. By the time they reached the center of the city, the sky was beginning to turn pale. The streets, usually deserted at that early hour on a Sunday, were bustling with people. Many were gathering with their families and friends for special Easter dinners of zakuski (appetizers), and kulich, a cake traditionally served with a sweetened, raisin-filled farmer cheese. Most probably sat feasting and drinking for hours, finally falling into bed late in the day.

But the journalist let Volodya off at a busy corner, where he could easily find a taxi. She had started her celebration of Easter as many young Soviets did, with a struggle to get past the police and inside the church door. But now she was too tired to finish it with an hours-long Russian Orthodox Easter dinner. She went home and climbed into bed.

The next day, she talked to correspondents who had attended services in the Yelokhovsky Cathedral, known among Russians as the "diplomatic" church, because it kept a special section roped off just for foreigners. Other reporters had driven to Zagorsk, the center of the Russian Orthodox Church, which houses a monastery and several beautiful onion-domed churches inside a towering brick wall. At both places of worship, the scene was the same: cordons of uniformed policemen and *druzhiniki*, the volunteer police corps, lined up outside and turning young people away. At Zagorsk, which attracted hundreds of visitors, the local police were reinforced by a company of young army recruits.

The authorities' rationale for these heavy-handed tactics was always the same: if all of the young hooligans out to catch a glimpse of the exotic costumes and rituals were allowed to attend church services there would be no room for the older worshipers who came in a sincere expression of faith. It was not a very artful dodge and it fooled no one; by consigning the large crowds of young Soviets to the ranks of mere curiosity seekers, the state was simply trying to hide from the fact that there were many believers among the young. Despite all of the hours of atheism lessons in school and in Komsomol, the authorities have failed in their Leninist mission of creating an atheist state.

ICONS AND CANDLES

Why, after more than seventy years of repression, do Soviets still believe? For some, the church is a spiritual alternative to red-and-white propaganda slogans and the state's intrusion into people's daily lives. The Russian Orthodox Church is an oasis of relief from numbing official ideology. Young people need something to believe in, because the dream of building communism has become spiritually unfulfilling. They attend classes, hold jobs, raise families, and go about their daily business. Still, there is something missing; many look to the church for solace and inspiration.

There is perhaps another reason that scientific atheism is doomed to decay into a gray, lifeless mass of ideology in the Soviet Union. Russians are, by nature, a spiritual and superstitious people. Their fascination with the spirit expresses itself in countless ways, from herbal cures to hours of prayer in the Russian Orthodox Church, astrology, numerology, and the occult. Coupled with a strong streak of sentimentality and emotionalism, the Russian national character simply is not very receptive to the Leninist philosophy of scientific atheism.

Lenin may have understood that his countrymen's peculiar psyche would make it difficult to impose the antireligious philosophy he preferred. He also must have known that his dream of communism would fail if any competing ideologies, like the Russian Orthodox Church, were allowed to get in the way. After the Bolshevik triumph of 1917, his government began a campaign of repression against the church. He nationalized church property and convened a council to discuss important issues in religion; it was under this council that the first of many bishops were murdered. During Stalin's rule, religion came under further seige. Fifty thousand priests, nuns, and monks were killed or exiled to labor camps. Most of the country's fifty-four thousand Russian Orthodox churches were destroyed or converted to museums, storage warehouses, or factories. The church became subservient to the state.

Antireligion statutes imposed in 1929 made it impossible for believers to carry their faith beyond the four walls of the church. Members of the clergy were prohibited from holding classes in religion for people under eighteen years of age. Ministers were allowed to visit the terminally ill, but only with the permission of local government authorities. Pilgrimages and religious funerals outside the church were prohibited. Religious proselytizing was illegal. In every Soviet classroom, atheism corners were set up to take the place of the Red Corners where religious icons had hung when the czars ruled Russia.

After the German army invaded in 1941, Stalin eased up on religion. To win support for the war effort, he reopened thousands of churches. But Khrushchev reversed that policy and launched a new crackdown on religious communities throughout the country. The State Council of Religious Affairs, a government agency, was created to oversee all church activities. No one was admitted to the seminary or ordained without the council's consent. Instead of acting as the head of his parish, each priest became an employee of the government. A flood of antireligious literature was published.

The Russian Orthodox Church became a mere shadow of its former self. All sense of community, so central to Western congregations, was stripped away. People stood for hours praying, crossing themselves, and bowing, prostrating themselves on the stone floor of the church. Then they went home. There were no other church activities—no Sunday school classes, no summer Bible camps, no picnics, no church baseball leagues. The church was infiltrated by informers; any worshipers who tried to organize their congregation into discussion groups or visits to local nursing homes were arrested and sentenced.

Believers were banned from the Communist party and their choice of careers was limited to the less prestigious professions. Applicants to the nation's elite institutes and universities were screened for religious beliefs; those found to be active in any faith were often denied entrance. Baptisms and church marriages were conducted in secret. Only the elderly attended worship services without fear of punishment; for the rest of the population, any open expression of religious belief or call for greater religious freedom brought trouble at work or in class.

Under Khrushchev, the biggest defeat for religion was the closing of ten thousand churches. After this crackdown, only about sixty-five hundred Russian Orthodox churches remained open in the entire country. The vast expanse of Siberia was left almost devoid of churches. For many people, going to worship services on Sunday became a hardship that involved hours of travel over bad roads to a neighboring town. Organized religion was no longer practicable; many people retained a feeling of faith, but they had no way of expressing it.

Many young Soviets who came of age under Brezhnev's rule saw the Kremlin continue its crackdown on religion, arresting activists and burning churches. The government also made cynical use of the church as an agent of pro-Soviet propaganda. Church leaders appeared on television, endorsing the "peace-loving" policies of the Soviet Union and criticizing Western governments. The Russian Orthodox Church donated many thousands of rubles to the Soviet Peace Committee, an officially sanctioned organization that was created to promote Soviet arms control propaganda. Orthodox churchmen even defended the Soviet human rights record. Many young people placed the church leadership in the same category as the corrupt bureaucrats they saw working at every level of government.

In school and at Komsomol meetings, religion came under steady assault. One woman who attended a general school in rural Russia said that her first-grade teacher started every Monday by asking which students had attended church the day before with their grandmothers. Anyone who raised his hand was grilled by the teacher: why had he gone, and what did he see there? The teacher criticized the child's grandmother as uneducated and ignorant and told each student, "Your grandmother is deceiving you, you don't need that. Next time, tell granny that you are an Octobrist and you don't go to church." Later, when parents came to school for meetings with the teachers, she demanded to know why they had allowed their children to be taken to church.

Parents of kindergarten students were encouraged to attend after-school lectures, with riveting titles like "Atheistic education is an inseparable component of ideological work," and "Religious remnants and their harmful effects." The Soviet media frequently complained that these evening lectures were poorly attended.

In the atheist corner of her school classroom, one young Soviet recalled a book and photo display entitled "Religion is poison." An atheist council was formed in her class. She said the school published an atheist magazine

modeled after the nationwide journal of atheism, *Science and Religion.*
Students who volunteered to work on the magazine were the most active
members of Komsomol.

She grew up hearing religion mocked and reviled in her classes. In
history, she was taught that Christianity had started wars, killed millions
of people, and made the masses blind to their own oppression. In art,
religious paintings were denigrated as inferior to other types of work. In
literature, teachers said that Tolstoy was persecuted for trying to oppose
religion, while Dostoyevsky had been a great writer who suffered from
only one weakness: religion. In Young Pioneer meetings, leaders told
stories about priests, portraying them as sly, tricky, and corrupt. Children
learned that the 1917 revolution had opened people's eyes to religion and
made them realize that the church had kept them in the dark for thousands
of years. The church was old and out of date—a mere relic from the past
that modern people had cast out of their lives.

One youth from western Siberia told about being raised an atheist by
parents who were opposed to religion. They were scientists and sent their
son to a special school, where he received a strong atheist education. He
was ignorant of the entire body of knowledge concerning religion. The
story of Mary and Jesus and the Bible were unknown to him. He was
mystified whenever he came upon references to religious figures in literature.

When in high school he went on an outing with his class to Vladimir
and Suzdal, two towns in central Russia that are an important part of the
religious history of the country. He tried to go into the ornately beautiful
churches there but was warned by a teacher, "You're a Komsomol
member—you don't belong in church."

He had been taught in school that religion was only for old people,
so the first time he went to the Russian Orthodox monastery at Zagorsk,
it came as a shock to see young priests there. "But when I entered the
churches, I saw the old ladies and it reinforced the stereotype that religion
was for pitiful, old-fashioned people—for old people wearing rags," he
said. The shadowy interior of the church and the sweaty odor of the
worshipers, as they stood together for hours, convinced him that religion
was medieval and backward.

Like his parents, he became a scientist and felt no pull toward the
church. It wasn't until he married a woman whose mother was religious
that the question of faith entered his life. His bride's mother wanted to
baptize their children and take them to church, but he was strongly opposed.
He found himself in ferocious fights with his mother-in-law, as he pledged
that his children would never become religious. The church, he said, was

something that should be gazed at from afar—a pretty image of golden, onion-shaped domes on a distant, snowy hilltop. "Religion wasn't part of my life, and I never expected it to be," he said.

For others, the decision whether to abandon religion was not so easy. One young Muscovite, the son of a Christian mother and an atheist father, told about his confusion and awkwardness as he tried to pick his way between the two competing ideologies within his own home. When he was five years old, his mother told him about God, but his father refused to allow his son to be taken to church. The boy listened helplessly as the arguments about religion roiled over his head. On Sundays, he would go with his grandmother for walks in a nearby park, where the two would sneak into a Russian Orthodox Church. He didn't understand the services, but he was fascinated by the church and treasured the secret he shared with his grandmother.

In school, he felt alienated when he heard religion ridiculed. "The other children didn't mind at all when our teacher stated flatly that God did not exist," he said. "But I couldn't be like them. I hated hearing the church attacked." As a teenager, he started going to worship services by himself. Every Easter, Komsomol members tried to bar him from entering, but when he lied and said that he had never been a member of Komsomol, they moved out of his path.

He became more knowledgeable about the Russian Orthodox Church and its teachings but was disturbed by the corruption of the priests. Even before the founding of the communist state, Russian Orthodoxy had always been the "official" church, and its patriarch and priests had served at the pleasure of the czars. They were still willing to acquiesce to the state's orders, in return for bigger food packages. He spoke with disgust about the state's understanding of the church's role in people's daily lives. "Soviet Communists have stopped believing in their ideals," he said. "They try to be close to God, which is forbidden to them. But what is better—people who believe in God, or people who believe in nothing? I think the answer is, people who believe in God *and* in communism."

PERESTROIKA GETS RELIGION

As *glasnost* allowed more open discussion of social issues, the press finally acknowledged that the government's policy of harassment and persecution had failed to eradicate religion. Orthodox services were crowded with worshipers every Sunday. The chairman of the Council on Religious Affairs estimated in 1988 that there were seventy million believers of various faiths in the Soviet Union. If the number was accurate, it meant that about 25 percent of the population was religious. Western experts set the figure even higher, however, at 40 percent.

Among nonbelievers, there was a broad tolerance for religion. A Moscow daily newspaper reported in 1988 that an opinion poll conducted in the city's suburbs showed that 44 percent saw no harm in religious ceremonies. The paper estimated that every third newborn baby was baptized.

Young people were increasingly interested in religion. A 1987 survey in the journal *Sociological Research* revealed that the majority did not consider religion harmful to society. Even though a third of the young people surveyed did not think of themselves as believers, they admitted taking part in christenings and said they sometimes read religious literature. Forty percent said they had visited working churches, temples, or prayer houses. The survey also found that young people with a higher education were particularly interested in religion.

As changes began taking place in Soviet society under Gorbachev, it became clear that religious believers were one more constituency that somehow had to be drawn into his plan of rebuilding the economy. Irritating a substantial minority group by attacking the church and assaulting them with a new round of atheistic teaching would hardly make them more amenable to *perestroika.* Many religious believers were hardworking, non-drinking citizens who were anxious for something they could believe in. In short, they were just the folks Gorbachev was seeking to help carry out his program of restructuring.

Under Gorbachev, the Kremlin moved to forge a new relationship with these believers, creating an atmosphere that was, at least on the surface, more tolerant toward religion. Soviet newspapers and magazines stopped publishing militantly aggressive articles against religion. Instead, they began carrying reports about infringements on the rights of believers, in most cases blaming local authorities for persecuting worshipers in small towns. The articles stressed that the Soviet constitution guaranteed freedom to worship and the right to build new churches.

There was other evidence of a thaw. Churches were allowed to ring their bells on Sundays and do charity work. Nearly half of the four hundred religious prisoners were released from Soviet labor camps, and arrests of activists slowed dramatically. The government permitted dozens of Orthodox churches to reopen and returned four monasteries to the church. In 1988, it claimed to have registered more than sixteen hundred new congregations, including churches of all denominations. The Pentacostal and Seventh-Day Adventist communities, which had long suffered under especially cruel repression, scored firsts: the opening of a registered Pentecostal church and a seminary for the Adventists.

The baptism of babies, a ceremony previously conducted in secret, was now allowed to take place out in the open. Under new state rules, passport numbers were not recorded when a child was baptized. Parents no longer needed to fear punishment at work for having their child christened; they were able to take their children to the baptism ceremony themselves rather than sending them with a grandmother.

Tiny inroads were made against the prohibition of religious teaching to minors. A youth newspaper announced that two high schools in the Latvian capital of Riga would offer Bible classes to tenth-grade students. The classes were strictly voluntary and open only to students in the two schools. As one school principal was quick to point out, the course did not offer religious instruction but focused instead on the Bible as a cultural document. Nevertheless, the course was a first: use of a government building for the teaching of religion to young people under eighteen was clearly forbidden in the 1929 antireligion decree. The move might have been an experiment by the state, to see if the closely controlled Bible classes incited broader interest in religion, or it might have been a concession to the Latvian Nationalist movement, which was linked with the Lutheran Church. Whatever the reason, the classes were allowed. Taught by a local Lutheran pastor, the Bible lessons were reported to be packed with interested students.

In Moscow, ancient religious relics that had been held in state museums were turned over to the church. Bibles, traditionally highly prized treasures that drew $50 to $150 on the black market, were made more available. The Russian Orthodox Church publishing house was allowed to print 100,000 Bibles, while the Baptists were given permission to import another 100,000.

More young Soviets were allowed to join the clergy. The government reported in 1988 that the number of students at the country's three Orthodox seminaries and two academies had more than doubled since 1973, to nearly two thousand. At Zagorsk, the state reported three applicants for every opening.

In a highly symbolic gesture, Gorbachev appeared on the main evening news program with the top hierarchy of the Russian Orthodox Church and called for a more tolerant attitude toward religion. The meeting was believed to be the first publicized reception for religious leaders in the Kremlin in more than forty years. In his televised remarks, Gorbachev welcomed the faithful into the ranks of *perestroika*, saying: ''Believers are Soviet people, workers, patriots and they have the full right to express their conviction with dignity. *Perestroika* and democratization concern them too.''

ATHEISM REVAMPED

While they began showing a new tolerance for religion in 1987, Kremlin leaders also searched for a more sophisticated style of handling atheism. Atheist teachings under Brezhnev and Stalin were roundly denounced. A return to Lenin's writings on atheism were called for, but there was confusion over exactly what this meant, since it was Lenin, after all, who had castigated religion as "the opiate of the masses." Conveniently, Lenin had written broadly on religion, so government experts searched the archives for an approach that would fit in with their newfound tolerance for religious faith.

The new government tack on religion was two-tiered. Crude attacks on believers were halted; at the same time, there were calls to improve atheist instruction. Under *glasnost*, atheism had to be transformed from an anemic, listless philosophy into a lively, vital body of thought that would be attractive to young people. Gone were the days when books on atheism, written in a turgid, uninteresting language, could be allowed to lie unread on store shelves. It was no longer enough for atheism teachers to proudly announce that religious faith was fading away in the Soviet Union; any young Soviet could look around and see this was a lie. Once he caught them lying on this point, he would be skeptical about everything his atheism instructors had to say.

Children and teenagers had to be shown that atheism was moderate and well reasoned—not only the preferred philosophy of loyal Communists, but popular all over the world. Atheism was not just the negation of God and the antithesis of religion; instead, it had to be presented as a complex of views and respected scientific knowledge. An atheist education, it was said, should serve to defend people from religion, not merely fight against it.

One Soviet television show for youth, "Program of thought," encapsulated the government's restructured policy on religion. Aired in late 1988, the program began with the obligatory reference to the "period of stagnation" under Brezhnev, saying that state persecution of believers in that era had been incorrect. During the show, students at the Moscow Institute of Pedagogy, the nation's top teachers' college, said that atheist training was effective only among the young, because their religious beliefs were not fully formed. If someone was already a firm believer, the show's moderator said, it was impossible to drive his faith out of him. One future teacher said that the history of religion should be taught alongside the history of atheism and that the teaching of atheistic propaganda should be on a higher level, made more complex and nuanced. But a young woman complained about the gaps in her own knowledge and said she was not prepared to teach either religion or atheism.

The show moved to the Moscow Theological Institute in Zagorsk, a seminary for Russian Orthodox priests, where the camera focused on a discussion among a class of young priests. One told about his path to God. As a boy, he said, he had been interested in religion and knew he could learn more about it if he entered the atheism faculty at Moscow State University. Instead of becoming a confirmed atheist, however, he decided that the church was his calling in life, and he entered the priesthood. The priest's story was a stunning indictment of Soviet-style atheism's failure to captivate young students. He had used his antireligious course work and textbooks to brief himself on religion, and ironically, his classes in atheism helped bring him to God.

BUDDHISM

Most young Russians in the Soviet Union who consider themselves religious believers are drawn to the Russian Orthodox faith, but a minority are members of other denominations. The Baptists, Protestants, and Buddhists in the Soviet Union often have an easier time learning about religion, because their churches are not as rigidly hierarchical as the Russian Orthodox is and their worship services can be held underground, with less pomp and ceremony. Many young believers, determined to defy their government's prohibition against the teaching of religion to minors, join their church choir. After each weekly choir practice, they stay on for classes and Bible study with their pastor. Others pray and study quietly in unregistered churches, with pastors who are not formally ordained.

Buddhism, with its heavy emphasis on individualism and hours of solitary meditation, has a large circle of underground followers, despite years of repression. Under Stalin, Soviet Buddhism was crushed with a severity experienced by few other religious groups. Accused of conspiring with the Japanese during World War II, Soviet Buddhists were considered the enemies within. Their lamas, once numbering ten thousand, were imprisoned and executed; by the late 1980s, there were only forty officially registered lamas left in the tiny area of the Far East where Buddhism had managed to survive. Only two monasteries, known as *datsans*, still functioned.

One was in Buryat, a remote spot near the border of Mongolia. When two reporters traveled across the country aboard the Trans-Siberian Railroad, they climbed off the train late one night in Ulan-Ude, the capital of

Buryat. The city was a strange mix of the ancient Orient and the modern Soviet Union. Its people were Mongolian in appearance, with dark skin, folded eyelids and high cheekbones; it was at first startling to hear these Asian people speak Russian. The city itself was typically Soviet, with nondescript apartment buildings of the type found all over the country and drab stores marked "Products," "Vegetables—Fruit," and "Milk." A huge cement sculpture of Lenin's bald head stood on the city's central square.

Ulan-Ude was so far off the Western tourist circuit that it had no Intourist Hotel, a standard fixture in most Soviet cities that caters to foreign tourists and accepts only foreign currency. Instead, the visiting reporters stayed in a hotel for Soviets. The room offered an excellent view of the cement Lenin's head.

Before leaving Moscow, the two had wired ahead to arrange a visit to the *datsan* and an interview with the high lama there. They were accompanied there by a member of the local Council on Religious Affairs and by a woman who worked in the party committee.

About twenty miles away from Ulan-Ude, they drove over a dirt road through a small village. Up ahead, the solitary *datsan* rose up from an empty plain, with the Khamar-Daban mountain range creating a dramatic backdrop. The brilliant scarlet, green, and blue and the exotic curves and flourishes of the monastery stood out boldly against the gray winter landscape. After the drab austerity of most Soviet cities, the garish beauty of the *datsan* was startling. In front of the temple, a sculpture of a snarling tiger bared its fangs. Inside the temple was a huge golden Buddha. The temple's walls were decorated with gold and red banners and pictures illustrating the story of Buddha. One of the young lamas stood at the back accepting donations from visitors and overseeing a smoking incense burner.

Later, the reporters were allowed an interview with the high lama, Bandido Hambo Lama, a wizened little octagenarian dressed in flowing saffron robes and high leather boots. The tour guide, the Council on Religious Affairs member, translated the high lama's words into Russian, with the explanation that he did not speak the language—a claim the reporters found difficult to believe, since he had spent much of his rather long life in the Soviet Union. It was never certain whether his translated responses were his own words or those of his overseer from the council. But it seemed likely that he had followed the government line, at least on that occasion, since it would have been unwise to deviate during a visit by two Western correspondents who obviously were under careful watch.

The high lama said that most of the 200,000 Buryats lived in nearby villages, where lay lamas practiced. Although they were informed religious leaders, the lay lamas had never graduated from the seminary where Soviet Buddhists were allowed to study, in Ulan Bator, the capital of Mongolia. He estimated that only four to seven lamas graduated annually and that there were only about three hundred surviving lay lamas, many of whom were elderly. The high lama said that thousands of believers made pilgrimages to the *datsan* every year.

The two correspondents were treated with deference there, and they were shown everything they had asked to see. Yet when they boarded the Trans-Siberian to reach the next stop of their journey, both were glad to be leaving Ulan-Ude. The party committee member who had overseen their visit had been a particularly clumsy and overzealous chaperone. Even more depressing had been the meeting with the high lama, who had assured them, in words that were probably not his own, that there was full religious freedom for Buddhist believers in the Soviet Union.

That was the last time they visited the Buddhist *datsan* at Ulan-Ude, and they never expected to meet Buddhists in other parts of the Soviet Union. But on another trip in 1986, a group of about twenty young Buddhists turned up in a most unlikely place: that most Western of all Soviet republics, Estonia. At first, it seemed incongruous to see young Estonian men, with their fair skin and blue eyes, wearing saffron robes, their heads shaved bald, worshiping at small homemade Buddhist altars. Upon reflection, however, it made sense that Estonians would be studying Buddhism; like millions of Westerners their age, these young men had turned away from Western religion and secular values and looked to the ancient traditions of the East as a source of spiritual enlightenment.

One member of the group, Velo Vaartnou, emerged as a leader. A tall, heavily built Estonian in his thirties with a penetrating gaze, Velo did not stoop to small talk. He had been expelled from the youth section of the Artists Union, and spent time in an Estonian prison and mental hospital as punishment for his activities. He had little patience for anything he considered trivial. Determined to win official status for his group, he petitioned the Soviet government for permission to build a Buddhist temple in Estonia. Velo submitted the signatures of twenty believers, as required by Soviet law; the local authorities turned down his petition.

That did not stop Velo from pushing ahead. He made many trips across the country to Buryat, where he stayed at the *datsan* and studied with the lamas. Velo once produced a faded black-and-white picture of himself seated next to the high lama. The contrast between the two men was striking—Velo, an imposing young man dressed in Western clothing, towered over the aging, diminutive Easterner swathed in robes.

Velo was so fiery in his determination that the lamas in Buryat considered him twice born (in his previous life, he had also been a Buddhist).

On each trip to the *datsan*, Velo and his fellow Buddhists were given books, drums, bells, statues, and other holy objects, which they carried back with them to Estonia. They studied Tibetan and the ancient Mongolian languages and built small altars in their apartments, where they sat in daily meditation and prayer. Lamas from the *datsan* monastery frequently visited Estonia to teach the fledgling society of Buddhists.

The group's activities extended well beyond silent home prayer. On the territory of a friend's house, they built four towering stupas—Buddhist shrines made of stone and cement and topped with conical metal ornaments. A flat disk on top, hung with brightly colored swatches of cloth, rotated merrily in the wind. Traditionally, such stupas are built over the remnants of saints and must be carefully constructed in accordance with laws that make them produce certain vibrations. With the help and advice of the visiting lamas from Buryat, Velo had seen that they were built properly. KGB plainclothesmen from Tallinn came out to stare at the stupas and ordered them torn down. When Velo refused, there was little the KGB could do. The stupas had been built in the garden of a private homeowner.

Velo and his group set up a small factory in the cellar of a building, where they printed Buddhist calendars and paintings. Their religious paintings on cloth, known as mandalas, pictured an eight-armed god surrounded by gold and red flowers. Other gods floated in the background on gold-tipped clouds. The mandalas' high quality and complexity were impressive; any of them could have been made in Buryat or another Buddhism center. It was clear that Velo and his group had dedicated a great deal of time to the paintings. But the clandestine production of religious objects without state approval was illegal and had to be kept secret. Velo's group was already under surveillance by the KGB. Outside Velo's apartment, a government car sat parked with two men who monitored the comings and goings of the young Buddhists and all of their visitors.

With the help of friends, the group bought a run-down farmhouse and a small plot of land on a collective farm in western Estonia. It was Velo's dream to turn the house into a monastery, complete with statues and stupas. The group also became involved in the Estonian nationalist movement that sprouted up in 1987. Velo and another young Buddhist signed a handwritten document calling for the creation of the first independent political party in the Soviet Union. The proposal stirred nationalist pride and alarmed the authorities.

Such a direct challenge to the supreme power of the Communist party, in combination with Velo's Buddhist activism, was too much for local officials. He was summoned to a militia station and given the choice: a Siberian labor camp or emigration to the West. Velo left the Soviet Union in 1988 for Stockholm and settled into the large émigré community of

Estonians there. He studied Buddhism without interference from the government and dreamed of traveling to Tibet or to India to meet with the Dalai Lama.

The Soviet authorities' move to force Velo into exile was effective; Buddhism's spread was checked in Estonia. A year after his departure, work on the new monastery had ceased and little was being done in the underground print shop. The Buddhists had stopped studying and meditating before their altars. They still shaved their heads and burned incense, but there were few other signs of religious devotion. Without their leader, the group was lost.

JUDAISM

Jews have been persecuted in other societies and other eras, but the Soviet Union has been especially adept at manipulating its Jewish population. An estimated two million Jews live in the Soviet Union. All of them have the word *Jew* stamped in their passports. People are identified as Jews on all official documents, from birth certificates to work papers. Jews are defined as a nationality, distinct from Russians, Kazakhs, and Uzbeks. A Jew born in Russia is not a Russian, he is a Jew. A young Jewish woman who emigrated to the United States in 1987 said that one of her strongest memories was of her high school records and university application, each of which carried the same heading: her name and the word *Jew*.

For years, Soviet discrimination against Jews has been a point of friction between the Soviet Union and the West. The official designation of Jewish birth as a separate nationality is unchanged, but other signs of increased tolerance toward Judaism have appeared under Gorbachev, in part to win better relations with the United States and other nations. Jewish activists have been released from prisons and no new arrests have been reported.

Emigration has become easier under Gorbachev. The state began by allowing about eight thousand Jews to emigrate in 1987; in 1988, the number grew to twenty thousand. Soviet officials in 1989 predicted that the number would top fifty thousand. Jewish groups claimed that more than three hundred thousand Soviet Jews wanted to emigrate, but Soviet officials set the figure much lower. Many in the West were suspicious about increased opportunities to emigrate. They pointed out that the authorities had allowed fifty-one thousand Jews to leave in 1979, but then the numbers had quickly dropped off after the Soviet Union invaded Afghanistan and U.S.–Soviet relations soured. Over the years, Jewish emigration has been turned on and off like a spigot regulated by changes in East-West diplomacy.

More significant for the younger generation of Soviet Jews was the permission given world-renowned Israeli Talmudist Adin Steinsaltz to form a state-approved yeshiva—the first to open in the Soviet Union in sixty years. The yeshiva operates in four units of an apartment building on the edge of Moscow and accepts about one hundred and twenty students who are taught by five American and Israeli rabbis. They study the Talmud, Hebrew, law, and "general Judaism." The yeshiva's backers have managed to import two hundred books and a Torah. Although it might not meet the standards for yeshivas in the West or in Israel, its opening was hailed by many as a milestone, because the training of rabbis has for so long been a problem among the nation's Jews.

Despite across-the-board improvements in the quality of Jewish life in the U.S.S.R., the spectre of pervasive anti-Semitism still haunts the faithful. Many say the source of a new and virulent outbreak of anti-Semitism is an ultra-nationalist group called Pamyat. The organization glorifies the Russian culture, language, and the Orthodox Church. Unfortunately, they go one step further by ostracizing anyone who is not Russian. Jews are seen as special threats to the Russian culture, and it is the group's anti-Semitic mission that many Westerners find most disturbing.

In early 1989, outside the red walls of the Novodevichy Monastery along the Moscow River, a Pamyat demonstration was held. The organization's leader, Dmitri Vasilyev, a paunchy, balding man in his mid-fifties, spoke through a megaphone. As the speakers became increasingly chauvinistic and zealously anti-Semitic, the police began to shift nervously. Eventually, Vasilyev himself called an end to the show.

Vasilyev hotly protests whenever he is interviewed by Western reporters that he is not anti-Semitic—he is, he insists, only anti-Zionist. His theories are extremely attractive to some young Russians, particularly those from blue-collar families living in small towns. Although its membership among young people is impossible to measure, many teenagers say they are active in Pamyat or sympathize with its goals.

Some young people do more than just attend the group's demonstrations and rallies. A circle of about a dozen young men have positioned themselves around Vasilyev to serve as his bodyguards and accompany him whenever he goes out in public. Each dresses in a black shirt that is chillingly reminiscent of Mussolini's black-shirted vigilantes. To accentuate their paramilitary duties, they cover their chests with medals, wear red belts, and don black army boots polished to a high gloss. At every demonstration and outing, they look toward Vasilyev; when he nods his head and raises his fist in approval, they mimic him. Mussolini was known by his followers as "Il Duce." Vasilyev commands similar fealty; he is known among his black-shirted bodyguards as *Otyets* or "Father."

Vasilyev has an adopted son named Seryozha, who lives in the Pamyat apartment headquarters on Moscow's busy Garden Ring Road. Seryozha, twenty-nine, is a ringleader among Vasilyev's bodyguards and representative of Pamyat's younger generation. A nervous young man with a painfully embarrassing stutter, Seryozha pours tea and politely offers cookies and homemade jam at a table cluttered with czarist memorabilia whenever visitors arrive. Russian Orthodox icons and portraits of the Russian czars hang on the apartment walls. Other black-shirted bodyguards occasionally slip in to stare threateningly at Western correspondents who venture into the closed, claustrophobic society of Pamyat.

The atmosphere in the headquarters is one of mistrust. As Seryozha speaks, Vasilyev carefully monitors the conversation and gruffly objects if his son reveals too much about the secret inner circle of Pamyat. When Seryozha let it slip that the group has a nine-member council of directors, his father hurriedly silenced him. "Seryozha," he commanded, "don't talk about our structure!" Seryozha frequently takes on an air of blind obedience and looks to Vasilyev to formulate all Pamyat policy. "Father is our spiritual leader," he said. "We read him and follow him."

Protecting the Russian Orthodox Church and the Russian language and culture are the group's most important goals. Like Hitler's Nazi youth, Seryozha and the other young members of Pamyat also stress physical fitness and able readiness to defend their motherland. Seryozha said they work out together and play soccer to keep in shape. When his watchful father once stepped briefly outside the room, the younger Vasilyev admitted that the group even conducts secret military drills in the forests around Moscow. Their drills are illegal under Soviet law, which empowers only the security organs and the army to hold weapons. "We're always spiritually and physically ready to sacrifice ourselves—for the sake of the motherland and the church," he said. When a correspondent asked him what Pamyat had to be ready for, Seryozha alluded to threatening forces that sought to exterminate the group. Lowering his voice to a conspiratorial whisper, he said, "Our main goal is spirituality—perhaps that's why people hate us and want us dead. You know, our enemies are all around us."

Seryozha identified the group's detractors as the KGB, the Communist party, and the Zionists. He said that the KGB keeps Pamyat under close surveillance and frequently summons Vasilyev in for questioning. Meanwhile, the Communist party's propaganda chief, Alexander Yakovlev, is a Jew and a Zionist and has targeted Pamyat for annihilation, Seryozha added.

He derided Judaism and said that Jews believe in God ''just for themselves.'' According to Seryozha, Christianity is the only religion that makes itself truly open to everyone. Seryozha hotly insisted that his fellow bodyguards are not anti-Semitic, even as he stood under a poster displaying the word *danger* over a six-pointed Star of David decorated with a skull and crossbones—a chilling image. As Seryozha struggled to show that personally, he had nothing against Jews, his overt anti-Semitism and the ghastly wall poster hanging behind him proved otherwise.

TWO SYNAGOGUES

In Moscow, a city of 220,000 Jews, there are only two places for Jews to worship: the ''official'' showplace synagogue, where visiting foreign delegations are brought, and a smaller synagogue that Westerners usually manage to find only if led there by Soviet friends. The official synagogue, with its ornate, colonaded entrance, stands on Arkhipova Street in downtown Moscow, just a few minutes' walk from the Central Committee headquarters. Its diminutive counterpart, a modest wooden building, is hidden away on a dusty back street in a northern suburb known as Marina Rosha.

The two synagogues serve as a metaphor of religious freedom in the Soviet Union. Moscow's ''official'' synagogue on Arkhipova Street is well kept, beautifully painted, and government sanctioned. The synagogue has a rabbi trained in a yeshiva in Hungary, for many years the only full-fledged yeshiva in the Eastern Bloc.

But Moscow's main synagogue remains a source of ambivalence and even disgust for many Jews. It has served as one of the only places that Jews in Moscow can go to express their Judaism; on the other hand, they know that the building is used by Kremlin officials to defend the government against charges of anti-Semitism. Like all religious leaders in the country, its rabbi, Adolph Shayevich, is under the direct supervision of the state.

In contrast to the official status accorded to Arkhipova Street, the smaller synagogue at Marina Rosha was for many years unsanctioned and under siege. Threats and pressure failed to discourage the synagogue's faithful, a devout group of Lubavitchers who dedicate a larger share of their lives to Judaism than did their counterparts on Arkhipova Street.

While dozens of other synagogues were demolished over the years, this one had somehow managed to survive the organized anti-Semitism of the Communist state. The aging building resembled an old shtetl synagogue, dwarfed by the slate-gray edifices of modern Soviet architecture that had sprouted up around it. Enterprises with strange names like the Supply Directorate of Metal Construction Work were its neighbors.

Inside, the synagogue was small and dark, a space simply furnished yet rich in character and religious feeling. Younger members of the congregation had taken over the top floor. Somber men in their twenties with earlocks and beards, they gathered in the evenings around a long wooden table, eating apples and bread and drinking tea from glasses as they discussed religion.

Most had applied years earlier to emigrate to Israel. One unhappy young man said his wife had been given permission to leave but he had been denied; she lived in Jerusalem with their child, a little girl he had never seen. The synagogue was clearly a gathering place for them; by applying to leave, they had become outcasts in their society, but the small synagogue was one place they could go to be together and be accepted. All they had to be was Jewish. They were doing what Jews had done through centuries of persecution. Despite a repressive atmosphere outside the synagogue, the young men had created a community of support inside to help one another survive.

The little synagogue jousted with the state until 1987, when the Soviet government moved to grant religion some breathing space. Under Gorbachev, the synagogue at Marina Rosha began to flourish. It has been transformed from an unobtrusive, shabby building quietly contained within its four walls, to a center of bustling activity. Inside, the walls of the synagogue's small lobby are plastered with handwritten notices offering classes, lectures, and other services. Once little more than an unpainted wooden cabin surrounded by trees and bushes and barely visible from the street, the structure has been painted a bright aquamarine and trimmed in white. Its Star of David, once boarded over, has been enlarged and painted white and stands out proudly against its blue-green background.

The Marina Rosha synagogue does not have a fully accredited rabbi, but a young man named David Karpov has all of the responsibilities of one. Only thirty-two years old, Karpov is a tall, thin man with earlocks and a beard. He dashes around the synagogue, carrying a faded, battered prayer book, answering questions, leading prayers and lectures, and greeting visitors. An intensely devout man, Karpov is well respected among the young people. He speaks Hebrew and has a good knowledge of Judaism, although he has never studied formally. Instead, he has met with visiting rabbis from America and is largely self-taught. Karpov started working at the synagogue in 1982 as a watchman, studying Hebrew and reading the Torah in his spare time.

While the synagogue seems to be thriving, Karpov explained that it still faces problems with the government. "The authorities are not sure what framework to place us in. They say we can do what we want, but there is actually little help from the government and many of the laws still block us," he said. As an example of the restrictions, Karpov said that although the synagogue was able to set up its own yeshiva in 1988 on the second floor, where about fifteen young men gather daily for lessons, it is hindered by the law that requires every Soviet citizen to hold a job. Because the yeshiva is not licensed by the state, the young men cannot be registered as students, which means they all must hold jobs, at least on paper. Karpov said that many feared they would be subject to the law on parasitism, which mandates a three-year jail sentence for anyone found to be unemployed.

GROWING UP JEWISH

After watching the government try its best for so many years to wipe out Judaism, Western Jews marvel over the fact that Judaism has survived in the Soviet Union. Like other minority groups that have been persecuted there, observant young Soviet Jews have managed to preserve their traditions by isolating themselves and creating a shelter within the dominant culture.

One member of this small circle was Yevgeny Prokhorovsky, or Genya, as he was known by most of his friends. Genya, twenty-two, a thin, dark-haired man with a full beard, had grown up in an observant family in Moscow and had become a regular at the Marina Rosha synagogue, where he studied at the yeshiva and taught three Hebrew classes a week to children from six to twelve years old. An intensely religious young man, he moved only between his apartment and the synagogue and rarely mixed with Russians. Having agreed to meet a Western correspondent for an interview in a small sidewalk cafe in Moscow, a look of revulsion spread over his face as he surveyed the cafe's filthy tables and floor. Moving to clear away bits of food and pools of discolored water from a table, he said, "How can you eat here? It isn't clean." Genya pulled open a bag and took out a bar of kosher chocolate and cheese that had been sent to him from friends in the United States. His yarmulke drew curious stares from other customers in the cafe.

Genya explained that his father had taught his two sons Hebrew at home. The family had always tried to keep kosher, as difficult as that had been in the Soviet Union. They avoided all meat, because they knew that Soviet meat processing facilities could not possibly be clean.

As he grew up in the regimented Soviet school system, his attentiveness to Jewish traditions had brought him a lot of grief. He had refused to attend classes on Saturday and went to school only a few hours every Friday, in observance of the Sabbath. Because his family considered the school cafeteria unsanitary, he had avoided eating everything there except for the bread. "To go for seven hours a day to school and eat nothing but bread—it's really hard for a little boy," Genya said.

He had found the lessons in atheism even more disturbing. "The teachers and school director wanted us to stop believing," he said. "They tried to foist off their psychology and it was really stupid and wasteful. When kids hear adults say that religion is bad and vulgar, it has a very harmful effect on them."

But Genya had found strength among other Jews. "Such problems are not just mine—all Jews share these problems," he said. "A Jew has to find ways around the laws to his own beliefs and traditions. We don't wait for the government to tell us yes or no. We formed our own yeshiva—we don't wait for official status." He spoke proudly of the synagogue's activities. "People come to us with problems and we help them. Marina Rosha is a place of comfort and warmth," he said.

Genya had been close to his father until 1987, when he fell in love with and married a Jewish woman who wanted to emigrate to Israel. He met his wife, Eugenia Meskina, at a party in a friend's apartment on one of the Jewish holidays. The two were quickly married in the synagogue and she emigrated to Israel in 1988. She gave birth to their daughter, Ida, in early 1989.

But Genya was trapped in the Soviet Union because his father refused to sign a document granting permission for his son to emigrate. The older man believed that Jews should remain in the Soviet Union. "My father thinks that Soviet Jews are a small group and they should struggle to preserve their culture. As more and more people are leaving, everything is becoming lost," Genya said. Besides, his father had disliked Eugenia and had disapproved of the marriage. Genya and his father had quarreled bitterly; more than a year had passed since they last spoke.

There was talk that the Soviet authorities might drop the law requiring all relatives to sign permission papers allowing would-be emigrants to leave. But Genya said that such rumors had circulated in Moscow for several years. In the meantime, he was left with nothing but a photograph of his wife and baby girl. "I was happy for my wife that she was able to leave—she's better off in Israel," he said. "She has an apartment there and enough food and good medical care and she can take care of the baby. If she were still here, I don't know where we'd live and since I don't work I don't know how I'd take care of her. I miss her, but I don't want her to come back—I want to go to Israel.''

Despite the signs of increased freedom of religion, Genya remained skeptical of Gorbachev's aims. Times had grown easier for young Soviet Jews, but their opportunities to follow their religion's teachings were still circumscribed by the state. Many wonder how long the breathing space they have been given will last, and they question the motives behind Gorbachev's increased tolerance for religion. Perhaps it springs from his drive to enlist every segment of his society, including the faithful, in *perestroika*. Or perhaps he simply wants to have a better country, in which people will have more freedom to do and think as they wish and where they will feel less inclined to leave. Gorbachev has made similar moves to meet the demands of many minorities, such as intellectuals, rock musicians, artists, and others.

The state's easier relationship with its religious minority may be among the most difficult to negotiate. After all, what can be gained for the Communist party by encouraging people to be more religious? As they grow more devout, they can only pull farther away from Soviet-style communism.

CHAPTER 7 CULTURE

BACK IN THE U.S.S.R.

 ARTISTIC FREEDOM in the Soviet Union of the 1980s has been transitory and mercurial; charting the ups and downs of rock music is perhaps the best way to make the cultural scene come alive. In 1983, rock came under a fresh assault in the Soviet press. Rock bands were denounced as "untidy" and "vulgar." Konstanin Chernenko, then the keeper of the party's ideological flame, scathingly dismissed Western culture as shallow and harmful to Soviet youth. The Komsomol obediently fell into line, declaring a war on "corrupting Western tastes that lure the young away from our rich communist ideals." Soviet rockers were given an ultimatum: clean up or break up.

Many went underground, recording surreptitiously in primitive studios with walls soundproofed by egg cartons. Others moved into the official milieu and found themselves confined to an ideological straightjacket, their lyrics purified and their costumes polite. The authorities decided to allow a few well-groomed groups to perform, rather than try to expunge all rock from the face of the Communist earth. The small island of official rock music that was allowed to exist in the Soviet Union was easier to supervise and control.

One of the sanctioned groups performed in the fall of 1983 in a youth club of a working-class suburb of Moscow. Arsenal was a jazz-rock band led by veteran saxophonist and composer Alexei Kozlov. The musicians played before an invitation-only crowd. Many of the young fans looked like well-scrubbed Komsomol members. Others wore clothes with foreign labels; they were "golden youth"—children of the elite who had traveled abroad and brought home Western goods. A few dared to be different. There were some punks in black leather jackets, their hair dyed in splotches of pink and orange. Where were these young people usually hiding? They weren't the same young Soviets that roamed the streets of Moscow. Most of the fans carried tape recorders; unlike Western concerts, there was no search at the door to discourage listeners from making bootleg tapes.

On stage, Kozlov and his men played a medley of Beatles hits. Their music was professional, but something was missing: the lyrics. It should have come as no surprise. Songs about drugs, such as "Lucy in the Sky With Diamonds," were taboo. But the young people in the audience sang along. They knew the words, just as they also knew that the band was not going to pronounce them.

During a break, a reporter went backstage to try to get an interview with Kozlov, a wizened man with a flowing beard and balding pate. He was polite but firm. "The last time I gave an unofficial interview and was quoted in the Western press, I got in trouble," he said. "I'm waiting for permission to go on tour in Czechoslovakia and I don't want to ruin things." He suggested calling the Ministry of Culture and going through the proper channels.

After submitting the necessary letters and making phone calls, the reporter was allowed to sit down with Kozlov one day, under the watchful eye of a ministry official. Kozlov spoke for the benefit of this cultural watchdog. He denounced other Western journalists who had dared to suggest that Soviet rock musicians enjoyed something less than total artistic freedom. And he criticized Frederick Starr's book, *Red and Hot: The Fate of Jazz in the Soviet Union*. The volume, according to Kozlov, was based on interviews with dissidents, émigrés, and dozens of anti-Soviet slanderers. His lip curled in disgust as he pronounced each name.

Kozlov droned on for a couple of hours. The visiting reporter served only as a backdrop; Kozlov was cleansing himself of his earlier sins. This interview must have cinched his trip to Czechoslovakia.

Four years later, Kozlov again became a mouthpiece for the state, but this time, he spoke for young Soviets as well. Seated on the stage at an officially organized news conference in the Soviet Foreign Ministry Press Center, Kozlov extolled the virtues of heavy-metal rock. It was, he said, an emotional outlet for underprivileged and unemployed young people, a way for them to work out their resentment toward the "golden youth." "If we forbid this music," Kozlov warned, "they will display their aggressiveness in other forms." His words fell neatly into line with the longtime Leninist struggle against class consciousness. Kozlov's statement was a facile excuse that the authorities could use for their about-face on heavy metal.

ENTER *GLASNOST*

Since Kozlov's statement on heavy metal, the rock scene has bloomed under the warming rays of *glasnost*. Rock has risen up from the underground, enjoying official tolerance. Alongside it, exhibits of art once considered dangerously anti-Soviet are showing officially in halls around Moscow and Leningrad. Soviet artists have found a Western market; their work is fetching respectable prices among American and western European collectors. Young filmmakers are producing films about the alienation of youth and treating other themes that were once off-limits.

On television, turgid documentaries on grain production in the Ukraine are at least broken up now by flashy music videos of some of the most popular rock bands. The traditionally rich veins of literature and poetry, long relegated to carbon-smudged sheets of tracing paper and passed around kitchen tables, are being tapped, and some works long banned in the Soviet Union have been released.

The cultural scene among young Soviet intellectuals is a thriving one. In a society steeped in the poetry of Pushkin and the prose of Dostoyevsky, the arts are highly regarded. Young people who scribble verse on scraps of paper consider themselves poets and hold strong opinions on the subject. Among young Soviets, being forced to study Marx and Engels has not eliminated their taste for the esoteric. It is a tribute to the exuberance of youth that, after more than seventy years of Leninist ideology, their heroes are writers, singers, and artists. They look to this class of intellectuals to push the limits and elude censors and bureaucrats. The government, recognizing the importance of the arts and their potential for social combustion, has kept a steady eye on everything published, painted, and sung.

Negotiations between artists and bureaucrats continue under Gorbachev, although the penalty for taking a false step has eased considerably. While people are not free, the boundaries have been extended, taking in previously forbidden themes and eras of Soviet history. Soviet artists and writers have charged into these newly open arenas. When, in a 1988 art exhibit, they placed a grand piano atop the once-honored visage of the late, great Soviet leader Leonid Brezhnev, nothing happened. At another show, a painting of four Gorbachev portraits, with a sassy commentary that said four Gorbys are better than one, was removed from the wall. The boundaries still exist, and the Soviet intelligentsia is struggling to define them without tripping over themselves.

There is a sense that anything is possible—or that it all might come crashing down tomorrow. Resistance to change runs deep in Soviet society and many artists fear that conservatives would prefer the old ways. Ultimately, they believe, the freer atmosphere can last only until *perestroika* is declared a failure. If and when that day comes, there may be a new crackdown.

In the meantime, the arts have entered a transitional phase. In song, film, art, and literature, Soviets are moving to fill in the blank spots, to deal with Stalin's purges and the years of stagnation under Brezhnev. Looking back on these once-forbidden times has been exhilarating, but now many are growing tired of the themes. The arts are in the process of catching up with the change that is taking place in society; they pause to adjust their focus as they search for new ideas.

A witness to the transformation from the harsh rule of Andropov to the easier times of Gorbachev felt fortunate to have watched the thaw. Knowing what came before has made the transition to *glasnost* even more remarkable.

✿   An early turning point arrived in 1986, when the British group UB-40 pulled off a string of concerts in Leningrad and Moscow. Formed when its eight musicians were jobless, the group took its name from the unemployment benefits form number 40 they filled out to claim government aid. UB-40's music was a blend of reggae and rock with brass, featuring lyrics that touched on unemployment, war, and racism. Its members disliked the politics of Margaret Thatcher and Ronald Reagan. When the band was mentioned to tour the Soviet Union, the authorities must have reviewed what little they knew and found UB-40 acceptably mild.

What they didn't know was that UB-40 was not just anti-Thatcher and anti-Reagan, it was antiauthority. The group's concerts, before crowds of twelve thousand in the Luzhniki Sports Stadium of Moscow, must have seemed like anarchy to the Ministry of Culture officials who oversaw the tour. Astro Wilson shook his long dreadlocks in time to the music. Lead singer Ali Campbell leaped around the stage, flanked by towering loudspeakers, while the group's four brass players swayed and rocked.

The crowd's behavior was unruly compared to most Soviet audiences, who usually show their appreciation by clapping slowly and rhythmically at the end of concerts and presenting performers with bouquets of flowers. Young people jumped out of their seats to dance and clap, evading the attempts of police officers to make them sit down in the rows of chairs neatly arranged across the vast floor. Black students from Patrice Lamumba University in Moscow crowded forward, dancing to the reggae beat. They were given special treatment which is usually accorded to foreigners, but Soviet fans did not fare so well. Some appreciative Russian fans were grabbed off the floor by police officers and taken backstage.

UB-40's lead singer shrieked at his fans to dance. The show's emcee, a pudgy, balding, confused-looking man, did not accurately translate his remarks. When Ali Campbell said, ''We'd love to see you dancing,'' the emcee said, ''The band loves movement.'' But the audience got the idea and swamped the stage. Campbell saw that he had to come between the police and his fans. He stopped the band, pointed into the crowd and angrily shouted, ''People are allowed to dance. Stop forcing them to sit down!'' The band's spotlight fell on an embarrassed policeman. As cheers rose over the stadium, he backed away from the young man he had been trying to shove into his seat.

As the band moved through its six Moscow concerts, Campbell honed his skills in police control. At the end of each ninety-minute concert, whole rows of people were on their feet and cheering. When UB-40 packed up to leave, Campbell was exultant. ''We've made a monumental achievement—getting people to dance in the Soviet Union,'' he said excitedly.

The UB-40 concerts were the first in which the Soviet authorities eased up on audiences of young people. It was beginning to dawn on them that allowing thousands of music lovers to dance, sweat, and holler would not bring communism to its knees.

✩ Scattered concerts were held in Moscow, but Leningrad emerged as the capital of Soviet rock. Moscow, being the center of everything, was also the center of control; there were more police, more plainclothesmen, and more KGB to keep a watchful eye over rock's rowdies. Leningraders said Muscovites were too materialistic and that musicians in the capital wanted only to play in huge stadiums where they could earn the big bucks—or at least the long rubles. Once they made their way into these giant arenas, the argument went, they forfeited artistic control and became sellouts.

Probably the best explanation for Leningrad's dominance over the rock scene was a simple one: a couple of creative geniuses, singer-songwriter Boris Grebenshchikov and jazz-rock experimentalist Sergei Kuryokhin, made their homes there. For years, the two lived in penury, providing spiritual sustenance and an emotional outlet for a generation of young Soviets. Under Gorbachev, they leaped to superstardom.

Only as recently as 1986, Boris and Sergei were caught in a struggle with the authorities. They were not interested in going official and joining the establishment, but they would have dearly loved to find themselves regularly on stage. The price exacted would have been an agreement to turn over their lyrics to the censors before every concert. They were unwilling to make the trade, so they remained unofficial and underground.

Boris's band, Akvarium, was known only through homemade cassettes, but these made their way to even the remote areas of Siberia. To his listeners, he was a spiritual leader. His apartment, in a sixth-floor walk-up on Sofia Perovskaya Street, was a musical mecca for his adoring pilgrims. The graffiti on the walls of the stairwell was a testament to his fame: "Boris, I love you—I can't live without you," one fan had scrawled on the faded, chipped plaster.

He lived there in a communal flat with his wife Lyuda and son Gleb. They occupied one room, while other young families lived in the rooms off a central hallway; everyone shared the kitchen and bath. Inside Boris's tiny, cramped home, an aging icon of the Virgin Mary hung over the doorway. One corner was reserved for Western artifacts: an emptied can of Campbell's chicken gumbo soup, a bottle of Black and White whisky, and a map of the United States. Posters of the Beatles, Mick Jagger, Keith Richards, and an Irish group called the Chieftains hung on one wall. There was a Red Corner for religious icons. Boris's collection of hundreds of audiocassette tapes stood along one wall. A rolled-up sleeping bag lay in one corner; the wallpaper and the ceiling were dark with stains.

It was hardly the life-style of a megastar, but the backdrop of poverty failed to choke off the ebullience of Boris and his band. Akvarium was lifting up millions of young Soviets. As guests sat around a long table that took up most of the room, Boris, shirtless and wearing jeans, with a large silver cross around his neck, explained the role of a rock star in Soviet society and retraced his career. Sergei, pianist and leader of a Leningrad cutting-edge jazz ensemble known as the Popular Mechanics, sat at one end of the table, his hands constantly moving, tapping out complicated rhythms on the table, a chair, or his tea cup. Boris spoke in the perfectly accented, nuanced English he had learned in a special school. He did his best to include his friend Sergei, occasionally calling him "Captain" and switching the talk into Russian. Alexander Kan, an English teacher and longtime observer of the world of Leningrad rock, translated and occasionally contributed an acerbic remark.

Boris explained that he had formed the group Akvarium in 1972, while still a student of math at Leningrad University. His songs ranged from brooding, Bob Dylanesque ballads to hard rock, reggae, and tangos. It was his heavily allegorical lyrics, with references to death, the boredom of life, injustice, and unfulfilled dreams, that most appealed to his alienated, cynical listeners. One song carried a message of hopelessness:

Friends, come on, let us all die
Why should we live this dreary life?
Better the grave, the humbling earth

Let's give ourselves to the blackness of death.
Friends, come on, let us all live
Let us strangle all the butterflies
And slap everyone else down
After all, life and death are just the same.

Another of his songs lashed out at the censors, the police, the authorities—all of the fixtures of Soviet life that maintained control:

You just wanted to climb higher
Rightly believing it's warmer
Up there than down here
Now you shoot people in the back,
Throw sand in their eyes,
You laugh in their faces.
You think if two people are silent,
The third can speak.
But you forgot one thing—
You sewed up his mouth.
Now it's time to say good-bye
But I won't give you my hand
I feel sorry for you,
Your fingers are covered in dirt
I won't forgive you,
But I won't judge you either
You are your own judge.
You even built your own prison.

After Boris played at the Tbilisi Music Festival in 1980, he was expelled from the Komsomol and forced out of his job as a programmer. So Boris found work as a night watchman; other musicians in his band labored as street cleaners and boiler room attendants. Undeterred, Boris kept writing songs and playing his guitar.

Boris became a rock hero, but he was nothing like the glitzy stars worshiped in the West by young people who look to their idols to live dangerously, use drugs, drive fast cars, and have crowds of adoring women flocking after them. Boris lived as simply as most of his fans did. He was revered not because he made lots of money, but because he was a poet and a spiritualist—a reflection of the age-old belief in Russia that an artist must minister to his listeners' spiritual needs.

He said he received postcards from young men and women all over the Soviet Union, many of them asking for his advice. Only a few days earlier, he said, he had received a letter from a young man in Siberia who asked, "Is the world an illusion, and if so, are the decisions we are making going to influence our karma?" Many young fans pleaded with him to be a leader who could offer spiritual values.

"In a country like Russia, someone like me can be a godsend," he said, unembarrassed about his explanation of his role. "When people don't have enough to eat or drink, to look at or to listen to, they try to find something to believe. Our deprivations make us a spiritual people." Boris reasoned that the Soviet Union had created conditions that made it easier to perform rock, blues, and jazz. "We're oppressed. You need it to sing the blues," he said with a half-smile.

In his lyrics, he mixed religious mysticism, social satire, and sentimentality. The words often got him into trouble; they were distinctly different from the bright optimism of most Soviet songs. Any verse not readily understandable was banned, because censors feared that the underlying meanings could be deemed objectionable by their higher-ups.

The authorities did not make it easy to be a rock star, but to their dismay, the nagging Leningrad rock scene did not fade away. Occasional concerts were allowed by unofficial rock bands that held the status of amateurs because they were not members of the musicians' unions. Boris and his friends gradually succeeded in persuading local officials to allow them to form the Leningrad Rock Club, the first club of its kind in the Soviet Union. The club, at No. 13 Rubenstein Street, was intimate by Western standards, seating only one thousand people, but it gave Leningrad bands a place to play. About seventy bands found themselves under its umbrella.

Still, the rules remained ironclad. Two young women worked as censors at the club, reviewing song lyrics before rockers took them on stage. Boris struck up a friendship with them, gradually reaching the point where they excised only the lines that would have cost them their jobs.

But Sergei found himself in trouble. His performances had always been more theater than music; in the tradition of the Russian serf markets, they included animals, jugglers, and poets. The noises they produced were often cacophonous. A moody and at times even capricious jazz man, Sergei played according to his feelings. He switched from vamp into scat and liked to take risks. Sometimes he was successful in what he created, sometimes not, but in any case, the authorities found his unpredictability objectionable. Summoned to the party secretary's office, he was lectured about having allowed a video to be made of one of his concerts. After that, he was banned from the rock club and expelled from the city's booking agency, *Lenkontsert*.

He and Boris were not interested in performing in stadiums. "It's not possible there to do the real thing," said Boris. "If I played in a stadium, I know I would pander to the pressure and start thinking about how to make the crowd react." Asked if he had ever dreamed of touring in America, he shook his head. "I choose not to—it's too fantastic to even think about."

But his music did begin to draw the attention of the American music industry in 1986, after a resourceful twenty-five-year-old Los Angeles woman named Joanna Stingray smuggled tapes by Akvarium out of the Soviet Union. Stingray, whose real name is Joanna Fields, had met Boris and other underground Soviet musicians while traveling in Leningrad. After eight trips there, she had enough material to put out a double album in the United States that was entitled *Red Wave: Four Underground Bands From the U.S.S.R.* By Western standards, the record quality was crude; the music had been recorded in a makeshift studio in an apartment. The bands earned no royalties from the record sales, but they had the satisfaction of knowing that their music was finally being heard in the West.

A short time later, Boris was interviewed and rehearsed by several recording companies who thought there might be a market for his music in the West. For both Boris and Sergei, 1987 was a watershed year. Their bands began playing in concerts all over the country, and for the first time, they came under almost no censorship. An Akvarium album was compiled from two underground tapes and issued officially on *Melodiya*, the Soviet Union's only record label. The first 200,000 copies sold out within a few hours; sales promised to top one million. Boris appeared on Soviet television and dozens of newspapers clamored for interviews. Many printed candid accounts of his early struggles with the censors.

SOVIET ROCK: A GROWTH INDUSTRY

Rock had finally come into the open. People attending concerts by Sergei's Popular Mechanics were allowed to slam dance. Bands with names like Cruise, Rondo, Bravo, Kino, and Black Coffee were well reviewed even by TASS, the official Soviet news agency. A heavy-metal group called Corroded Metal gave a concert that turned violent and destructive; just like concerts in the West, fans tore up the seats and stage. In Moscow, there was one rock concert every night.

A concert by a Leningrad group named Televizor and another band, Alisa, was typical of the rock music scene under *glasnost*. The two groups performed one evening in the summer of 1988 at the Luzhniki Sports Palace, a huge, domed arena on the Moscow River. Unlike the punks and fans who gather at the feet of Western rock bands, this crowd was a mixture of generations. Elderly men in suits and ties and grandmothers in flowered dresses sat stiffly, staring at the antics of the group on stage. Nearby, young punks wearing black leather, their heads shaved, stabbed their fists into the air and stomped their feet, shouting "Fascist!"

On stage, Televizor worked its way through its repertoire. Televizor's music was neither inspiring nor varied, but its nihilist lyrics were occasionally interesting. One song, called "Three-four snakes," cursed the small circle of establishment figures who ruled rock and, therefore, all of life, as these young musicians saw it. A raucous blend of tortured instrumentals and caustic shouting, the song was a fugue of hopelessness, despair, and anger vented toward all authority figures. "Those who have climbed up rule everybody / It's impossible to rise to that level with clean hands," the band sang.

Another number, "Your father is a Fascist," electrified the crowd. With their calls of "Fascist," a word even more laden with political and cultural significance in the Soviet Union than it is in the United States, the audience had hoped to goad the band into playing it. The song took a slap at the older generation; everyone who had come before was guilty of fouling the earth with their notions of society and order. What had been accepted was now detested. The refrain lumped everyone in the older generation together: "My father is a Fascist, our father is a Fascist, your father is a Fascist."

Dozens of fans streamed down the aisles toward the stage, screaming the defiant lyrics and shoving their fists into the air. Police officers tried to push the dancing young people back into their seats, but the crowd was too much for them; they could only watch with resignation as Televizor finished its act and filed off the stage.

After the break, the band Alisa was up. The group played a punk-pop synthesis. Its lead singer, Kostya Kinchev, was dynamic. His face was smeared with theatrical black-and-white makeup that gave him a vampiric cast, and his lips were painted red. He wore a dramatic black cape that he whipped around the stage, yelling and gesturing at the audience and striking seductive poses. Compared to the energetic Kinchev, Televizor was less polished; despite Televizor's daring verse, they had neither Kinchev's stage presence nor his flare for entertainment.

With each song, his fans charged toward the stage, only to be driven back to their seats by a barricade of police officers and civilian volunteers. Most submitted obediently; they were enthusiastic rockers, not soccer fans. But then Alisa's encore, "We're together," provoked an avalanche. Young people moved in waves toward the stage while the police struggled mightily to push them back. One young woman lunged toward Kinchev, and as an officer moved to grab her, Kinchev abruptly halted the song and ordered the police to let her go. As hundreds of young people crowded around the stage, singing and dancing with Kinchev, the officers lost control. In a final crescendo of shouts and brutal shards of noise, Kinchev called out for change:

> I begin to sing in my own langugage
> I am convinced there is meaning to this
> I am writing poems for those who are not waiting
> For the answers to present-day questions
> I am singing for those who go their own way
> I am glad if someone understood me
> We are together.

After Alisa left the stage, the house lights blazed on and fans straggled toward the doors. The arena was awash with the spent energy of a rock concert just ended. Some fans stood together, shouting the lyrics of Kinchev's last song. A few diehards hung around, forlorn, hoping that he might return to whip the audience once again into a frenzy of adulation and rebellion. Finally, they were herded away by police.

It seemed that Soviet rock'n' roll had been given carte blanche; they snarled at the authorities and cried out for anarchy, just as rockers did in the West. But many Soviets worried that they would grow soft in the newly permissive conditions. The outbreak of *glasnost* was making them nervous. Boris Grebenshchikov became such an establishment figure that he wondered whether fans would think him a sellout. In an interview with *The New York Times* in 1987, he said, "Nobody can believe that the system has changed. They think we must have changed." Even though officials were not tampering with his lyrics, he worried that rock would be co-opted as it was drawn into the mainstream.

Many remained suspicious about the authorities' motives. Concerts sponsored by the Komsomol, they said, were attempts by the state to lure disenchanted youth back into the fold. Rock's acceptance was only part of Gorbachev's goal of getting Soviet youth to shed its cynicism and apathy.

On a practical level, the authorities knew that rock concerts were a good source of revenue. Bands were no longer restricted to playing only for government concert agencies, such as *Moskontsert* (Moscow) or *Lenkontsert* (Leningrad). They were hired for one-night stands by private entrepreneurs and cooperatives eager to earn the fat profits that a famous rock band could bring in; the state and the artists received their cuts. Some were paid as much as several hundred rubles, a vast improvement over the pitiful ten-ruble fees they had earned only a few years earlier.

Soviet rock was forced to mature. In the early 1980s, it was easy enough to be a hero by simply proclaiming something boldly; there was no need to pay attention to musical form. In 1988, the unprofessional noises that Soviet rockers made were beginning to sound silly. The focus shifted from the political content of their music to its aesthetics. It had become necessary to match boldness with musical polish.

As in so many other areas of Soviet life, deficits stood in the way. The shortage of high-quality, Western equipment was a handicap for Soviet musicians, but the dollars needed to buy the instruments were carefully doled out by the Ministry of Culture. The only way many could get new instruments was through the black market, where prices were soaring. The average electric guitar that cost roughly three hundred dollars in the West ran as high as three thousand rubles on the Soviet black market.

Melodiya, the state's official label, suffered from a shortage of recording studios and pressing equipment. Rock was given the lowest priority; only ten rock albums were released from 1980 to 1985. Musicians often turned to friends who worked for *Melodiya* and had built recording studios in their apartments or had access to equipment they could lend.

Many musicians pushed to perform abroad, where they could earn the foreign currency they needed to overcome their shortages of equipment. While abroad, they also picked up a few of the consumer goods they longed for. Besides the financial considerations, most musicians simply wanted to get a glimpse of what was beyond their borders. Soviet authorities gave their approval, reasoning that rockers might put on a good public relations show for *glasnost* and bring in some dollars as well.

But those who have managed to go on concert tours have encountered several roadblocks to fame and fortune in the West. They play on ancient guitars and wheezing amplifiers, and many lack the polish of Western bands. Tamed by Soviet standards of behavior, many heavy metallists do not know how to be as lewd as their Western fans demand. The biggest obstacle is their Russian verse. Most Americans think the language of rock is English, and they have no interest in deciphering Soviet rock lyrics. Thus, the best that Akvarium and others have to offer—their poetry—is lost on American audiences.

The first Soviet rock musician to get a chance at success on the world stage was Boris Grebenshchikov. It was the logical choice; Boris was well spoken, photogenic, and charming; his blond-haired, blue-eyed good looks led people to compare him to David Bowie and Mick Jagger. His talent and song-writing ability won him a multi-album contract with CBS. Boris agreed to write nine of the ten songs on the album in English, to make himself more accessible to the American market. Just for good measure, he dropped a couple of troublesome consonants from his name. The result, Grebenshikov, was more pronounceable for Americans.

His record was underwritten by David A. Stewart of the Eurythmics, with background vocals by Annie Lennox, also of the Eurythmics, and Chrissie Hynde of the Pretenders. But even close friends who heard Boris's finished product gave it negative reviews, pronouncing it too commercial and overproduced. Boris's voice had been buried somewhere under many layers of synthesizers. Soviet musicians, jealous of Boris's newfound fame, predicted that it would be his last Western album. But it was Boris's first try in the West. He is probably the type who will keep at it until he gets it right. After all, Boris had met other challenges that were just as difficult. He had managed to survive in Leningrad's rock underworld for years, when just daring to sing certain words on stage meant risking arrest.

His buddy, Sergei Kuryokhin, leader of Popular Mechanics, also traveled in 1988 to the United States, where he sat in Frank Zappa's living room and met several of his longtime jazz heroes. He played in dozens of concerts and competed in a Thelonius Monk contest in Washington. The precision of the other pianists must have had Monk rolling in his grave; it was Monk, after all, who said, "If it's wrong, it's right." Sergei was too avant-garde, too innovative, to fit in there.

Later, he sat in a northwestern Washington living room as he surveyed the current state of rock music in the Soviet Union. In 1988, he said, most rockers were doing the same thing they had been doing five years earlier. The only difference was that they were doing it for much larger audiences. Their themes were the same; most bands were still singing about their Stalinist uncles or their scrapes with authority. "There are no new topics, only *glasnost* and *perestroika*," he said with a grin. "Many people are waiting for the coming of the next cultural messiah."

Sergei at first drew a blank when asked what he wanted to do next and how he wanted to grow. "Play as much as possible, I guess, as much as I can, using a lot of different styles," he replied. Sergei agreed that his style had changed little over the years, but that now he had more resources to call upon. Five years ago, he played with a string quartet; under *glasnost*, he had been given a symphony orchestra. Once he had brought in a live chicken to "sing" in his band; later he was allowed to have ten. "Soviet power has given me everything," he said wryly, echoing a government slogan.

Under previous regimes, he had encountered problems with officialdom; lately, the government had become more permissive, so he had had to invent the difficulties himself. He laughed about how he had wanted to bring a horse on stage, which drew protests from animal lovers and from the stagehands who worried about cleaning up after it. When he proposed to drop chunks of wood from the rafters as his orchestra played Shostakovich, fans of the classic Russian composer objected.

He shook his head in disbelief over his change in status. Only a few years earlier, he had been disciplined by the party. Recently, one of his band members had come to him for his signature on an exit document he needed to apply for permission to travel abroad. A word of approval from Sergei had become a sign of sound moral character.

It was Sergei who offered the wisest theory on why rock was no longer considered Western poison under *glasnost*: the party had discovered that there were more important tasks ahead than trying to put a leash on rock'n'roll. "With our economy in such bad shape that it is even questionable whether the country can continue to exist, people have stopped caring what our rock bands sing about," he said.

THE EMERGENCE OF UNDERGROUND ART

Like the rock scene, art in the Soviet Union has been sprung from its hiding places by *glasnost*. What was called "underground" art has emerged from basements and apartments into the open. The terms "official" and "unofficial" art no longer have currency. State shows, once the preserve of the Artists Union, exhibit the works of members alongside those of nonmembers. Artists are expressing ideas that would have once brought swift punishment. Limits exist, to be sure, but the strongest reaction an artist seems to be able to elicit these days is the removal of his painting from the wall of an exhibit, and even that is rare.

Opportunities to show work, once caught in the vicelike grip of the Artists Union, have grown exponentially. Under the government's cooperative laws, artists can form their own clubs, rent exhibition halls for shows, stage performance art, and schedule cultural evenings. One group of young Moscow artists has formed an independent gallery, with a foreign currency account that enables them to sell Soviet art to foreigners.

Like their counterparts in rock music, visual artists are no longer content to stay home; the world beyond their borders beckons. Soviet art has found its way into the galleries of western Europe and America, and many of the artists have been allowed to accompany their work, enabling them to get their first views of the West. The art has been warmly received, and a few paintings have even fetched six-figure prices. Once some of the glow from *glasnost* fades away, the prices may fall, but many collectors have begun to think there might be a stable Western market for Soviet painting and sculpture.

The current flurry of artistic activity in the Soviet Union was unthinkable only a few years ago. During the brief rule of Yuri Andropov, art slipped into a deep freeze. Many Soviet intellectuals remember it as the worst time for them. Unofficial art was denounced as a mold growing on socialist art and a fabrication of the Western press. Soviet newspapers reported that Western correspondents bought so-called alternative art with money from the CIA; the artists, in turn, put on exhibitions exclusively for Westerners. And they supplied the foreigners with slander about the suppression of creative freedom in the Soviet Union.

The official Artists Union and the Ministry of Culture were run by a group of established, older professionals who ruled that, since there was a shortage of exhibition and studio space, it was in their best interests to keep their numbers small and exclude young interlopers. Its members formed an all-powerful monopoly. The KGB and Soviet authorities were not the only enemies of younger, more innovative artists. It was the union that ran Soviet art.

Writers could function in this repressive atmosphere by typing up their work and passing it around to their friends, but artists were at a special disadvantage. Without studio space or exhibition halls, it was practically impossible to be an artist. These unofficial artists occupied the fringes of society, their numbers decimated by the massive Soviet emigration of the late 1970s and early 1980s.

But one group of unofficial artists, mostly men in their twenties, were unfazed by the frigid cultural atmosphere under Andropov. They staged regular exhibits, which got them into frequent scrapes with the authorities. There were arrests, the occasional summons from the KGB, and even forced exile into the army. Calling themselves the Toadstools, they lived at a breakneck pace, staying up late, debating philosophy over many cups of strong tea, always on the lookout for available studio space, a party, or a meal. There were the usual rivalries among artists, but basically, they trusted one another and, at a time when there was little room to hope that their lives would improve, they worked together more than the other non-conformist elements of Soviet society did.

In 1985, when the Western correspondent happened upon the group, lapel buttons bearing the word *Aptart* were all that was left of these artists' last show. It had been a tribute to the exhibitions of art within apartments—a tradition among many generations of artists, since government galleries had been closed off to them. The show took place in the apartment of Nikita Alexeev, a Muscovite who, as a young art school graduate, had experienced the 1974 ''bulldozer exhibit,'' named after the bulldozers that were sent in by the authorities to clear out an unofficial exhibit from a field in a Moscow suburb. It was a formative experience for Nikita, one that had made him determined to pursue his own aesthetic and philosophical goals. He was a tall, thin man, softspoken in manner, but with the capacity to become a ringleader of sorts.

Nikita lived in a nondescript building made of the tan bricks used in most of the construction of the Khrushchev era; the neighborhood was known as *Yugozapadnaya*, or "Southwest." On the ground floor of his building, there was a women's clothing store. Nikita's flat was one flight up, past an elderly woman concierge, down a long, cavernous hallway, and into a single room at the end.

At first, *Aptart* was an environment more than a show. Instead of hanging one painting on one wall and another on a facing wall, *Aptart* was a structure of one hundred paintings suspended in the air and working together. Later, the show became more conventional. Nikita announced that *Aptart* would be considered "the first avant-garde gallery on this one-sixth territory of the globe."

Shows continued there for more than a year. During that time, several young artists developed their own distinctive styles. One young conceptualist named Yuri Albert, for example, showed a series of paintings full of whimsical references, in which he defined himself in terms of what he was not. One painting was titled "I am not Jasper Johns," and another was given the name "I am not Kabakov," a reference to Soviet painter Ilya Kabakov, who at that time was largely unknown but whose work in 1988 commanded the attention of the New York art world.

Aptart occasionally drew crowds of three hundred people in a day. Admirers went trooping up the stairs, past the quizzical concierge, and down the hall. Nikita's neighbors were curious but polite; he said they never complained, despite all of the noise and foot traffic. They only occasionally visited, and when they did, they seemed interested, although a bit puzzled, by what they found there.

The effect of *Aptart* on the Moscow intellectual community was lasting; it energized what had been a timid group and set up lines of communication between them. *Aptart* was an outlet, a means of expression for young artists who had chosen not to emigrate. Through their work, they sent a message of defiance to the authorities. The hum of activity around *Aptart* also drew a response. Early one morning, two KGB plainclothesmen knocked on Nikita's door and announced that they had come to search the place. They rummaged through his belongings for hours. As they left, they warned him against telling anyone about the search.

Nikita promptly crossed the courtyard to the apartment of his longtime friend and fellow artist, Misha Roshal, where he found the same men conducting a similar search. Misha, a dark, bearded gnome of a man with a mischievous smile, lived in an apartment that was large by Soviet standards; the thorough examination of the contents of its many rooms kept the police occupied for the rest of the day and into the night. Friends and artists, hearing of the search, dropped by. By the time the police were finished with their work, a loud party was going on in the kitchen. Nikita was summoned to a local police station, questioned about his contacts with Westerners, and ordered to stop using his apartment as a gallery.

Nikita rebounded once again. *Aptart* moved into a field outside of Moscow and was suitably renamed *Aptart in Plein Air*. The event took place on a warm spring day in a grassy field bordered by trees and lakes. It was supposed to be "the symbiosis of the natural with the artificial." At least a hundred guests showed up; when they got off the metro train at the nearest station, the organizers handed them maps showing the path to the field. Unlike the bulldozer exhibit that took place outdoors and was broken up by police almost a decade earlier, this one ended peacefully.

But shortly thereafter, the authorities decided they had had enough. Three members of the *Aptart* group were summoned to their local draft boards and forced into the army. Nikita's close friend Sven Gundlakh, a bearded young man with a droll sense of humor and a rapid-fire chatter that resembled a machinegun, was sent to Sakhalin Island in the Soviet Far East for two years. Two other artists were given terms of eighteen months; Volodya Mironenko was shipped off to Kazakhstan and Kostya Zvezdochetov went to the Kamchatka Peninsula. Nikita himself was spared a stint in the army, but he suffered a deep sense of loss in watching his friends shipped off to these hardship posts. He slipped into a period of mourning.

The avant-garde movement of young artists in Moscow had been dealt a stern blow. If it was not possible to have exhibits in official galleries, they reasoned, they would have them in their apartments. When that avenue also was closed to them, they moved into the open air. They had poked fun at the rules, but the security organs showed that they could not take a joke. People worked quietly in their own small apartments, but there were no shows, no public demonstrations. The *Aptart* group ceased to meet or to function formally. Its members had done all they wanted with the concept and began looking for new means of expression.

Young artists in Moscow kept up with Western trends, including new wave, German expressionism, works from New York's East Village, and other aspects of the art scene, through art journals sent to them by friends and supporters. It was a bit like gazing at the world through a keyhole, but their art was not derivative. Many developed their own characteristic styles that did not rely on Western ideas. Because there were no Soviet art magazines, people swapped treatises and debated philosophy through samizdat writings.

Work was a problem for most. They were not members of the Artists' Union, which meant they had no official status as artists. To protect themselves against charges of parasitism, they looked for employment that could be listed on their work documents. Many joined *Gorkom Grafikov*, the

City Graphic Arts Committee, an off-shoot of the Artists' Union. Founded in 1929 for book illustrators, *Gorkom Grafikov* gave artists a social cover and a marginal source of income. But just being in *Gorkom Grafikov* did not guarantee them work. They still needed to bid for contracts and meet with book editors. Since many of these editors were hardly inclined to work with young maverick artists, members of the *Aptart* group were forced to look for other sources of income. Like young painters and sculptors in the West, most of them held day jobs and worked on their art at night.

✸   Then a gold mine landed in their laps—well, not actually in one of theirs, but it came close enough that it could be shared by all. In the fall of 1985, a young sculptor was hired to work as a guard in an abandoned building that was once a kindergarten in downtown Moscow. He was paid a small salary to keep an eye on the place, clean ice from the walks, and rake the leaves. The kindergarten was the property of the Central Committee, whose monolithic gray headquarters were nearby. Moscow's main synagogue, the state visa office, several military institutes, and the Komsomol building were in the same neighborhood, so the police kept the area well patrolled.

The sculptor's art was of a traditional sort; in the style of Edgar Degas, he fashioned ballerinas and dancers out of wax. This work took up a lot of space, but there was plenty of extra room in the kindergarten. The two-story building held a half dozen high-ceilinged classrooms that had been used for years to bring up thousands of little Soviet children. He brought in his tools and wax figures and cleaned up a small room which he turned into his living quarters. There was no hot water, but the price was right; he wasn't required to pay rent and the place even had a telephone.

The artist looked around at his friends. Many of them were working at home in cramped apartments and desperately needed studios. So he invited several to join him, including Kolya Filatov, who painted large canvases in the style of the German neo-expressionists, and another young man named Andrei Roiter. Roiter appropriated some of the teaching aids and posters that were left over from the building's years as a kindergarten; they made useful icons of pop culture, which he combined in brightly painted canvases. In another room of the kindergarten, Garrick Vinogradov, an intense young man with a shaven head and boldly striped shirts, labored away on an installation of musical-mobile sculptures illuminated by Bunsen flames.

Other artists came to work and live in the kindergarten, each taking his own room. For several, it was the first time they were able to work on large canvases and concentrate on their art without frequent interruptions from wives, children, and parents. They called themselves the Kindergarten Group.

Their home quickly became known among unofficial artists in Moscow and Leningrad. But it was more than just the scene of parties and one-night shows. The kindergarten represented the spirit of their generation. It was their attempt to grab a little piece of what was available at the time and make it their own, before the inevitable crackdown came from the authorities. They knew their *kife* would have to come to an end, but they meant to enjoy it as long as they could. For the community of young Moscow artists, it was their Zeitgeist—a sort of kiddie-pool Zeitgeist, because it was only a tentative step forward, and a short-lived one at that.

As expected, the building and its young residents drew the attention of the police. One day before what was to have been a large show by the Kindergarten Group, the building was frenetic with activity. Its small kitchen, where countless glasses of dark, strong tea had been consumed over gossip about the Moscow art scene, was alive with young artists who had dropped by to help set up the show. Artists were putting up paintings in the classrooms, on the ceilings, and in the hallways.

The night of the exhibit was windy and rainy. Nikita, who by that time was painting on vinyl tablecloths as a reference to the abundance of intellectual life that took place around the nation's kitchen tables, had arranged to meet a visitor outside the tall metal fence that surrounded the building. But when his guest arrived, the heavy gates were locked and the building was dark and silent. A small group of people stood outside, huddling under umbrellas. The authorities had let it be known that the exhibit should not take place; they had also pointed out that the Kindergarten Group was using state property without authorization.

A week later, the kindergarten was closed. Police arrived at the door one day and ordered everyone to leave in thirty minutes, as if clearing out a family of squatters. Dispirited over their eviction, the Kindergarten Group went back to working in their cramped flats. This was difficult for many, because their canvases had grown larger. The avant-garde art scene had suffered a loss with the closing of the kindergarten, because it was their only exhibition space.

Nikita was quietly philosophical. "If this had happened ten years ago, I would have called up a lot of foreign correspondents and asked them to write stories," he said. This time, he didn't bother to alert anyone; the "dissident" story had dried up and few correspondents bothered to follow it. Besides, the rules of the game had changed. When outside pressure was applied, the authorities rarely responded. Young artists were beginning to sense new forces of liberalism within their own cultural establishment, and they looked toward them for change.

In mid-1986, a decree was published in the Soviet press that electrified the Moscow intelligentsia. It granted people the right to form "informal associations" that were allowed to be "self-financing." What did it mean? people wondered. Artists, poets, and musicians began phoning one another at night, trying to interpret how far the decree would allow them to go. It was one of Gorbachev's first steps toward loosening control over the right to free assembly—a means toward freeing up his society and getting people engaged in *perestroika*. Special-interest groups of all kinds were allowed to gather, pay dues, open bank accounts, and plan events.

The decree was translated into action by Moscow's cultural community. A group calling itself the Association of Moscow Artists, Poets and Musicians began collecting dues of three rubles a month from each member. They opened a bank account and set up an eleven-member board of directors. With their dues, they rented a small downtown auditorium for one evening from the Union of Tobacco Workers. At the opening, there was an air of excitement in the place; people had the feeling that they were pioneers. In the lobby, the club's artists showed their postmodern work; on stage upstairs, a jazz band played, a half dozen young poets read their poetry, and Garrick Vinogradov fired up his metal performance sculpture and Bunsen burners. The group's president, conceptual artist and writer Dmitri Prigov, concluded the evening with a reading of his bitingly satirical verse.

A bespectacled man with a goatee and an acid tongue, Prigov was frenetically busy. He set out to beat the authorities at their own game and emerged as a leading force in Moscow cultural circles under *perestroika*. As *glasnost* took hold, Prigov's fortunes rose and fell in the rapidly shifting cultural climate. Only a few months before being allowed to rent the tobacco workers' auditorium, Prigov had been denounced in the press. One night he was giving a public poetry reading; a few days later he was arrested by the KGB, transferred to a police station, and finally sent to a mental clinic before he was allowed to go home.

Undeterred, he and his fellow poets and artists began organizing a busy schedule of shows at the House of Artists on Kuznetsky Most. The Kindergarten Group, the former Toadstools and *Aptart*—all were there with their work. They still had problems. Older, more conservative artists called the hall and complained that it was full of drug addicts and homosexuals. They said there had been pictures of naked women on the walls. It was suggested to the young artists that they stop working together.

In other parts of the city, *glasnost* was gathering steam. On the southern edge of Moscow, artists began showing their work every Sunday in Bitsa Park. It was the first time that artists were allowed to sell paintings and drawings outside the official salons reserved for the Artists' Union. At first, the work shown there was largely traditional landscapes and water colors. Much of it was kitsch and handicrafts. But as more artists recognized the park as an opportunity to show their work, it became possible to find some daring themes. There was nudity, religion, a few mildly disrespectful swipes at the party—all of the no-nos.

Bitsa quickly drew the attention of the authorities. The local district council moved to regulate it, forming a "comradeship" of artists who drew up a complex legal document containing forty articles and subarticles. The art market was to be fenced off and all artists who wanted to show their work there were to be charged ten rubles. Visitors would have to pay thirty kopecks to enter the area.

Members of the Association of Moscow Artists, Poets and Musicians were determined to show that despite all of the talk of openness, the authorities still exercised control. One Sunday, they stormed into Bitsa Park and staked out their territory, tying their canvases to trees. On the snowy ground, Nikita Alexeev stretched a long piece of black construction paper. Drawn there in colored chalk was his story of "The black square." Appropriating the symbol of the Russian minimalist painter Kazimir Malevich, Nikita used the adventures of the black square as a satiric commentary on the ups and downs of artistic freedom in the Soviet Union under various regimes since the 1917 revolution.

His friend and neighbor, Misha Roshal, set out a pat of butter on top of a small red velvet–draped table and stretched a lengthy roll of blue-and-white cardboard milk containers between two birch trees. The red velvet symbolized Soviet power; the butter and milk cartoons were Soviet production. It was conceptual art: Misha's way of making fun of the propaganda slogans that boasted of the nation's ever-burgeoning productivity.

Many older Russians insisted that Misha's sculpture was not art at all, but an insult to their nation. He stood in the snow wearing his heavy coat and Russian fur hat, smoking one cigarette after another, arguing and joking, waving his hands in the air, patiently discussing his concept of art. But the visitors to Bitsa Park that Sunday were not convinced. They grabbed the string of milk cartons and ripped it in half, removed his table and stomped on his pat of butter. The people had decided: Misha had gone too far. In this case, the authorities were not the final arbiters. They might have allowed the exhibit to take place, but the people themselves were too conservative.

Members of the comradeship arrived and there was a confrontation between the directors and the young interlopers. Nikita and his friend and fellow artist Nicola Ovtschinikov were appointed to speak for the avant-gardists. Standing in the forest under the birch trees, they faced the directors. They were informed that their brand of art was unsavory and out of step with the goals of the art mart. The young artists, well satisfied, took down their canvases and left the park to celebrate at a rowdy party. They had succeeded in proving their point: artistic freedom under *glasnost* was a sham.

Meanwhile, events were moving forward at the Manege, a vast yellow stucco vault of a building outside the Kremlin. Once used to exercise the czars' horses, it had been converted into a palace for official Soviet art. A typical example was an exhibit in late 1986 that was called "We are building communism." The paintings were repetitive, unoriginal, and superficial; works with such titles as "Acceptance into the Komsomol," "Welders," and "Builders of the Novosibirsk Metro" were hanging there. The Manege was virtually empty of visitors each day, until a group of young people put on a show of performance art at the back of the cavernous building.

On the afternoon of one performance, the small stage was covered in brown and yellow leaves. Onstage, four young musicians made random noises. One whistled atonally into the microphone. Another worked at an ancient metal sewing machine. A melancholy young man played at an upside-down cello. A butler dressed in black tie and tails appeared with a tray of drinks. Several women wearing black scraps of lace and silk waded through the leaves.

Their brand of performance art was outdated—a style that had long ago run its course in the West. More interesting was the public discussion that followed. As the microphone was handed around the room to each speaker, one elderly man said, "You know, I'm just an engineer from Voronezh, and I don't know much about art, but it seems to me that you people have no sense of tradition or culture. Where are your traditions?" A young woman jumped to the group's defense. Shaking her fist, she shouted, "You have no right to dictate your idea of culture to us. Let us find our own." In a country where culture had long been defined by the establishment, her call came as a bold challenge.

A few nights later, an official happening took place at the Manege. The host for the evening was Andrei Voznesensky, a once-rebellious young poet who had grown into a flag bearer for *glasnost*. Voznesensky had invited artists, actors, poets, musicians, critics, and architects. Boris Grebenshchikov and his group Akvarium came down from Leningrad. A poetry reading featured verse about Soviet travel restrictions. Pop star Alexander Gradsky sang a ballad with lyrics by Vladimir Nabokov, whose works were only then beginning to show up in Soviet publications.

A public discussion was the centerpiece of the evening. "Who gives you the right to say what is good art and what is bad art?" one young man asked Voznesensky. "What criteria do you use? You closed my exhibition last year; who gave you the right?" Voznesensky defended the changes under Gorbachev. He read a list of long-banned works about the Stalinist period that were set for publication. "To say that this is like Khrushchev's time is not true," he said. "Two years ago, most of the people performing here were not allowed. Now they are performing, and we are reading Nabokov."

But it had not been as easy as Voznesensky's glib defense made it out to be. Before the start of that evening's entertainment, the former Toadstools and *Aptart* groups had been hanging their canvases around the hall, when the Manege director, an elderly man in a gray suit, had charged in and loudly ordered the removal of all of the art from the hall. The building's artistic council had surveyed the works and pronounced them ideologically unacceptable. Vadim Zakharov, who painted giant gray canvases of elephants outlined in white, with their wise pronouncements preserved in balloons floating overhead, had looked around in disbelief. His works were so large that he'd had to rent a truck to transport them to the Manege. Arguing with the official had been out of the question; if they had put up a fight, he would have summoned the police. All he could do was load up the paintings and take them away. It was symptomatic of the spotty, show-no-show atmosphere that artists later jokingly called "early *glasnost.*"

Nikita Alexeev, a veteran of numerous struggles with the authorities, grew weary of the unpredictability and wanted to see life in the West. He married a French woman and applied to emigrate. After only a short wait, he was given permission to leave. Many of his friends marveled at the ease with which he received his exit visa, but it really should have come as no surprise. To the authorities, Nikita was a troublemaker, and they were glad to be rid of him.

His departure came as a devastating blow to the former *Aptart* and Toadstools groups. Nikita had been a leader, always devising new ways to test the rules. With his inspiration, the young artists had pitted themselves against the authorities. After he left, his friends floundered for a time. They were beginning to lose their marginal status, and they could not enter the mainstream.

A few began making wise use of the new rules. Sven Gundlach, Dmitri Prigov, and another young artist named Josef Bakhshtein formed a new organization that referred to itself, with a dose of irony, as the Avant-Gardists Club. Together, they found a regional hall in the Auto Factory Region of Moscow and negotiated with its director, then went to the city cultural section and told the authorities: "Look, you've allowed people to form these informal groups for joggers and knitters, so what about us? If you don't allow it, we'll behave like teenagers and drink port wine in your doorways." The authorities had little choice but to grant them permission. The hall began hosting shows.

In the summer of 1987, the Avant-Gardists Club was one of the busiest informal groups in Moscow. They rented a riverboat for a daylong exhibition on the Moscow River. Small paintings and drawings were awarded as door prizes. Dmitri Prigov read his poetry. Their club's rock band, Central Russian Height (a pun that may be understood as a geographical area of the average Russian's intelligence level), played on board. Led by Sven, with his hair tied up in a half dozen ridiculous ponytails, the band was musically inept but fun to listen to, with songs like "House of Stalin" and "Spaceship Heroes."

An even bigger milestone was Moscow art historian Leonid Bazhanov's formation of the Hermitage Society, a coalition of artists, historians, architects, photographers, and filmmakers who rented an empty library building in the distant suburb of Moscow in early 1987. The irony of its location was that the building was in the Belyaevo Region, where the bulldozer exhibit had taken place more than a decade before.

The society charged a small admission fee, which was used to pay the building rent and the salaries of two employees. Members had earned enough from admissions to purchase a film projector, and they were saving up for a VCR. The building had become the setting of many cultural evenings of art, poetry, and public debate. There were studios for several young artists in the basement.

Misha Roshal's blue-and-white milk cartons and red velvet with butter was on the floor. On one wall, an oil painting by Kostya Zvezdochetov showed a party official glowering over a slice of watermelon; he bore a strong resemblance to the late Konstantin Chernenko. The colossal gray elephants and forbidding expressionist landscapes of Vadim Zakharov and the satire of conceptualist Yuri Albert also were there. For more than six months, the works rotated, with new selections of paintings coming in from as far away as Georgia.

Kolya Filatov, a society member formerly with the Kindergarten Group, defended the gallery to a visiting elderly artist. "What do you think you're doing—setting out independently to have a museum?" the critic asked angrily. "You need the collective. You must have it—everyone must have a collective." Kolya spoke patiently to the man, trying to explain the group's goals, but he made no headway and finally turned away in frustration. It was a classic confrontation. The older generation wanted to nudge these mavericks back into the *kollektiv*, but the young Soviets clamored for anything that was fresh and nontraditional.

The Hermitage exhibit was finally forced out of its space in late 1987, after it sponsored "Resurrection," a thirty-year survey of unofficial art. It was attacked in the Soviet press for including the work of artists who had emigrated from the Soviet Union in the 1970s. Other artists said the reasons for shutting down the hall were more commercial than ideological; they criticized the society for failing to put together shows that were professional and thoughtful rather than merely provocative.

If the show had been organized a year later, it might not have encountered problems. In the summer of 1988, as the U.S.–Soviet summit unfolded in Moscow, there was a new level of tolerance for unofficial art. The public and the bureaucracy were assimilating cultural change at a rapid pace. Even conservative party organizations like the Komsomol were hosting exhibits by informal groups. The Komsomol's Palace of Youth opened its first show, entitled "Labyrinth." About 250 artists exhibited there, representing 30 different informal associations with names like World Champions, Key, and End of the Century. The Avant-Gardists Club occupied a large section of the exhibit.

This show included the entire spectrum of unofficial art, from abstraction to conceptualism, photo-realism, impressionism, and new wave. There was plenty of what had become known as Sots-Art—pop art turned Soviet by its ridicule of communism's symbols and icons. Two works judged disrespectful were removed: a self-portrait by a young artist named Yuri Surikov that showed him flanked by Lenin and Christ, and an oil painting of four Gorbachev portraits, by Konstantin Latyshev. The first had to go because the artist had dared to equate himself with Lenin; furthermore, he had placed Lenin in the same frame with Jesus. The second was objectionable only because of its accompanying commentary, which wondered, Why not have four Gorbachevs, which would surely pave the way for even more *glasnost*? The authorities had not yet reached the point where they could tolerate a young artist poking fun at the general secretary.

One of the groups that showed their work in the "Labyrinth" exhibit had taken *perestroika* one step further. They called themselves the First Gallery and formed a cooperative, similar to the restaurants and clothing factories that had sprouted up around Moscow but with one distinction: it dealt in art. As its name implies, it was to be the first privately owned gallery under the new cooperative laws.

The First Gallery was organized by Zhenya Mitta, Sasha Yakut, and Aidan, a young woman who preferred to be known only by her first name.

A darkly exotic woman with the determined gaze of a serious business-woman, Aidan is the daughter of Tair Salakhov, the first secretary of the Artists Union. As she sat in her studio on the upper floor of a crumbling building around the corner from her future gallery, she explained how she had gone into business with Mikhail Kruk, the founder of Moscow's first cooperative restaurant. She said Kruk had helped the artists find an empty building at No. 7 Strastnoi Boulevard, not far from Pushkin Square. The interior had been gutted and it was being prepared for a full remodeling job, which was to cost 150,000 rubles, or about $250,000. Kruk came up with the money by putting together a joint venture with the Belgian beer company Stella Artois, which would have the right to sell its beer in the gallery.

The First Gallery was affiliated with Intourservice, a government travel agency allowed to handle foreign currency. This meant that the gallery would be able to sell Soviet art for dollars and keep dollars in a bank account. Aidan and her partners could spend their earnings on foreign goods, both for themselves and for the gallery. They could even show and collect art by foreigners, although that path would lead them into the ups and downs of art as an investment—a distinctly capitalist undertaking.

Aidan said her real hope was to develop collectors among Soviets wealthy enough to buy art. That, she suggested, would create an alternative to government support of artists through the tyrannical and stodgy Artists Union. Years ago, this system divided artists into two groups: one approved by the state, and a separate, much larger group of misfits who lived outside the establishment, working at odd jobs and painting in their spare time. Under *glasnost*, the line between the two groups blurred considerably—so much so, in fact, that in 1989, it was almost impossible to tell the official from the unofficial. If the First Gallery fully lived up to Aidan's expectations, it would make the distinction even fuzzier.

✶ In the brief span of only a few years, some of the barriers to artistic freedom were torn down. One of the last to fall allowed young Soviet artists to take their work out to the West. Young painters and sculptors who were not members of the official Artists Union suddenly began receiving permission to travel abroad. Some sold their work to Westerners for six-figure sums.

The successful sale of one such painting, entitled "Fundamental lexicon," won it a place on the front page of *The New York Times*. It was an oil painting that had been sold at the Sotheby's auction in Moscow in July 1988 for $415,000—the highest price ever paid for a work of contemporary Soviet art. The work was painted by Grisha Bruskin of Moscow;

five other paintings by Grisha brought him another $450,000. Sotheby's had transformed him into a millionaire—or close to it, anyway. A photo in *The Times* showed him bearing an expression of rumpled disbelief.

It was easy to understand why. Two years earlier, Grisha had been a struggling artist in a cramped studio on the top floor of a ramshackle building on Gorky Street. A small group of correspondents who climbed the stairs to his work space found Grisha, a small, dark-haired man with a full beard, laboring in front of a striking assemblage. The painting showed wholesome boys and girls engaged in patriotic activities; each was painted as a white marble statue in the Stalinist style. The work was "Fundamental lexicon." Another painting hanging nearby was made of small canvases of character types drawn from Judaism and folklore and then assembled into a huge canvas.

Grisha said that both works had been shown once in an official exhibit but then had been quickly removed. The first had been pronounced too pessimistic and had been criticized for taking swipes at many of the Soviet Union's treasured symbols; the second had come down because it dealt with religious themes. Grisha gave out his telephone number and invited the reporters to return, but he cautioned them against calling on a telephone in a foreigner's apartment or office. The last time he had entertained Western correspondents, he said, he had been visited afterward by the police.

Two years later, Grisha was an internationally known artist. His works, along with 113 paintings by 29 other contemporary artists, sold for a total of $3.6 million, more than three times Sotheby's preauction estimate. Under the rules set by the government, the painters were to receive 60 percent of the purchase price, with ten percent of that in dollars and the remaining 50 percent in special gold rubles, which are worth about four times the official rate.

The high bid that Grisha's painting fetched at the auction was a rags-to-riches story; the stage seemed set for the truly talented among Soviet artists to compete in the world's top galleries. But there were ominous signs as well. Some Soviet artists and Western collectors were concerned that bids at the Sotheby's auction had been driven up by the novelty of *glasnost*. If prices were not similarly high at future events, they worried, Soviet art would lose the tiny foothold it had gained. Collectors would not consider it a sound investment if its value fell, and it would quickly lose its appeal as Western excitement over Gorbachev's *glasnost* waned.

Another difficulty that Soviet artists faced was that they could not be paid directly in dollars, pounds, or marks. All of their foreign earnings had to go through the Ministry of Culture, which took its cut and set the rate of exchange from each sale. More than six months after the Sotheby's auction, none of them had received even a kopeck for their works. A number of the artists threatened to file suit. Their predicament came as a sad lesson; despite *glasnost*, they were still at the government's mercy. Many learned to circumvent the government apparatus by signing with a Western dealer, going to Paris or New York City, making their art, and going back home.

Despite the occasional dark cloud, the young artists in Moscow were full of hope. Much more than the young people who worked in offices or factories, their lives had been transformed by *glasnost*. For the first time, they could earn respectable money. Even though the government had held back payment from the Sotheby's auction, many figured that eventually they would get their cut, which could add up to thousands of rubles. Some began dreaming about buying cars and cooperative apartments. Their standard of living soared. These young artists had finally found *kife*.

THE PRINTED WORD

As *glasnost* brought great change to Soviet music and art, the literary establishment experienced upheavals as well. The printed word was enlisted to win over the Soviet intelligentsia as an ally and a friend—one that would be fully involved in reforming Soviet society.

For the first time, the works of many longtime literary outcasts were published. The short stories of Vladimir Nabokov, condemned as an anti-Communist pornographer for his novel *Lolita*, became available to Soviet readers. *Children of the Arbat*, a novel by Anatoly Rybakov chronicling Stalin's terror, was excerpted in the proreform weekly magazine *Ogonyok*. Excerpts from the labor camp memoirs of Nadezhda Mandelshtam, wife of the poet Osip Mandelshtam, were carried in another publication. Boris Pasternak was restored to the Writers' Union and arrangements were made to publish his novel *Doctor Zhivago*.

Literature by living émigré writers, such as Vladimir Voinovich, found its way into the pages of the Soviet press. Excerpts of his novel *The Life and Extraordinary Adventures of Private Ivan Chonkin*, a satire long banned in the Soviet Union, were published in the journal *Youth*. A magazine named *Krokodil* reprinted a short section of Vasili Aksyonov's memoirs *In Search of Melancholy Baby*, but then appeared more interested in publishing the outraged letters that followed. In 1989, the leadership appeared poised to publish even the most controversial works of Alexander Solzhenitsyn.

These momentous decisions—to print or not to print—were made over the heads of Soviet youth. The publication of such books was determined by bureaucrats, censors, and historians. The Kremlin gradually began to withdraw from its role of chief literary censor. But the decisions touched the lives of young Soviet writers. By allowing more voices to be heard, they created a more liberal climate for literature. The blank spots of history were being filled in by a more vigorous press and newly released works of literature.

Young, unconventional Soviet writers, meanwhile, are still excluded from the literary establishment. Censorship has been eased and long-suppressed works published, but the Writers' Union often still stands in the way of far-reaching liberalization. The head of the union was kicked upstairs in 1986 and his post was filled by a slightly younger, more liberal man, but the ten thousand poets, authors, dramatists, and critics there continue to be a powerful force for conservatism. These members, many of them aging dinosaurs, are comfortable with the Brezhnev-style system in which their books, verse, and plays are readily published. They have established a comfortable monopoly and are not receptive to the idea of turning over any of the nation's scarce paper for novels by young mavericks.

Book publishing bears all of the trademarks of the socialist way of doing business. Profit and loss have long been irrelevant. Readers' interest are not taken into account when decisions are made about what should be published. While people clamor for more well-written, contemporary books, huge stacks of dull, gray literature and dry political tracts continue to go to the printers.

The waste is astounding. At least 10 percent of the 2.5 million books produced every year remain unsold. Up to 50 percent of the books in Soviet libraries are checked out only once or not at all.

Public taste in literature is still considered untrustworthy. Young people cannot simply buy the books they want; their tastes have to be molded and they have to be given an ideological education. It is useless to point out that tedious volumes are lost on young readers, who refuse to cast a glance at them.

Favoritism and cronyism play large roles. A handful of powerful officials in the State Committee for Publishing and Printing, known as *Goskomizdat*, hold control over publishing. Even though they are poorly read, the works of these bureaucrats and their friends, allies, and longtime colleagues appear in large editions. They are also reprinted and translated into other languages for sales abroad, where they reap foreign currency for their authors.

Occasionally, studies are carried out about young readers. *Literaturnaya gazeta* reported on a 1986 survey that found that young people were turned off by Soviet fiction. They complained that the characters were too hard-working, dependable, and loyal—in short, stereotyped heroes of socialist literature. Young readers who responded to the poll said they preferred to read newspapers, because characters there were sensational and multidimensional. The survey carried an example of the type of story young people found intriguing. It was about a seventeen-year-old boy, a good student and secretary of his local Komsomol committee, who stabbed a girl to death to prevent her from telling people that he had once struck her. Such gossip, he feared, would have spoiled his chance of entering a university. *Literaturnaya gazeta* urged writers to deal with more contemporary themes, or risk losing all of their readers to newspapers.

There were calls for reform. Articles in the Soviet press in 1988 urged that *Goskomizdat* be dissolved. Some authors suggested that publishing houses should follow the Western system of keeping a book in print only as long as there was a demand for it. They said writers' earnings should be based on sales.

There was talk in 1988 of establishing cooperative publishing houses as a way to wrestle some control away from *Goskomizdat* and give young writers an opportunity to appear in print quickly. With an eye toward the millions of rubles it stood to lose if forced to compete against cooperatives, *Goskomizdat* quickly crushed the debate over new publishing ventures. When new regulations for Soviet cooperatives were published in late 1988, private book publishing was outlawed.

A few writers published books in the state printing houses at their own expense. The first self-financed volume came out in 1988 in Moscow. A scientific text, it was written by a chemistry professor who paid 600 rubles (about $960) to bring out 400 copies of his book. But this is not an option open to most young writers, because they cannot afford to pay such high fees.

More important, many young writers do not care to grapple with the state publishing apparatus. They do not focus their energies on getting their work published officially. It is their dream instead to publish abroad.

This does not keep them from writing prolifically in their spare time. Writing is more of a pastime for young people in the Soviet Union than it is for American youth, who are distracted by videos, fast-food restaurants, and football games. In the Soviet Union, there are fewer diversions. Many young people spend long hours sitting in their apartments; not surprisingly, their thoughts tend to turn inward. They write to entertain themselves and their friends.

Poetry, prose, and lengthy essays are written out in longhand; after revising their work, they type it on old typewriters, with sheets of carbon layered between flimsy pages of tracing paper. The resulting manuscripts, often faint and difficult to read, are distributed among friends, admirers, and competitors. They are pored over and discussed around kitchen tables. There is plenty of competition. Manifestos clash with countermanifestos. Some of the nation's finest literature is passed around this way. Editing comes through the comments and criticism of readers, whose tastes are often discriminating and sophisticated.

The dialogue is rich. This intellectual underworld is one of the most stimulating and attractive elements of the youth subculture. Writers and poets often write all their lives without being published in their own country, but some hardly seem to care. Just writing for their own friends and relatives is challenge enough.

Sergei Anufriyev, a young man from Odessa, was one such writer. Seryozha, as he was known by most, joined forces with two other young Muscovites in late 1987 to collaborate on collections of prose, poetry, and philosophy. They staged their works together in strange, ambivalent productions that were a cross between poetry readings, performance art, and theater. They called their group Inspection, because, as Seryozha said, they were like inspectors, visiting parties and cafes, being inspected, and inspecting their audience. They pulled reactions from onlookers and asked to be assigned grades 1 through 5, as in the Soviet grading system. Inspection even performed several times in 1988 at a student revue for Moscow State University.

Seryozha, twenty-four, was a short, wiry man with the swarthy skin and coal-black hair that are the trademarks of his hometown. He once explained that getting published in the Soviet Union had never been his desire. "It's possible to write something, but it's impossible to do something with it. I am very lazy," he said in a self-mocking voice. "You must know all the official avenues. We are artists, not dealers."

Seryozha's talents showed themselves in a number of ways. Besides being a writer, he was also an artist, theoretician, and clothing designer, his specialty being outlandish and comical clothing. Sometimes he appeared at openings in voluminous costumes which he said were from outer space. At other times, he showed up in women's brightly colored pantaloons. He once sang with the band Central Russian Height, wearing an androgynous, well-padded dress that he combined with men's pajamas. Seryozha was occasionally partial to women's makeup and a very curly black wig; at other times, he shaved his black hair into bald patches which were interspersed with dangling braids.

One of his partners was Pasha Peppershtein, twenty-two, the son of master painter Viktor Pivovarov, who lives in Prague and works in the style of conceptualist Ilya Kabakov. Pasha had begun writing at age thirteen and turned out novels, short stories, and poetry in a style that is both mystical and strange. He occasionally worked as an illustrator of children's books.

The third member of Inspection was Yuri Liderman, twenty-five, who also began writing in childhood. He completed his first novel at the age of seventeen. One of his best-known works was an epic poem describing Lenin as a spiritual holy man.

The three young men met regularly and spoke into a tape recorder. After a year of collaborating, they had made nine cassettes. One of their biggest problems was finding a way to print them, since typing is time consuming and the three did not own a typewriter. They wanted to buy a computer, but that remained simply a dream. Their goal was to get their cassettes translated and then printed in the United States.

Seryozha was at a loss to describe the work of Inspection. It was, he said, "like a schizophrenic china, a kind of mental structure." It was not exactly a short story, but it was like a short story—sort of halfway toward philosophy, but not at all professional. "We try to understand the next level of culture and imagination," he said in a far-away voice. "Ours is a strange, ambivalent presentation of understanding." Seryozha said the three have devised a new language, terminology, and text to break the borders of thinking.

They sent a collection of their stories and essays out to the West in 1988. One tale was given the title "Vera, Nadezhda, Lyubov," three girls' names in Russian. It was the story of a little girl raised in a family of nobility in prerevolutionary Russia. The girl had a treasured cat, which was punished by a family maid after it killed a chicken. In a surrealistic final scene, the maid appeared with a bundle in her arms, unwrapped it, and revealed a plate with a gold star. On the star was a poem, which read:

In the last monastery of salt and tears,
Don't ever forget me, never.
Not in gardens, where there are wings of dragonflies,
Where there is green water flowing under bridges,
Made of my pale suffering.
Your snow-white umbrella
Will blink in the distance,
The dust will fly in the air and
The trembling rhythm of a black pine tree
Is fluttering in the sand as a black stick.
The gold light in navy blue heaven will light again,
In the sky of black-blue, in the dark blue heaven,
Will lighten again as a farewell star,
To squeak and to sob.

Their other short stories were similar. They included lengthy dream sequences laden with symbolism, imagery, and surrealistic twists. The point of view constantly shifted and the language was at times pretentious. Their plots were heavily allegorical. One story was about the early years of Adolph Hitler. The boy grew up in a serenely wealthy family, but he was told by an uncle that he should find some living being to sacrifice for the sake of his motherland. Young Hitler chose to kill a wild cat living in a forest near his home. After chasing the animal through the trees, the two fell into a violent struggle. When the cat escaped, the infuriated Hitler cursed loudly, calling the animal ''Jewish shit.'' The theme was a bit too heavy-handed: evil Hitler was raised in a polite home lacking any sense of morality, while the cat symbolized the millions who suffered for the purity of his motherland.

Another story, written by Pasha Peppershtein, was titled ''From a Certain Correspondence.'' It was an exchange of letters between Lenin, from Siberian exile, and his wife, Nadezhda Krupskaya, in Paris. The story offered an intimate portrait of Lenin, as if he were talking to himself; its language was both intellectual and disarming. But the work was derivative. Alexander Solzhenitsyn had, years before, written the original story, called *Lenin in Zurich*. Like Pasha's story, it was never published in the Soviet Union. Pasha's account contained more dream sequences and its plot had a surrealistic quality, but it was too similar to Solzhenitsyn's work to be truly original.

This collection of stories offers an intriguing glimpse into the kind of literature that is passed around among young Soviets. As in the art they hang on their walls, surrealism is popular; much of it seems like surrealism for surrealism's sake. Their writing at times veers toward humanism and philosophy, but it is mainly self-disclosure. Writing is a hobby for them that has not yet grown into literature. Pasha, Seryozha, and Yuri are now in their early twenties; as they grow older, their work is sure to mature.

THE VIDEO REVOLUTION

The Elektronika shop, Moscow's only store for videocassette recorders, was housed on the ground floor of a drab apartment building on Leninsky Prospekt in the suburbs. After the store opened in 1986, it began selling the VM-12, then the only domestically made VCR in the Soviet Union. The store was mobbed with customers, but the machine itself was not on display; only a picture of one could be seen in a pamphlet on a counter. Its price was listed as twelve hundred rubles, or about two thousand dollars—a year's salary for many young people. Anyone wanting to buy a VM-12 was advised to put his name on a list. Although a clerk said buyers would have to wait only two or three months, some people later said they had been promised a VCR in no less than a year.

There were a few cassettes of Soviet-made films on display, including mainstream productions such as *Train Station for Two* and *Moscow Doesn't Believe in Tears*, which won an Oscar for best foreign film in 1981. Their price tags read 100 rubles ($160 at the official exchange rate).

The state had set a production target of only sixty thousand VCR's per year through the 1990s. VM-12s were for sale in only four Soviet cities, and the press was full of customer complaints about the quality of these units. Of every one hundred that reached the Moscow store, twelve had to go straight back to the factory for repairs. One young Soviet told about buying a machine after waiting a year; he returned one unit and got another, then had to send that back to the shop, too. His third broke down after only a few hours' use.

Two video lending libraries were established in Moscow. One of these opened on the Old Arbat and showed films on a VCR in its front window, drawing curious crowds every day. There was also a small theater inside; each screening, or séance, quickly sold out. The Arbat library rented only Soviet films and a few carefully evaluated movies from Western and Eastern Bloc countries; its entire stock totaled five hundred. Video libraries opened in nine other Soviet cities, but they were reported to be similarly undersupplied.

Despite the government's inability to keep up with demand, video fever has swept the nation. VCR's are much preferred to the state-run cinema houses because they offer Soviets a peek at the West in films that are not shown at their local theaters. Young Soviets are seeing a wide variety of Western films on video, including some that are so ideologically objectionable they may never be shown in official movie theaters. One young man from Voronezh, the city where Soviet VCR's are manufactured, said he had seen Stanley Kubrick's *Clockwork Orange*, a tale of violence among London street toughs who appropriate Russian words to form their own private language.

Soviet diplomats, journalists, and businessmen who traveled abroad were the first to own Western VCR's and films. Many came home and sold their Western-made VCR's in second-hand shops for thousands of rubles. Others were brought in by Westerners; students and diplomats from Third World countries proved to be an especially rich source of VCR's.

The police, KGB, and customs officials worked to control the spread. They carefully checked cassettes that came through Moscow's Sheremyetevo Airport and had a list of titles that were not allowed into the country. Any unauthorized cassettes were confiscated.

There was a two-year prison term and a three hundred-ruble fine for illegally copying videocassettes, but some Soviets risked the dangers. Entrepreneurs bought high-priced Western video equipment and quickly recouped their investments by showing films in their apartments. The standard price of admission was ten rubles.

A whole underground industry developed around the public's craving for videos. Mechanics converted foreign VCRs so that they could be used with Soviet televisions. Video samizdat has come into vogue. Soviets fluent in foreign languages are hired at twenty rubles an hour to dub Western films into Russian. Private libraries boasting hundreds of cassettes are uncovered by police.

One of these underground libraries produced a hilarious version of Sylvester Stallone's *Rambo: First Blood, Part Two* on a Soviet-made videotape. Dubbed into Russian by a woman, the tough-guy image of Stallone, uttering obscenities and grunts, was rendered in a squeaky, feminine voice. To make it even more funny, the translator had understood the name Rambo to mean ''rainbow,'' so throughout the film, she referred to him as *raduga*, the Russian word for ''rainbow.''

The authorities have gradually come around to accepting VCRs and videocassettes as permanent fixtures of information technology. In 1986, the first Soviet film made especially for videocassette appeared, starring pop singer Alla Pugacheva on board a paddle steamer on the Volga River. Video-cafes have begun to appear around the country. One opened in the cavernous October Cinema Hall on Moscow's Kalinin Prospekt in 1987. Inside, tables and sofas are carefully arranged around the cafe's sixteen monitors. Customers buy tickets that allow them to stay for up to two hours.

Video theaters have cropped up all over the country, but they are most common among the trend-setting Baltic republics. Young Balts have reported seeing video-cafes with as many as twenty employees scurrying around to wait on groups of young people watching films from all over the world on twenty-one-inch television sets. The police takes a hands-off approach. In the more conservative central Asian republics, a newspaper reported that the local police had confiscated a film about Islam, saying it undermined atheistic propaganda and stirred up nationalism.

Despite regional variations in tolerance, Soviet video fever had grown into an epidemic. In 1988, the VCR was named by the media as the most popular consumer item, especially among young people. Some Soviets say they want a VCR more than a car. Owning a video is *kife*. Instead of trying to stifle video, the government has adopted the if-you-can't-beat-'em,-join-'em philosophy. The Council of Ministers set a production target of two million units by 1995, up from seventy thousand in 1988, although it seems unlikely that Soviet factories will meet that goal.

The authorities also have moved to allow Western manufacturers to fill the gap. Customs duties have been cut, enabling more Soviets to import videos, although there is still a limit on the number of machines they can bring into the country. Soviets also are given permission to receive VCR's and videocassettes from abroad.

This newly liberal approach to video is in keeping with the *glasnost* philosophy. The leadership can hardly open up Soviet cinema and at the same time move to check the spread of home videos. The Kremlin-approved video revolution is another step toward drawing more converts to *perestroika*.

★ It's ten o'clock Sunday morning in Moscow—time to switch on the television set and watch "I Serve the Soviet Union." A group of army veterans just back from Afghanistan proudly talk about the training school they have set up for teens in Zaporozhye, a city in the Ukraine and the site of one of the nation's largest car factories. Dressed in camouflage outfits, the boys are organizing mock troop movements, and learning how to use weapons and fight karate style. A vet says proudly that he is helping rehabilitate juvenile delinquents "who might otherwise be on the streets."

Cut to a large group of young people. A reporter carrying a microphone wades into the crowd. The camera focuses on one boy with a punk haircut, a jean jacket, and an earring. Puffing on a papirosa, he says defiantly, "This is our area. We call it Little Paris. We named it that because France is the most cultured country. This is like Paris—we're the most progressive people in Zaporozhye. Here we have punks, hippies, heavy metalists, and Greens." A girl nearby wears an expression of indifference, until she is asked about her relationship with the Komsomol. Then her face switches to a look of disgust. "I feel that the Komsomol, as an organization for youth, is worthless. Earlier, Komsomol might have been a kind of happiness. But for us, now, it's just something for the resume." Another girl pipes up, "I've been in Komsomol for five and a half years, I pay my dues, and that's all, nothing more. I don't want anything from the Komsomol. It doesn't mean anything to be in it."

Cut back to the club of Afghan vets. Says one vet, "In our country, there is a shortage of things to do that are open to young people. Many join gangs or become punks. We need to restore the moral values in our youth." The show also features shots of soldiers running into battle and a discussion with young people on the banks of the Dnieper River, in which one factory worker complains bitterly, "We say the period of stagnation under Brezhnev is over, but beyond *glasnost* there are no signs that it's over."

The show's format is bouncy, dodging from one topic to the next, even including a rock music video to keep its audience tuned in. This is the new, improved Soviet television—television given an injection of *glasnost*. Shows are lighter and zippier, more entertaining, and fast-paced. Much of the programming is educational, dedicated toward raising good Communist citizens, but it is repackaged in a way that is supposed to make it attractive and, at times, even fun.

Apparently, the leadership has realized the medium's vast power to bring millions into line with *perestroika*. When Gorbachev became leader in 1985, television ownership among Soviet citizens had already skyrocketed—partly because television sets were readily available and also because Soviets spent so much of their leisure time at home. Ninety-three percent of the Soviet population, or 260 million people, now own television sets. Soviet television reaches 86 percent of the country's territory, across eleven time zones. Even in rural areas, where people live without running water and indoor toilets, television antennas rise up over the wooden rooftops. Television is the nation's only truly mass medium, reaching many more people than do the nation's daily newspapers. Elderly scientists in Moscow and youthful collective farm workers in far eastern Buryat receive the same, standardized government message, transmitted at lightning speed.

Before it was freshened up under *glasnost*, television's vast power to inform and indoctrinate was being squandered by party functionaries who saw it as their duty to safeguard the airwaves from ideological pollution. The bulk of its programming was mind-numbing: a ten-and-a-half-hour special from Novosibirsk explaining how to operate milking machines; a musical about building roads in central Asia, with a truck driver as leading lady and a drill operator as leading man; and so forth. The Soviet press pronounced such shows "a great success" and party leaders labeled television "an active tool of Communist education."

Young viewers knew better. For most, Soviet television was background noise, something that could be listened to with only half an ear. Soviets glanced up at their sets when a classic film came on, or a musical variety show, or the news, which could be counted on to carry shots of Westerners striking, demonstrating, and living on the streets. For young people, television had little to offer. Like school, work, and the Komsomol, it was irrelevant.

One of the first changes made by Gorbachev was the speedy retirement of the aging chief of *Gosteleradio*, the State Committee for Television and

Radio. Television's role in promoting the objectives set by the party went unchanged; instead, it was the party's objectives that changed. As Gorbachev fixed his sights on the restructuring of Soviet society, state television was enlisted to help.

A new philosophy took command at *Gosteleradio* and a new generation of reporters, producers, and writers were installed to carry it out. Leonid Kravchenko, the new chief there, called on television to possess "perfect pitch with regard to the truth." Beamed into people's apartments and families, Soviet television invaded people's privacy; thus, it had to be trustworthy. As veteran Soviet television commentator Vladimir Pozner said, "The best propaganda is the truth."

Truth was even more crucial, the leadership believed, in capturing the youth audience. In a series of articles that pondered ways to make television more gripping, a Soviet magazine said in 1988 that young people were always adept at spotting hypocrisy; if they saw a television commentator dissembling, they rejected everything else he said. Reforming society, the articles said, would be impossible if young people were educated in lies. Like their canceled history exams and rewritten textbooks, television programs for young people had to be revised.

Change was spearheaded by a special department, the Editorial Office for Youth Programming. Elderly moderators there were replaced by men in their thirties—younger than the gray-haired men of the past, yet still old enough to command the respect of teenagers. The pace picked up; serious discussions were interspersed with music videos and man-on-the-street interviews. Most important, the list of approved topics was expanded to include the former taboos. Drug addiction, sexually transmitted diseases, prostitution, alcoholism, draft dodging—few subjects were left untouched.

One of the shows that received a souped-up format under *glasnost* was "Up to 16 and Older." The title is meant to imply that it is intended for all age groups; actually, its target audience is unmistakably youth. It focuses on young people as they relax, after school, on park benches, and in discos. When they talk about their despair, the camera records it. Soviet television, the show seems to be saying, is on their side.

Each segment of "Up to 16 and Older" begins with the image of a long-haired teenager running down the slender white center line of a highway, as if teetering between childhood and maturity. Nikolai Korovin, a journalist who looks about thirty-five—neither too old nor too young—is the commentator. Professional and comfortable on camera, he assumes a style that is both nonchalant and serious, and he never talks down to his audience. Korovin sometimes starts by reading mail from viewers. At other times, the program begins with a series of quick shots: a rock band on stage, a youth in a cut-out T-shirt, a boy wearing black leather and heavy chains, a fashion show with leggy models, a couple locked in an embrace on a park bench, a group of teenagers flashing grins as they hold up their internal passports.

A typical show carried a discussion between Korovin and students on the steps of their school. One boy said that Soviet people are not able to express themselves freely or take the initiative to change things. Another spoke of the distrust he feels toward adults. "Grownups lie and rewrite history," he said angrily. "We young people are alienated."

Another scene showed a confrontation between a soldier in a military band and a long-haired rocker pounding on a guitar. Sneering, the soldier said, "It's not music. You call that singing?" Replied the rocker in a stony voice, "We sing and we will sing."

A group of teachers discussed their students. Said one: "There are good students and there are bad students. But most kids have a low cultural level. They are interested only in silliness." The teacher was the authority figure who castigated everything young people care about as "silliness." The theme was adults versus youth, documented by television.

The show is far from light entertainment. It occasionally includes the shocking, grotesque, and tragic. There have been scenes of gang fights in Kazan, with young people using clubs and homemade bombs, and close-up shots of the horribly beaten faces of young gang members. In one hospital scene, people injured by bombs had their burns cleaned. Abandoned children were filmed in an orphanage and a handicapped woman was shown struggling up the steps of her apartment.

The show moves out into the countryside. In one episode, the camera cut to a rural school where a student was beaten to death by a teacher. Collective farm women, their heads bound up in scarves, joined in a modern-day self-criticism session; many were weeping. In an interview outside the school, students said corporal punishment was common. "They beat me and they beat my friend's brother. All the teachers hit the students," one boy complained.

"Up to 16 and Older" occasionally jumps behind Gorbachev's an-tialcohol campaign. In the most popular cafe in Smolensk—which just happens to be a nonalcoholic establishment—younger students confronted older ones who had been drinking. They were charged with "setting a bad example." One young teetotaler said the drinkers should be forced to pay fines.

☆ A great premium is placed on trendiness in Soviet television. Even dull shows like "I Serve the Soviet Union" are sliced up by music videos. Often the technique does not work; it is tough to imagine young people sitting through the lengthy discourse of a retired World War II veteran, his chest clinking with medals, just to catch a glimpse of a pop singer. But that is Soviet television in early 1989.

MTV, Soviet style, has come into its own. Many movie videos appear on the musical show "Morning Mailbag" and are slow moving and romantic, featuring gently crooning pop singers. The camera follows handsome young men strolling through Moscow's International Hotel, a backdrop quickly recognizable as the place where Soviet television always goes to get the foreign look. As in all popular Russian music, the verse is more important than the driving rock beat. Their lyrics are mushy and sentimental; ballads and Italian loves songs are the most popular.

Only a few have the pounding beat and fast pace of a Western rock video. One of the best is a song called "I Don't Love You," by the group AVIA, or Anti-Vocal Instrumental Ensemble, which plays an amusing synthesis of kitschy pop tunes, jazz rock, and performance art. The video is social satire that pokes fun at many stock Soviet images, including a row of elderly ladies who sit rigidly in their seats at rock concerts, looking annoyed and offended. In one shot, a bald party functionary endures a denunciation session by his party committee. Throughout the music video, AVIA sings about their beloved things—the sun, the sea, the moon. But each refrain ends in a shout: "I Don't Love You!"

Another rock video features Viktor Tsoi, lead singer of Kino. Tsoi, wearing a black leather jacket and blue jeans, tells the camera that he does not like being a rock star. The lack of privacy, the fame—it is simply too much. "People look at me—but they don't really see me," he says plaintively. A few scenes are shown from his 1988 film *Needle*, named for his heroin-addict girlfriend. Tsoi, whose great-grandfather was Korean, has the black hair and Asiatic looks of a Bruce Lee, with the karate chops to match. He uses kicks and punches to fight off a gang, then, bruised and shaken, laughs in relief, leaning his head back against a fence. Freeze frame.

Soviet television also has added late-night news and entertainment, from 11:00 P.M. to half past midnight, to appeal to the younger audience. The show *Vzglyad* or "View" appears in that time slot every Friday and has become one of the pioneers of television *glasnost*. Among its firsts was a segment on three neo-Nazis. "This country is threatened—as is the whole world—by overpopulation. Women are giving birth to children with defects and the nation is becoming weaker," the group's spokesman said in a bland monotone. *Vzglyad* also showed clips from a documentary film about the Solovki labor camps, the prototype for the nationwide gulag system that killed millions of people under Stalin and still exists today under Gorbachev.

One of the biggest changes under *glasnost* is television's honest assault on even the most squeamish subjects. Journalists on a show called "Health" courageously invade drug hospitals and VD clinics and chase poppy growers through fields. One segment in late 1988 showed interviews with syphilitic prostitutes in Leningrad. After a young woman admitted that she made money by accepting "rides" with unknown truck drivers, a clinician berated her for having an "immoral" life-style. Another segment of "Health" started with the desperate screams of drug addicts behind the dark bars of a jail. In an interview, one young addict admitted he had murdered for drugs. Close-ups were shown of hideously deformed babies born to drug addicts. The hyperbole made the message clear: don't do drugs. Such images had been out of the question during the pre-*glasnost* era, when the Soviet Union did not even admit the existence of prostitution or drug addiction.

Not all of Soviet television has been transformed. In 1987, the government news agency TASS estimated that one-quarter of the programs on Soviet television had been replaced and another one-half had been revised. Many old standbys remain, like "Your Very Own Lenin Library," "War and Peace—Chapters from the Novel," and "Harvest Time." One classic title was "The Exhibition and Demonstration Orchestra of the U.S.S.R. Internal Affairs Ministry's Internal Security Troops."

Public service programs are arguably the most boring on Soviet television, and they follow the government's habit of speaking to citizens as if they are children. One regular series, called "Safety Tips," offers lessons on how every good samaritan should behave. If, for example, a Soviet motorist finds himself driving down a highway and a large box falls from a truck in front of him, the driver should promptly pull over, stop his car, and remove the box from the roadway so that other motorists won't have accidents. The announcer added helpfully, "While picking the box up from the road, don't forget to avoid getting hit by a car."

Soviet television remains virtually commercial-free under *glasnost*. In a society plagued with shortages of consumer goods, it seems pointless to advertise items that are not for sale. But Soviet television even has a special department, known as SoyuzReklamFilm, which devotes itself to creating commercials. There is one for a car radio, another for a miniature tape recorder with earphones, and a third for a Western-style ghetto blaster—all items that are extremely difficult to find in stores.

Western correspondents with children praise the absence of commercials on Soviet television. Unlike their American counterparts, Soviet children's shows allow viewers to be children instead of little consumers. These programs are also free from the violence that pervades so many American television shows for children.

"Goodnight Little Ones" is a staple of children's television, appearing nightly at 7:30. Starring a woman clown and her top-hat-attired straight man, the show teaches positive lessons about the honor of work and the duty of keeping a clean apartment. One typical show was about the importance of always telling the truth. It began with the tale of an elephant who grew smaller with each lie he uttered. Fortunately, he reformed himself before he disappeared.

Young Soviets, like their counterparts in the West, rely increasingly on television for an idea of what is going on in the outside world. *Gosteleradio* learned in one survey that nearly 90 percent in one sample group gave television as their primary source of news; 63 percent considered television to have the biggest influence among the news media in shaping their opinions.

Many young people prefer the news program *Vremya* over newspapers for their daily dose of news. *Vremya*, or "Time," appears nightly at nine o'clock and continues for about forty-five minutes, although it can drag on for an hour and a half to accommodate lengthy speeches by Gorbachev or other politburo members. Its format is stodgy; there is no sound bite, no fluff, and no snappy kicker. Despite the show's dull pace, its audience is huge, numbering 150 million—more than 80 percent of the adult population and twice the combined audience for all three major networks' evening newscasts in the United States.

A typical program begins with the leadership's activities. There is ample domestic news: a Siberian power station is given a new generator unit, a textile factory has overfulfilled its plan, the cotton harvest has been completed in Uzbekistan, and so forth. Until very recently, news about earthquakes, plane crashes, and crimes rarely made it on the air. Now they are prime-time fare.

Vremya also devotes a large chunk of time to international news. Before television became more interesting under Gorbachev, many young Soviets said they tuned in exclusively for that; they were hungry for any information they could find about the West. The news slant of international news reflects the status of Soviet relations with each country that is covered; stories about the United States were bleak during the early years of the Reagan administration. America's image then was black and white: there were fabulously wealthy capitalist businessmen alongside poverty-stricken street people.

Young Soviets have developed great peripheral vision when it comes to watching television news. In these quick glimpses of the West, they note how people are dressed, what their cars look like, and what is on display inside store windows. Sometimes negative news coverage creates the opposite of the desired effect. One young man recalled watching scenes of students throwing paint and rotten eggs at the White House in the antiwar demonstrations of the 1970s. Instead of joining along in disapproval of U.S. policy, he felt only a strong desire to visit the country that would allow its young people to hurl insults at the very seat of power.

Vremya got a facelift under Gorbachev. Directors of *Gosteleradio*, realizing the show's tremendous impact, brought *glasnost* to news reporting. In domestic news, the Chernobyl disaster of 1986 was a turning point. At first, the leadership responded to the crisis as it had always reacted—with stony silence. For two days, the Kremlin denied there had been an explosion at the nuclear power plant. Finally, a terse, forty-four-word report was read on *Vremya* acknowledging that an accident had occurred, that people had been injured, and that they had received aid. The story was buried toward the end of the program.

Meanwhile, the rest of the world clamored for more information and condemned the Soviets' handling of the accident. As radiation from the stricken plant spread into western Europe, news accounts streamed into the Soviet Union over "Voice of America" and other radio broadcasts. The reports on *Vremya* grew by a few sentences, revealing that two people had died in the fire at the plant. Then the May Day celebration intervened and there was silence once again.

When the government got back to business after the holiday, it was obvious that there had been a change of heart. News of the accident poured forth in newspapers and on television. *Vremya* showed a government commission touring the plant as well as pictures of the surrounding area. There were man-on-the-street interviews in nearby Kiev. Produce grown on surrounding farms was checked for radiation and evacuations were described. Soviet commentator Vladimir Pozner admitted that waiting for two days to report the accident had been "a mistake."

Apparently, the Kremlin agreed. Since Chernobyl, news of disasters is carried regularly on Soviet television. There are stories about train wrecks, fires, floods, and collisions of ships on the Black Sea. Even a story about young drug addicts who hijacked a plane made the evening news. Following the earthquake in Armenia in December 1988, television reporting was quick and thorough. The reports are less sensational than those shown on Western television, but the coverage is a tremendous improvement over pre-Chernobyl days.

International news has also changed. As U.S.–Soviet relations improved, America took on a more detailed image. Vladimir Dunaev, the *Vremya* correspondent in Washington, took to the road and gave America a human face. He covered a twins' contest in Iowa and farmers racing on lawn tractors in Illinois. Dunaev also took his viewers to Wisconsin, where he showed a Soviet collective farmer working alongside American farmers. Instead of showing the long-suffering faces of the poor, Americans were seen laughing and praising their Soviet visitor as a great worker. But there was a downside to all of this "happy" news. Dunaev also took his viewers to a wooden bridge in Portsmouth, New Hampshire, and said ominously that the area at the other end was off-limits for Soviet correspondents. He never bothered to report that there were cities in the Soviet Union similarly closed to his American counterparts. Propaganda against the United States has become more subtle, and the negatives still outweigh the positive.

Still, it would be a mistake to dismiss the changes on Soviet television as only slight moderations passed down by the Kremlin. The announcers, editors, and producers themselves have a degree of independence undreamed of only a few years ago in making decisions about which topics are safe and which are not. At times, the boundaries of the acceptable shift rapidly; what is forbidden one month is fine the next. Television producers are taking risks and testing the unknown, and young audiences are eagerly tuning in to all that is new.

GLASNOST COMES TO THE WIDE SCREEN

Assa, a film about gangsters, rock, and rebellion, was in the can in September 1987. It was shown in private screenings before enthusiastic crowds in Leningrad, but five months later, it still had not premiered in Moscow. The authorities, nervous about the reaction it would generate, had postponed several openings. It was to show first in the Shock Worker, a well-known theater on the Moscow River across from the Kremlin. The opening was advertised on billboards around the capital—an unusual thing in itself—and T-shirts and posters were printed. There was an air of eager anticipation; finally, the long-awaited *Assa* was to premiere.

Then, the night before the screening, inspectors entered the theater and pronounced it a fire hazard. *Assa* followers were once again told that they would have to wait, and its producers began searching for a new theater. In February 1988, they were told they could have their screening, this time in the House of Culture of the Moscow Electric Lamp Factory. An unlikely spot for a movie premiere, this building was located in the distinctly unfashionable district known as the Power Plant Region.

But that evening, it was the chic place to be. If you were anybody, you had to be there. All of the cultural glitterati from Moscow and Leningrad converged for the Hollywood-style opening. Teenagers stood outside, politely begging for the chance to pay fifty rubles for a ticket. Others tried to push their way in. The police put up metal barricades to protect the doors.

Inside were several rooms of art. One, called the iron curtain room, had a sheet of scrap metal hanging over a piano wrapped in foil. Underneath the piano was a giant poster of Leonid Brezhnev. A Stalin room was dominated by a triptych modeled after the socialist icons of the Stalinist era. In one panel, a little girl wearing her Young Pioneer scarf looked out with expectant eyes. The next panel featured an imposing portrait of the old dictator himself. The third panel featured a giant hole, a symbol of the girl's grandparents, the generation wiped out during the Stalin years.

As stars of the movie paraded around the hall, they were trailed by a crowd of paparazzi. Sergei Bugaev, the leading man, wearing a Napoleonic tunic with epaulets, posed next to the works of art with his lovely, leggy girlfriend. Tatyana Drubich, who played the movie's female lead, was more demure, but she had her groupies as well.

Posters and T-shirts were selling rapidly. Even the Soviet reporters were covering the event like a real opening. When director Sergei Solovyov arrived, he was mobbed by curious journalists. A short, stocky man with a beard, Solovyov said, ''What's it about? Well, it's a sort of romantic model of the times—the setting of spiritual forces in society. You'll just have to judge for yourselves.''

The film itself was a letdown. Some compared it to an early ''Monkees'' television show, with Jean-Luc Godard's direction of *Breathless* thrown in. It dragged on for two and a half hours. The actors were an uninspiring bunch. Rock music written especially for the film by superstar Boris Grebenshchikov was its high point. The film attempted to be trendy, using English slang like ''daddy-o,'' ''momma,'' and ''broad'' and defining them in subtitles, but the technique fell flat.

Assa, street jargon for ''madness,'' ''turmoil,'' and ''confusion,'' is set in winter in a Black Sea resort, amid palm trees covered with snow. Bugaev, the star of the film, is a young Leningrader known to the cognoscenti as Afrika. Western filmgoers are mystified by him. His acting talent is limited and he has an uninteresting singing voice, but Afrika is the first Soviet pop star in the Andy Warhol tradition. He is a teddy bear, an easily manipulated toy—a joke on the uncomprehending audience. With the success of *Assa*, Afrika became a sex symbol for millions of Soviet women.

In the film, he is the lead singer in a rock 'n' roll band. He becomes involved with a gangster's moll named Alika, who is portrayed by Drubich, a pretty young actress whose leaden expressions and childishly whining voice provide a poor counterbalance to Afrika's wiggy sappiness.

The hopelessness and corruption of the Brezhnev era is the theme of the film. In one scene, a giant poster of Brezhnev stands alone and absurdly out of place in a deserted, windswept park. In another, Afrika is arrested for wearing an earring and hauled into a police station, where he is beaten and called a ''queer.'' He surveys his badly bruised face, then goes home to find his mother and grandmother contentedly watching Brezhnev receive medals on television.

No wonder Afrika and his generation are alienated; the police are out chasing kids for wearing earrings, while the real criminals are killing innocent people. Meanwhile, the older generation sits at home watching television, lulled into complacency by Brezhnev's promises.

Just in case anyone missed the film's point—that the older generation has wrecked everything and young people are fed up—Solovyov tacked on a final scene. Viktor Tsoi, leader of the Leningrad rock group Kino, tries to enter a music academy and encounters a barrage of rules. He storms out, jumps on a stage and sings a harsh, angry song: ''It's time for change, you can see it in our eyes, we can feel it in our hearts, we want things to change.''

Assa drew long lines wherever it played. Brezhnev's appearance was greeted with boos and catcalls, and young audiences broke out in cheers at the film's calls for change. *Assa* spoke to them about alienation, and it offered a sympathetic portrayal of Afrika, a nonconformist who questioned society's rules.

The film also contained all of the Gorbachev-approved themes: Brezhnev was to blame for the period of stagnation, corruption had to be cleaned up, the system must be made to work. It was another effort to clean out the cultural closet. But Soviet youth were blind to the film's flaws and knew that such a movie could never have been made before *glasnost*. It was at least a step toward something refreshingly new, which was enough to stir the enthusiasm of most young people. *Assa* was an historic event.

Before *glasnost*, filmmakers had grown used to dodging the censors. They created subplots and symbols, feinting at controversial themes and hoping their audience would understand. A young Soviet actor once explained filmmaking in his country by saying, ''For us, everything is like this,'' he said, circling his arm up and over to touch the ear on the opposite side of his head, ''—roundabout and indirect. We're not used to saying things in simple ways. We have to be satisfied with allusions.'' Directors submitted their screenplays to *Goskino*, the State Committee of Cinematography. When Goskino banned a film, there was usually no recourse.

An inevitable consequence of this censorship was that Soviets were bored with their movies. The press reported in 1985 that more than half of the films made every year drew audiences of only one-fourth the expected size. *Mosfilm*, one of the nation's biggest studios, had lost half of its moviegoers over a ten-year period.

Although many young people complained that their cinema was dull, they made up a huge portion of the film audience, probably because going to the movies was one of the cheapest forms of entertainment available. A movie ticket cost only twenty kopecks, or about thirty-five cents. *Komsomolskaya pravda* reported in 1986 that the vast majority of moviegoers were between fourteen and thirty. Young Soviets, the paper said, averaged thirty-five to fifty visits to the cinema every year.

The leadership must have realized that cinema was one of the best ways of educating young people, but that, like television, it had to be made relevant. They set out to make Soviet films more attractive, by easing state censorship and allowing directors to bring out more engaging, honest works. Many long-banned films have been removed from the shelf and shown in state cinema houses. With cinema reform, Gorbachev was serving his goal of wooing the intelligentsia and enlisting new converts to his cause.

A few areas remained off-limits for Soviet film. No directors dared take swipes at either Gorbachev or Lenin. What changed most in Soviet filmmaking was the more honest treatment of life in the Soviet Union. Directors no longer had to polish their work with a patina of optimism. Films started taking a hard look at Soviet society and didn't always end on a cheerful, uplifting note. When *glasnost* found its way into film, one of its first targets was youthful alienation and rage.

Is It Easy To Be Young? a documentary-style film directed by a Latvian filmmaker named Juris Podnieks, packed cinema houses across the Soviet Union when it was released in 1987. The film touches on the despair and anomie of youth in a way that is new to Soviet cinema. It takes its name from a segment in which a young Latvian asks, "Is it easy to be young? No. I walk out on the street and the militiaman sees this"—he stops to show his long ponytail—"and takes me down to the station." In one scene, punk rockers spray-paint hostile graffiti on the walls of buildings. In another, a teenager professes the need for unquestioning submission to his guru. One episode documents a rambling conversation with several young people who say that the only worthy goal in life is having heaps of money.

The film has several narratives, but one of its strongest documents the odyssey of a group of young hoods through the Soviet legal system. After attending a rock concert, they tear up the seats in a railroad car late one night and are charged with vandalism. One young man is defended by his mother, who tearfully begs the court's lenience. When he is sentenced to many years of hard labor in a camp for young offenders, both mother and son break down in sobs.

Another segment of the film focuses on veterans after their return from the war in Afghanistan. They describe the brutality they witnessed but still pay lip service to the justice of the Soviet cause. An air of lethargy and bitterness hangs over them; they are as angry as any American veteran of Vietnam. "We return home at the age of twenty and we want to return to the past—to the way we lived before," one says wistfully. "But to the distant past—we want to return to our childhood. It's no way for a young person to live." Another muses about how the war has changed him forever. "The feeling that I have done something dirty, something not really human, will remain with me," he says. "A stain is sure to remain on me."

The film's detractors said that its mixture of documentary and drama was contrived. Some scenes, including a melodramatic visit to the apartment of a male nurse after his death, look rehearsed. Its courtroom scenes, in which the three young Latvians are sentenced for vandalism, are documentary. The movie's impact may have been weakened by this shifting style, but its bold honesty is refreshing. Like *Assa*, it draws cheers from the young audiences that stand in long lines to watch it. The film's director, Podnieks, is held up as a national hero in Latvia.

Two other 1987 films about youth are more lyrical. *Plyumbum*, which in English means "Lead plug," deals honestly with the hypocrisy of role playing and immorality in Soviet society. *The Messenger Boy* focuses on the helplessness many young men feel as they look toward two years of mandatory army service.

Plyumbum, directed by Vadim Abdrashitov, portrays a young man raised in a supposedly ideal Soviet family. His parents are intelligentsia who spend their spare time listening to the famous Soviet bard singer Bulat Okudzhava. They teach their son to be an activist and often quote from *Izvestia* and other newspapers. At the age of fifteen, when he says he has volunteered to become a *druzhinik*, or volunteer policeman, his parents congratulate themselves for having brought up a morally fit young man.

Plyumbum, as he calls himself, gets to know everyone in town by hanging out in bars and restaurants and working at the local vegetable storehouse and railroad station. He is a despicable little informer who uncovers the illegal schemes around him and, after gaining the trust of those involved, turns them over to the police. He tries to worm his way into the police department, but the officers refuse to accept him, saying he is too young and small.

One policeman asks Plyumbum why he calls himself lead instead of a stronger metal like steel. Plyumbum remains silent, but the audience is supposed to infer that steel is too rigid. The film implies that society's new heroes are like lead—dangerous and heavy, yet so soft that they can adjust themselves to any new idea that comes along. Although their names are never mentioned, it is an allusion to the succession of Soviet leaders —Brezhnev, Andropov, Chernenko, and Gorbachev—and the Soviet bureaucrats who, like malleable lead, change their beliefs to match each newly approved official line.

In another scene, the chief of the local mafia is arrested and Plyumbum blackmails the man's girlfriend. The two go together to a beach in a rainstorm, where he forces her to undress. Thinking she might be able to save her boyfriend from jail, she complies with Plyumbum's orders and takes him into the rough, cold sea, where she teaches him to swim. It is a classic moment in Soviet cinema: the two are supposed to be having sex, but the film only makes the allusion. Later, the woman realizes that instead of helping her boyfriend, she has only been used by Plyumbum.

After the incident, the police are convinced that he is good enough to work for them, and they give him his first assignment. Plyumbum stakes out a lake and waits for people to hunt illegally there. He arrests one poacher and then discovers the man is his own father. Plyumbum takes him to the police station anyway and coldly issues his report.

The movie is a modern-day tale of Pavlik Morozov, the young martyr to communist purity who informed on his father, only to be murdered by his uncle and grandfather. For years, the Pavlik Morozov tale was used to teach Soviet youth that their loyalty to the state should outweigh family ties. But lately, the Soviet establishment has been trying to rewrite the fable by making Pavlik out to be less of a hero.

When the director of *Plyumbum* attempted to do the same, he found that the old myth dies hard. Reaction to *Plyumbum* was the opposite of what Abdrashitov had hoped. Appearing on "Kinopanorama," a popular television show about film, he explained that he had made Plyumbum a repulsive character. To his surprise, he received letters from some young people saying they admired Plyumbum and wanted to model themselves after him. Some young filmgoers cynically believed that to succeed in Soviet society, they should become like him. Following his path would, they thought, lead to *kife*.

The Messenger Boy is a film that deals with the feeling of entrapment some Soviet young men experience as they wait to be drafted into the army. The film's leading character is a seventeen-year-old Leningrader whose parents are divorced. His father lives abroad and his mother is a busy professional woman who rarely has time for her son. He hangs out with his neighborhood buddies, break-dancing, roller skating, and drinking cheap wine in the doorways of buildings. After he fails his entrance exams and is turned down for entry into an institute, he takes a low-paying job as a messenger.

His aimless wanderings are poignant and sorrowful; the young man has nothing to occupy himself with, other than cruel jokes and a boring job. His friends' lives are similarly bleak. One who returns from two years in Afghanistan is distant and quiet; he wears the expression of a soldier who has experienced the cruelties of war but is unable to discuss what he has seen. The young man wants to rejoin his gang of break-dancing friends but finds he cannot be like them. Nor can he reinhabit the old self that existed before he left for war.

He bears witness to the despair that young Soviet men feel about losing two years out of their lives. Like the messenger, they are unable to focus on a career or an education as military service looms ahead. They worry that they will return home like the Afghanistan veteran—psychologically maimed and unable to fit into civilian life.

Two films, *Little Vera* and *The Burglar*, both released in 1988 underscored the bleakness of life for Soviet youth. Unlike their predecessors, these films pulled no punches. A sex scene was not transformed into a night on a stormy beach; instead, the director of *Little Vera* simply turned his cameras on two young people unabashedly making love. Such boldness drew harsh criticism; fights even started up in a few theaters. Young people, impressed by the honesty of the film, turned out in droves.

The Burglar, directed by Valery Ogorodnikov, stars Kostya Kinchev, lead singer of the rock group Alisa. Although Kinchev has no particular talent for acting, his performance in the film is uncomplicated and sincere. And since he is well known to fans of rock music, his presence is a big draw. Kinchev portrays a young Leningrad rocker, also named Kostya, who lives in a communal flat with his ten-year-old brother Senka and their father, an alcoholic ladies' man. The father's life-style draws the disapproval of their snoopy neighbors. Their mother is dead.

Kostya and Senka try to watch over each other, but the eldest brother has already fallen into a bad crowd of punks. He owes money to one street tough named Howmuch, a greasy, black leather type with the looks of Elvis Presley. Howmuch turns threatening but suggests he is willing to accept the synthesizer from a local community center as payment for the money Kostya owes him.

There are lengthy scenes of Kostya in concert, singing the popular song "We're Together." A row of old men in business suits looks on with blank, uncomprehending expressions, while teenagers in black leather and chains shout and dance to the music. Backstage, an elderly woman says his lyrics have drawn complaints; a committee is on its way. Senka sits in the audience, applauding, screaming, and obviously very proud of his big brother.

Kife is a catchword for Kostya. It is his concept of heaven and his definition of a good time. As he stumbles through a field, he splutters about his gang's turf, which is also *kife*—something he cannot live without. "We can't change, we can only be annihilated," he tells his brother hopelessly.

Senka, believing that his brother is becoming more desperate, grabs the synthesizer before Kostya can make off with it. After he confesses the next day, he takes the police home, where he finds his father in the middle of a drinking bout. The neighbors protest that the little thief has destroyed the collective's honor.

Senka spends the night in juvenile detention, but his father picks him up the next day. As soon as Senka is free, his father slides into a phone booth, where he calls up a drinking buddy and urges him to quickly come around "with a couple of bottles." Senka slips away, unnoticed by his father. In the final scene, he sits in an alley, his back up against a crumbling, ugly wall, hopelessness written across his small face.

Although *The Burglar* is all too predictable, it incorporates several themes that make it appealing to Soviet youth. Scenes of punks getting busted in the local police station for their nonconformist clothing and hairstyles give the film currency. Young people are at odds with the adults, who are blamed for creating a sordid, uninhabitable world. For every rock concert, there is a scene of formal musical training—a contrast between the spontaneity so appealing to Soviet youth and the enforced conformity they find in their schools.

Little Vera is even more frank. It was made by a twenty-seven-year-old director named Vasily Pichul and his screenwriter wife, Maria Khmelik, also twenty-seven. Khmelik wrote the screenplay in 1983 for her final project in film school. When she turned it in to her professors, her work won lavish praise, but no one ever thought it would be produced in the Soviet Union.

The film is a damning depiction of ordinary family life in a grimy provincial city in the Ukraine. The title of the film, translated to mean "Little Faith," alludes to the pessimism some young Soviets feel about their system. It opens with the panorama of an industrial city, including blocks of run-down apartments and rusting factories with chimneys belching sulfurous smoke.

Vera, played by the beautiful and sultry Natalya Negoda, is a shaggy-haired teenager. She lives with a truck-driving alcoholic father and uncomprehending mother in an apartment overlooking a noisy, polluted railroad yard. Like any teenager, Vera battles with her parents about her friends, her clothes, her smoking, and the Western posters that plaster the walls of her room. The fast crowd of young people she runs with has nothing better to do than join gangs and get into fistfights with the local police.

In merciless detail, the film dissects the cruelty of her life. When her father becomes drunk, Vera undresses him and puts him to bed, then makes her mother's bed in the living room. The older woman complains that Vera has forgotten to scrub the floors, and she curses her daughter as "an ungrateful bitch." During a family quarrel, Vera learns that her parents had decided to have her only so they could get a larger apartment. But Vera's listless life changes when she meets good-looking, blond Sergei at a dance. They share many afternoons and evenings in bed in his room at a seamy hostel for workers. On a lark, Vera and Sergei resolve to get married. To win their consent, they lie to her parents that she is pregnant. Later, the two are shown making love.

Although many young Soviets might have watched more explicit scenes in Western films, this is the most daring they have seen in one of their own. The interlude prompted hundreds of Soviets to line up for hours to buy tickets. In Moscow, the lines of moviegoers were so long that authorities banned *Little Vera* from downtown theaters. The scene comes as a new first: with the making of *Little Vera*, sex too has been placed on the list of taboos broken under *glasnost*.

When Sergei moves out of his workers' hostel and into Vera's apartment, his relationship with her father quickly worsens. Like so many Soviet families suffering through bad housing arrangements, their close quarters are too much for them. A violent hatred develops between the two men. After a screaming quarrel, Sergei locks his father-in-law in the bathroom. When the older man finds his way out, he picks up a long knife from the kitchen table and plunges it into Sergei. The stabbing is muted by Western standards, since the violence takes place around a corner and out of sight. But in a country that has only rarely shown domestic violence in films, the scene is all too shockingly realistic.

Vera's mother, worried that her husband will be sent to prison, convinces the girl to tell police that Sergei was threatening her father when the stabbing occurred. Her brother, a physician from Moscow, writes out a prescription for tranquilizers, and the family joins in a conspiracy to keep Vera drugged and silent. Unable to handle the situation any longer, she attempts suicide.

After discovering that Vera has consumed an overdose of pills and *samogon*, her brother hauls her into the bathroom and forces her to vomit. In a moment of searing bitterness and pent-up frustration, Vera's brother screams at his parents, "I hate you—I hate you all." After their mother asks what has happened, he turns to her and says with venomous sarcasm, "Don't worry. Everything is OK." It is a stock Soviet answer and a lie that young moviegoers have heard countless times before; yet in their lives, everything is decidedly not OK.

Little Vera was another first in Soviet cinema—a signal that some filmmakers no longer intended to keep silent about the problems that have long lurked beneath the surface in their society. By making *Little Vera*, Pichul and Khmelik let it be known that they were not satisfied with murky allusions and half-truths. *Glasnost* had given them an opening and they intended to use it.

Khmelik, who traveled to New York in early 1989 to prepare the film for its American release, gazed out the window at the skyscrapers of midtown Manhattan as she talked about *Little Vera*. She was a pretty, dark-haired young woman, the daughter of a Moscow theater director. After the release of *Little Vera*, Khmelik had become a star. She and her husband ranked among the nation's most talented filmmakers.

Producing *Little Vera* in the Soviet Union would never have been possible, she said, before the congress of the Cinematographers Union in 1986, when the union's geriatric leadership was replaced with a new generation of filmmakers. "The bosses realized that the way films were made had to be changed," Khmelik explained. "At that point, there was a revolution; unfortunately, the revolution has swallowed itself."

Pressed to explain this statement, Khmelik said that the goal of the congress was to eliminate pressure on directors. Now, directors are not only pressured by censorship, she said, they also are supposed to produce films that will be commercially successful.

Bitterness edged into her voice when she spoke about the financial side of filmmaking in the Soviet Union. All filmmakers, she said, receive a set fee for their films, no matter how successful. In the case of *Little Vera*, she and Pichul received enough money to buy a used Soviet car. Negoda, the film's leading actress, was able to purchase a new bed with her earnings; she also was given her own small apartment—no small prize for a single young woman living in Moscow. But their earnings were pitiful considering the film's huge success. *Little Vera* had been seen by fifty million Soviet filmgoers in the first three months after it opened; it was the most popular film in Soviet cinematic history. Khmelik said it had cost only about 300,000 rubles, or less than half a million dollars, to make. The film's fat profits went almost entirely to the state.

Hoping to keep more of the money their films make and to guarantee themselves full artistic control, Khmelik and Pichul formed a filmmaking cooperative after they completed work on *Little Vera*. Their next project, a psychological thriller set in the Black Sea resort city of Sochi, was to be made by the co-op, which they had named Pride. They had already rented equipment and space from a state studio in Gorky, lined up a distributor in the Russian republic, and arranged to have the film shown abroad.

Just when it looked like this remarkable private project would go through, the state stepped in. A decree was published in December 1988 that prohibited the making, showing, or distribution of films by cooperatives. Their cooperative was taken over and the movie became a state-owned project. No matter how successful their next film is, Khmelik and Pichul can expect to see only a small portion of the profits.

The loss of their co-op was a major setback for Khmelik. Her face took on a pinched, tense expression and her voice went flat when asked about the future of cinema under *glasnost*. "People everywhere are worried that the situation will change and things will go back to what they once were," she said. "The population is divided into two groups—one that believes in a bright future and one that doesn't." She hesitated to include herself in either group. "As for me," she said, "I just want to do as much as possible and see what happens. The way my life is shaping up right now, I wouldn't want to say what I'll be doing after tonight." Still, she ended on a guardedly optimistic note. "We made our first film out of enthusiasm; we got no reward other than our moral satisfaction," she said. "I imagine we'll keep on doing that."

But Khmelik sounded tentative. As a twenty-seven year old, she wanted to make the best films possible, even though she wouldn't be paid a high salary or have the control over her art that she so badly wanted. How long would her dedication last? Would she grow tired of not receiving greater financial and artistic rewards because she lived under a system that refused to relinquish profit and control?

Khmelik and her film-director husband Pichul embodied the essence of Gorbachev's dilemma. In a nation where self-reliance and independent thought have always been feared by the organs of authority, Gorbachev must nevertheless confront some of the kinds of challenges posed by Khmelik and Pichul. As more barriers are broken, expectations grow and the possibilities of creative expression seem greater to people who are used to tight controls. To ensure the future of his reform, Gorbachev will have to find ways to allow the nation's young, creative geniuses to stretch themselves in new ways. Otherwise, they can never develop the independent minds that Gorbachev so badly needs. Khmelik and Pichul have already proven themselves adept at making a world-class film, yet the state has shown itself unwilling to allow the real freedom that controlling the financial side of their movies would give them. Just when they thought they would be truly free to take risks, the state pulled them back, making them dependent again.

It is the nation's young people who will pull the Soviet Union into the twenty-first century. Khmelik, Pichul, and other bright young Soviets could become the new-style leaders envisioned by Gorbachev. But there is the risk that they could be as cynical as the Brezhnev generation or as fearful as their grandparents who grew up under Stalin. In the eyes of young Soviets, the balance is fragile.

INDEX